D0857702

Apartheid Unravels

SOUTHERN AFRICA

▭ SADCC Countries

— Railroads

APARTHEID UNRAVELS

Edited by R. Hunt Davis, Jr.

UNIVERSITY OF FLORIDA PRESS
CENTER FOR AFRICAN STUDIES
Gainesville

Maps by Jill Dygert

Copyright © 1991 by the Board of Regents of the State of Florida
All rights reserved
Printed in the U.S.A. on acid-free paper ∞

Library of Congress Cataloging in Publication Data

Apartheid unravels / edited by R. Hunt Davis, Jr.
    p.   cm.
  Includes bibliographical references and index.
  ISBN 0–8130–1069–1
  1. Apartheid—South Africa.   2. South Africa—Politics and
government—1978–   I. Davis, R. Hunt.
DT1757.A66   1991   91–469
305.8'00968—dc20   CIP

The University of Florida Press is a member of University Presses of Florida, the scholarly publishing agency of the State University System of Florida. Books are selected for publication by faculty editorial committees at each of Florida's nine public universities: Florida A&M University (Tallahassee), Florida Atlantic University (Boca Raton), Florida International University (Miami), Florida State University (Tallahassee), University of Central Florida (Orlando), University of Florida (Gainesville), University of North Florida (Jacksonville), University of South Florida (Tampa), University of West Florida (Pensacola).

Orders for books published by all member presses should be addressed to University Presses of Florida, 15 Northwest 15th Street, Gainesville, FL 32611.

CONTENTS

LIST OF MAPS

FOREWORD

Apartheid Unravels is the third volume of Carter Lectures published by the Center for African Studies, and the second in a series that the center is co-publishing with the University of Florida Press. The first volume in the jointly published series is *Structural Adjustment and African Women Farmers,* edited by Christina Gladwin.

The Center for African Studies honors Gwendolyn Carter (1906–91) by hosting annually either clusters of lectures in a conference format or a series of thematically related individual lectures. The Carter Lectures have come to be widely recognized as a means of important discourse on some of the most critical issues facing Africa today. *Apartheid Unravels* is both a timely and an in-depth analysis of the crumbling underpinnings of the South African system of apartheid today.

Peter R. Schmidt, director
University of Florida Center for African Studies

PREFACE

It is especially fitting that this edited volume, analyzing as it does the fundamental and deep-seated changes taking place in Southern Africa, should appear as part of the Carter Lectures on Africa series. For more than four decades Gwendolen M. Carter played a central role in the growth and motivation of Africanist scholarship in the United States. In particular, her name has been associated with the study of South Africa. Beginning with her landmark analysis of apartheid politics, *The Politics of Inequality* (1958), she has been the author or coauthor of innumerable books, articles, and essays that serve as the foundation for the work of other scholars who have engaged in research and writing on contemporary South Africa. Sadly, Gwendolyn Carter died at her home in Orange City, Florida, on 20 February 1991, as this book was in production.

The authors originally presented the papers collected here at the University of Florida lecture series entitled "The Exploding Crisis in Southern Africa," which was composed of two symposia in 1987 and a separate single lecture in 1988. Gwendolen Carter presented the after-dinner address for the first symposium, speaking on *"The Politics of Inequality—A Retrospective View."* Neither her address nor the papers of three contributors to the symposia are part of the present volume. J. Mutero Chirenje of the University of Zimbabwe addressed the issue of "Zimbabwe: The Ordeal of a Frontline State." Unfortunately, his untimely death in September 1988 prevented the preparation of his paper for publication. The other two papers were by Thomas G. Karis, City University of New York ("Who Will Rule South Africa? Emerging Black Leadership and the Problem of Democracy"), and Winston P. Nagan, University of Florida ("International Law, Legitimacy, and Crisis"). Conversely, Karl Beck and Robert Shanafelt did not present their chapters as papers for the original lecture series but instead prepared them specifically for this volume. All the authors have thoroughly revised and updated their chapters, most as recently as summer and fall 1990.

The Carter Lectures on Africa Committee and the Center for African Studies, University of Florida, sponsored the lectures that led to this volume. Members of the committee contributed significantly in helping conceptualize the overall theme for the lecture series and in selecting those to be invited to present papers. Funding for the 1987-88 Carter Lectures on Africa came from the Center for African Studies, including its Title VI National Resource Center Grant from the U.S. Department of Education, from a grant the Ford Foundation provided for the lecture series, from the Public Functions Policy and Lectures Committee and from the President's Concession Fund of the University of Florida, and from individual contributors to the Carter Lectures on Africa account at the University of Florida Foundation. The provost of the University of Florida provided additional funds to help defray publication expenses for this book.

Cody A. Watson provided valuable assistance in preparing the final manuscript. Thanks are also due the two outside reviewers for the University of Florida Press who made helpful suggestions for both the authors and the editor. In recognition of Gwendolen Carter and its own long association with her, Indiana University Press granted permission for adapting the first two maps. Lisa Compton greatly enhanced the final appearance of the book with her careful copyediting.

R. Hunt Davis, Jr.

Introduction: Apartheid Unravels

R. HUNT DAVIS, JR.

Nelson Mandela's internationally televised walk through the gates of Victor Verster Prison to freedom on 11 February 1990 demonstrated in a most dramatic fashion that South Africa's apartheid order is unraveling. The last decade of the twentieth century opened with South Africa's political sphere in a state of flux. Not since the events leading up to the watershed election of 1948 has there been a similar potential for new political forces to bring about a fundamental realignment of South Africa's political structure. To be sure, the apartheid era has not yet ended. One of the conclusions that emerges from the contributions to this volume is how structurally embedded apartheid is throughout the institutions of South African society. Indeed, the prolonged spate of intra-African violence in Natal that began in the late 1980s and the outbreak of extensive fighting in August 1990 in the Transvaal townships constitute striking manifestations of apartheid's structural legacy for South Africa. Yet apartheid is ideologically bankrupt and a spent force.

There have been for some time numerous indicators of the crisis of the existing order. White politics has fragmented. The governing National party (NP) reached its zenith in the late 1970s, increasing its parliamentary majority from 116 to 135 (out of a total of 164 seats) in the 1977 election and, according to an opinion poll, garnering the support of 67 percent of the electorate in 1978 (Schlemmer 1980:263–64). Although the NP managed to hold onto its overwhelming parliamentary majority until the end of the 1980s, winning, for example, 123 of 166 seats in the 1987 election, its hold on the electorate has steadily slipped. As Kenneth Grundy notes in his chapter, the NP began to lose its claim as the voice of the *volk* with the formation of the Conservative party (CP) in 1982. Its share of the total vote fell steadily, so that in 1989 it received only 48 percent of the votes cast and returned to power with only 93 seats. International pressure on South Africa to end apartheid has progressively mounted and, with the exception of England (at least while Margaret Thatcher was prime minister), remains unified even with the release of Mandela. The economy has been in the doldrums for several years, suffering from a weak currency, major structural weaknesses, and international sanctions. Most important of all has been the resurgence of black political power even before the beginning of 1990. This resurgence took several forms, including the articulation of black political thought, the emergence of a strong and militant labor movement, a successful quasi-military offensive that has deprived the government of control of the black townships, and aboveground political organizations such as the United Democratic Front (UDF) and then the Mass Democratic Movement. Furthermore, this black resurgence gathered momentum in the face of determined government efforts to quash it.

It was against this background of a mounting crisis, both internal and external, that President F. W. de Klerk took the series of steps that led to the unbanning of the African National Congress (ANC), the Pan-Africanist Congress (PAC), the South African Communist party (SACP), and other organizations and the freeing of a number of political prisoners, the most widely known of whom was Nelson Mandela. Following this has been the beginning of face-to-face negotiations between the government and the antiapartheid opposition, most notably the ANC.

To help clarify the relative positions of the contending parties, this introduction first examines the historical context in which the dramatic events of late 1989 and early 1990 took place. It then discusses the insights that the chapters provide into the unraveling process that is taking place within South Africa and how events within that country affect the Southern African region as a whole. Finally, it presents certain conclusions arising out of the chapters about the future that looms ahead for South Africa as the apartheid era draws to a close.

The Context

South Africa has clearly been in the grips of a profound crisis since the mid-1980s, a crisis that originated with the open revolt against the apartheid state that broke out in September 1984 and led the government to declare a state of emergency in parts of the country in July 1985, to be followed by a nationwide state of emergency in June 1986. It is, most immediately, this crisis that has undermined the apartheid order and produced the pressures that led to the government's decision to release Nelson Mandela.

The heart of the crisis lies in the demography and political history of South Africa. It is a country of some 36 million people, 85 percent of whom are black (11 percent Colored and Asian, 74 percent African) and 15 percent of whom are white. Over the course of the twentieth century, white South Africans have developed an absolute monopoly of political and economic power through which they have managed to reserve the overwhelming share of the country's wealth and income for themselves. In 1980, for instance, whites earned 65 percent of the national income while Africans earned only 25 percent (Wilson and Ramphele 1989:20–21). Due to South Africa's domination of the political economy of the entire Southern African region, whites have also managed to divert much of the resources of neighboring countries to their own purposes. While the whites have been the beneficiaries of the apartheid political system, it is the Africans who to a significant degree have provided the labor that has made the wealth possible. Yet they have derived little economic benefit from this labor. Indeed, their lot has been largely one of poverty, which is deep and widespread and is a result of "inequality that is as great as in any other country in the world" (Wilson and Ramphele 1989:4). The white monopoly of power has come under increasing challenge in recent years, both from within and without the country. For a long time the government's response to this challenge has been to persist on the apartheid course it had first charted in 1948, but under the new state president, F. W. de Klerk, it came to the conclusion that it could no longer maintain an overt apartheid order.

The critical questions, then, are, what are the causes of this crisis that seems to have finally broken the apartheid order, and why did the crisis erupt in such dramatic fashion in recent years? Or, put another way, why did a crisis of such magnitude not grip the country so fully and thoroughly after the upheavals associated with the Sharpeville massacre in 1960 or the Soweto student revolt in 1976? Yet another way to pose the question is to inquire into why white rule has continued in South Africa long after it disappeared elsewhere on most of the continent—the early 1960s for most countries; the mid-1970s for Angola, Mozambique, and Guinea-Bissau; 1980 for Zimbabwe; and, finally, 1990 for Namibia.

In seeking an answer to the central question of the timing of the crisis in South Africa, it is necessary to examine the complex set of internal and external factors that have produced the current situation. The internal factors refer to domestic pressures on the South African government; the external factors are the international pressures on the apartheid system. Although these factors are, of course, interlinked both across and within the two broad categories, they are discussed here as discrete categories and subcategories strictly for purposes of analysis.

Internal Factors

Important though the external factors have been in undermining the apartheid order, the internal factors have been far more significant. Indeed, if it had not been for the internal pressures on the apartheid system, the external pressures would never have been brought to bear. For purposes of analysis, we will focus on four sets of internal factors: demographic changes, political processes, administrative control, and economic realities.

Demographic changes in South Africa have done much to make the apartheid system ultimately untenable. One critical dynamic is the growth, both absolute and relative, of the country's population groups. When the first census for the Union of South Africa was taken in 1911, there was a population of approximately 6 million, of whom 4 million (67.3 percent) were Africans, 1.3 million (21.4 percent) were white, and about 650,000 (11.3 percent) were Asians and Coloreds. In 1960, at the time of the Sharpeville crisis, the population had surpassed 16 million, with nearly 11 million (68.3 percent) Africans, some 3 million whites (19.3 percent), and nearly 2 million Asians and Coloreds (12.4 percent). The estimated current population is 36 million, of whom nearly 27 million (74 percent) are Africans, 5.4 million (15 percent) are whites, and 3.6 million (11 percent) are Asians and Coloreds. As the percentage of whites in the total population shrinks, so does the ability of the privileged minority to maintain control over a steadily growing majority.

The second dimension of demographic change is that of African urbanization. Throughout the twentieth century, a majority of white South Africans have lived in urban areas (53 percent in 1904, 88 percent in 1980), as have a majority of Coloreds (51 percent in 1904, 77 percent in 1980). The African population has been much slower to urbanize, largely because of stringent government barriers to this process. In 1904, only 10 percent of black South Africans lived in urban areas, and the figure had not yet doubled by the eve of World War II. By 1980, however, 33 percent of the country's Africans were urbanized (Wilson and Ramphele 1989:26). To this figure, however, must be added a phenomenon peculiar to South Africa—that of large-scale "displaced urbanization." A massive urbanization has taken place in the bantustans, the officially designated African "homelands," with perhaps as many as 56 percent of the inhabitants of these supposedly rural areas having been urbanized. Some of this concentration has occurred within officially designated towns, but most "has taken place in huge rural slums which are 'urban' in respect of their population densities but 'rural' in respect of the absence of proper infrastructure or services" (Murray 1988:117). The ability of Africans to contest the government's authority has risen in almost direct proportion to their increased urbanization.

The third dimension is that of social mobility, involving as it does growing levels of education and professional and skilled job opportunities. While educational opportunities for blacks are severely limited in comparison to those for whites, and while levels of educational attainment are heavily skewed in favor of whites, Africans have nonetheless made great educational strides. In 1927, for example, 53.6 percent of those enrolled in South African schools were white; by 1977, only 16.4 percent were white. Furthermore, the number of Africans at the secondary level has shot up dramatically, rising from 35,000 in 1955 to 658,000 in 1979 (Marcum 1982:16–17). Increasing levels of education also mean that the black professional class, though still very small, has been expanding, thus providing, in turn, an enlarged leadership cadre. For example, Steve Biko, the central figure in the emergence of the Black Consciousness Movement, was a medical student, and Mamphela Ramphele, codirector of the Second Carnegie Inquiry into Poverty and Development in South Africa, is a medical doctor. Finally, there is the growth of semiskilled and skilled employment opportunities for Africans. The pool of migrant workers remains vast, and hundreds of thousands of blacks receive sub-subsistence level wages for their labor. But the steady industrialization of the South African economy has led to the broadening of improved job opportunities (and wages) for blacks, since the number of white workers available to fill these positions has long been insufficient. One hallmark of this process has been the rapid growth of African labor union membership, increasing from 603,000 in 1969, when the government was still actively repressing the organization of African workers, to 1,616,000 in 1984 (Adam and Moodley 1986:183).

In the political realm there have been several processes at work that have interacted upon each other. The first has been the exclusion of Africans from constitutional politics and then from citizenship. This process began with the Act of Union (1910), which established the political and constitutional structure for modern South Africa. Under its provisions membership in Parliament was limited to white males, and blacks had the franchise in only one of the four provinces. Next came the Separate Representation of Native Voters Act (1936), which removed African voters in the Cape Province from the common voting roll and provided them with three (white) representatives in Parliament. In 1960 the government enacted legislation that abolished the Cape African vote altogether, and then in 1963 it pushed through self-government for the Transkei bantustan. Having eliminated all vestiges of African participation in the constitutional politics of the country, the government then began to remove Africans from the ranks of its citizens. The so-called independence of the Transkei in 1976 stipulated that all Africans who supposedly originated from the Transkei were henceforth citizens of that state and had forfeited any claims to South African citizenship. Three other bantustans soon followed the Transkei to "independence"—Bophuthatswana (1977), Venda (1979), and Ciskei (1981)—while the other six were to assume self-governing status. The 1984 constitution completed this process by setting up three separate houses of Parliament, one each for whites, Coloreds, and Asians, while relegating the African political future to the bantustans. In 1985 the government backed off somewhat from the implications of the 1984 constitution when President P. W. Botha promised to restore South African citizenship to those who lived permanently outside the "independent" bantustans and to consider dual citizenship for the remainder. At the same time the government reiterated its commitment to the bantustans' role in the constitutional order.

The African revolt against the government over, among other issues, the new constitution, which broke out in late 1984 and continued on into 1986, had compelled Botha to revise his stand on African citizenship. This revolt also exemplified the progressively intensifying African militancy that was a response to the government's exclusion of Africans from the constitutionally sanctioned political process. The origins of this militancy lay in the 1940s with the revival of the ANC and the formation of the African National Congress Youth League (ANCYL). With the adoption of the Programme of Action (1949), the ANC moved into a phase of boycotts, strikes, and demonstrations that brought it into open conflict with the government. The Freedom Charter (1955) set forth an alternative vision of the future, in which South Africa "belonged to all who lived in it, black and white." The formation of the PAC in 1959, with its claim that South Africa was an African country, heightened the level of African political militancy. This militancy escalated even further when, in response to government banning in 1960, both the ANC and the PAC adopted the strategy of sabotage and then armed struggle. The emergence of the Black Consciousness Movement in the late 1960s, the widespread strikes by African workers in the early 1970s, the 1976 revolt that broke out first in Soweto and then spread to the rest of the country, the renewed revolt in the mid-1980s, and the formation of the United Democratic Front in 1983 all symbolized the intensification of African efforts to throw off the yoke of apartheid. Furthermore, the process of grassroots "empowerment" that began with the Soweto revolt and gathered steam in the early 1980s served to institutionalize the antiapartheid revolt and make it the dominant political force in South Africa. In large part the unbanning of the ANC, the PAC, and other organizations and the release of Nelson Mandela from prison in February 1990 are a direct result of this African political militancy.

The third element in the political context is that of increasing government repression of those opposed to apartheid. This process began with the Suppression of Communism Act in 1950 and continued with the passage of increasingly draconian legislation that A.S. Mathews

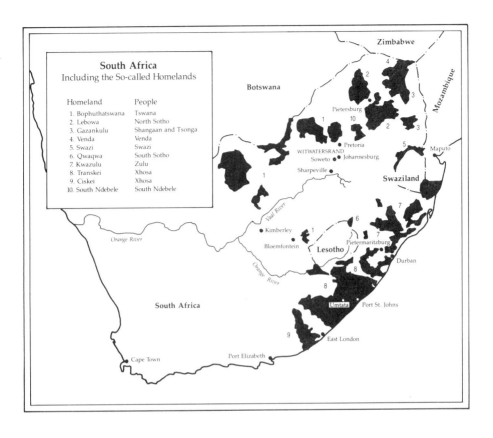

South Africa
Including the So-called Homelands

Homeland	People
1. Bophuthatswana	Tswana
2. Lebowa	North Sotho
3. Gazankulu	Shangaan and Tsonga
4. Venda	Venda
5. Swazi	Swazi
6. Qwaqwa	South Sotho
7. Kwazulu	Zulu
8. Transkei	Xhosa
9. Ciskei	Xhosa
10. South Ndebele	South Ndebele

Zimbabwe

Botswana

Mozambique

Pietersburg

WITWATERSRAND
Pretoria
Soweto ● Johannesburg

Maputo

Sharpeville

Swaziland

Kimberley

Bloemfontein

Lesotho

Pietermaritzburg

Durban

Orange River

Orange River

Vaal River

South Africa

Umtata
Port St. Johns

East London

Port Elizabeth

Cape Town

describes in his contribution to this volume. The nationwide state of emergency declared in 1986 and the further crackdown on political organizations in 1988 represented yet further intensification of this process. As Mathews indicates, while the government justified its actions in terms of national security, what in fact occurred was that the regular flow of harsher and harsher security measures intensified rather than stemmed internal conflict. South Africa has perhaps reached the end of this road under President de Klerk, since for the first time in the history of National party rule the government has relaxed rather than further intensified internal security measures.

A third set of internal factors are those related to the administrative control of the African population. Since the formation in 1910 of the Union of South Africa, the government has steadily tightened its control over the African population. Two key pieces of earlier legislation were the Natives Land Act (1913), which limited African land ownership to 7 percent of the surface area of the country (later increased to 13 percent), and the Natives (Urban Areas) Act (1923), which established the legal basis for strictly limiting African urbanization. After the 1948 election, the process of exerting administrative control over Africans intensified. In short order, the government passed the Population Registration Act (1950), which classified people according to race; the Group Areas Act (1950), which enabled the government to limit occupation of an area to a specific population group; and the Bantu Education Act (1953), designed for better control of Africans through their education. In addition, the pass laws were strengthened for more effective control of the movement of individual Africans. The development of the bantustan program, designed for more effective political control, was also a part of this process. While effective to some degree, ultimately the increasingly rigid administrative control structure failed in its purpose. It was, after all, an anti–pass law demonstration that sparked the Sharpeville massacre in 1960, and widespread unrest and popular opposition against authoritarian administration gripped the bantustans in early 1990.

Economic factors have contributed significantly to the unraveling of the apartheid order. In many ways, the success of apartheid has been dependent on the success of the bantustans, but their increasingly desperate poverty has undercut their viability. For example, in 1975 the mean annual income of Africans in the bantustans was less than half that of Africans in the metropolitan areas (R925 compared to R2,017; Wilson and Ramphele 1989:25). Since then, many hundreds of thousands of Africans have been resettled in the bantustans, having been forcibly removed from the rural white areas. Such individuals were usually completely destitute, thus adding another heavy burden to the already tottering social and economic structures of the bantustans.[1]

Another significant economic factor contributing to the weakening of the apartheid order is the changing position of African labor. One facet of this has been the broadening and diversification of the South African economy, which has expanded from its earlier agricultural and mining base into manufacturing. As Pearl-Alice Marsh notes in her chapter, there has been as a consequence a shift away from migrant labor and toward a more stabilized labor force. A measure of this change is the emergence of the strong African trade union movement, which in turn has led to an upsurge in strikes. For instance, the number of person-days lost to strikes nearly quadrupled between 1974 and 1984 (Adam and Moodley 1986:183, 186).

Just as the changing nature of the South African economy led to an expanded and more diversified role for African labor, so too has there been an alteration in the economic "need" for Africans. As long as the economy rested on mining and farming and thus was export oriented, as was the case for the most part up to the 1960s, the purchasing power of Africans was of negligible consequence. As manufacturing assumed a more prominent role, however, the economy became increasingly dependent upon the domestic and regional markets where South African products could compete effectively. As a leading economist of South Africa has noted, over time, as manufacturing and commerce "have become more capital-intensive and mechanised, their need for skilled labour and for longer production runs has increased, and this has raised the costs to them of apartheid, which keeps skilled labour scarce and expensive, and limits the domestic market [and here one could add the regional market] because of low black wages" (Lipton 1988:53).

The economic factors we have been examining so far involve those related to deeper structural shifts that have placed the apartheid economy under severe strain. The more recent economic downswing has provided further aggravations. For most of the 1980s, South Africa has faced a situation of "low growth accompanied by high inflation, low investment and rising taxation." Domestic economic problems have been further complicated by the country's weakening international position, and the late 1980s has seen "the economic noose tightening around the South African economy." Of particular importance was the 1985 refusal of U.S. banks to roll over their credits, thus forcing the South African government to declare a partial moratorium on its foreign debt repayment (Robinson 1988:205–06).

External Factors

Basically, the external set of factors concerns South Africa's eroding position in the global community. The country emerged from the

Second World War with an enhanced international standing because of its important contribution to the Allied war effort. Furthermore, its domestic politics were not subject to criticism, let alone opprobrium, in an era when the major Western states were all colonial powers and the United States had its own legislated as well as social segregation. Prime Minister Jan Smuts also played a key role in the founding of the United Nations, for he was the person who drafted the original declaration of aims in the U.N. Charter's preamble (Davenport 1978:312).

South Africa's international position began to erode in the postwar era primarily because of two factors. The first was the emergence of the former colonial countries to independent status; the second was the accession to office of the Nationalist government in 1948. This government, with its nearly exclusive focus on domestic affairs, was isolationist and thus far less responsive and attentive to foreign affairs than its predecessor had been. It was, of course, the Nationalists who were responsible for institutionalizing apartheid. The result was the juxtaposition of newly independent countries that expressed a deep-seated repugnance for any political order based on racial privilege and exclusion with a government in South Africa not only committed to such principles but also embarking through apartheid on entrenching white supremacy even more systematically and fully than it had been in the pre-1948 segregation era. South Africa was well on its way to becoming "a skunk among nations."[2]

There have been a number of crucial steps in the process of South Africa moving from its position as a member in good standing among the so-called community of nations to that of a pariah state. The first of these involved the enlargement of the community of nations itself in the late 1940s and early 1950s as former colonies became independent (e.g., the Philippines in 1946, India and Pakistan in 1947, Burma in 1948, Indonesia in 1949, Egypt in 1952). The Bandung Conference, convened in 1955 with twenty-nine Afro-Asian states in attendance, symbolized the emergence of the anticolonial bloc of nations, a bloc that was decidedly anti–South African. Next came independence for sub-Saharan Africa, beginning with Ghana in 1957 and taking a quantum leap in 1960 when fourteen French colonies became independent along with Nigeria, Somalia, and Zaire. These African states dedicated themselves in their foreign policy to the eradication from the continent of colonialism and its associated racial domination.

In the 1960s South Africa's international position deteriorated still further. First came South Africa's withdrawal from the British Commonwealth in 1961. Then came the onslaught of "U.N. resolutions condemning South Africa's policies wholesale, with massive majorities and almost no defending votes.... The formation of the Organization of African Unity [in 1964] ... provided the decolonization crusade with a central organization, if not a high command" (Davenport 1978:318). The World Court's decision in 1966 to revoke South African trusteeship over Namibia marked yet another defeat on the international front. South Africa's biggest international success during the 1960s was to prop up and support the barrier of white-ruled states (Angola, Mozambique, and Rhodesia) that lay between it and the African-ruled states to the north. The 1974 military coup that toppled the Portuguese government and subsequently set the stage for the independence of Angola and Mozambique partially destroyed South Africa's buffer. The independence of Zimbabwe in 1980 finished off the rest of it.

South Africa entered the 1980s more isolated than ever before. It did find some temporary solace in the election of Ronald Reagan to the U.S. presidency, for his administration's "constructive engagement" policy implied that the U.S. government would work through, rather than against, the existing white government to bring about change. The British government under Margaret Thatcher took a similar stance. By the middle of the decade, however, the growing anti-apartheid movements in the West overcame the opposition of conservative governments to implement economic sanctions against South Africa. The most dramatic event in this process was the 1986 congressional override of President Reagan's veto to enact the Comprehensive Anti-Apartheid Act. Sanctions in turn led to severe economic problems for South Africa, as James Cobbe describes in his chapter. In the end, the international pressures on the South African government proved too great for it to adhere unalterably to apartheid, a point that Nelson Mandela noted when crediting international sanctions in part for his release from prison (*New York Times*, 12 February 1990).

The Interaction of External and Internal Factors

How do all of these factors come together? Externally, South Africa emerged from World War II as a respected member of the international community. As a consequence, its handling of its domestic affairs received little meaningful challenge from other members of this community. By the 1980s, however, it was almost completely isolated internationally, with its domestic policies under severe censure and its economy subject to a broad range of economic sanctions. Internally, the 1984 constitution helped trigger a major revolt that the country's changing demographic patterns helped sustain and make much harder to control than was the case with either the Sharpeville crisis in 1960 or the Soweto rising in 1976. Furthermore, events in South Africa were much more in the international spotlight than they had been during the previous crises. The condition of the South African economy also made it more difficult for the government to contain the revolt, given the increasingly complex dependence on skilled and stable African labor and domestic and regional markets. At a point when the South African government needed economic growth to provide it with the flexibility and resources to respond to the rising tide of black demands, its international isolation and the tightening economic noose undercut its ability to do so. Finally, the government had placed all of its bets, so to speak, on the bantustans. In doing so, however, it had wagered on a fading horse, for the bantustans proved incapable of sustaining the apartheid order.

Where does all of this lead? South Africa remains a powerful state with the strongest economy on the African continent. Yet its future is more questionable than at any time since the 1948 electoral victory of the National party. No longer will we see a scholar writing, as did R. W. Johnson (1977:16), that "the most striking feature of the demise of white South Africa...is that it has constantly been prophesied and that it has not come about." Instead, as the contributors to this volume clearly demonstrate, the apartheid order, while not yet finished, is most decidedly unraveling. Furthermore, the far-reaching changes now underway have decided implications not only for South Africa itself but for the entire Southern African region.

The Papers

The papers fall into five categories. The first of these, consisting of the paper by A.S. Mathews, focuses on the nature of the South African state and the type of control it has sought to exert through its security laws. Looking toward the future, Mathews raises the problem of attempting to build a postapartheid order along democratic lines in the context of a legal system that for so long has increasingly resembled a police state.

The second category of papers is concerned with the beneficiaries of the apartheid order—white South Africans—who for the first time in more than four decades confront a situation that seems certain to destroy the political economy under which they have prospered. As Kenneth Grundy notes, this is producing a situation in which white politics, reflecting the broader fortunes of the apartheid order, finds itself in a state of transition and multidimensional uncertainty. According to C. J. Driver, those white liberals who over the years have opposed the totalitarianism inherent in the apartheid state, if not as equally the benefits they have derived from it, find themselves, Kerensky-like, caught in a tightening vise between increasingly militant opponents and defenders of the existing order.

A third category of papers examines the black opposition, which, as C.R.D. Halisi notes, developed along three lines during the 1970s in a context in which the established liberation movements (the ANC and the PAC) were banned. The groupings that emerged were those of neo-ethnicity, radicalized youth, and the labor movement. Among the youth in particular Black Consciousness thought became especially significant. Karl Beck's paper illustrates how in the mid-1980s, with the emergence of the UDF (founded in 1983), the ANC position of multiracialism reasserted itself in organizational form in a widespread reaffirmation of working toward a future South Africa built along the lines of the Freedom Charter. Yet, as Halisi argues, Black Consciousness thought remains a powerful current in the black political opposition.

The fourth category of papers discusses black labor, which finds itself in a stronger economic and political position than ever before in its history. The strongest single union is the National Union of Mineworkers (NUM), and its leader, Cyril Ramaphosa, has become one of the most powerful African political figures. As Robert Shanafelt notes, however, there are deep fissures within NUM along lines of both occupational differentiation and ethnicity that threaten worker solidarity and provide openings for both large-scale capital and the state to play various factions against each other. The evolution of NUM into a powerful organization whose membership includes a large element of migrant workers from outside South Africa belongs to the wider context of the organization and mobilization of black labor that Pearl-Alice Marsh analyzes in her chapter. The origins lie in the emergence of a white-based interstate system in Southern Africa that in turn produced a regional labor structure. During the last two decades, national-based economies have steadily displaced the earlier race-based regional economy, leading in turn to significant changes in the pattern of migrant labor. Black labor unions such as NUM have as a consequence achieved sufficient power to participate in shaping the labor system of the present and the future.

South Africa's domination of a regional race-based labor system brings us to the final category of papers, those that examine the country's presiding role over the politics and the economy of Southern Africa as a whole. As James Cobbe notes, South Africa continues to overshadow and dominate the newer national-based economies of the region. The emergence of the Southern African Development Coordinating Conference (SADCC), however, along with the emerging structural weaknesses of the South African economy itself, has served to weaken the country's hold over the economy of the region as a whole while at the same time creating uncertainty and holding the potential for widespread economic insecurity in Southern Africa.

The implications of attempting to establish a national-based economy with control over labor and other resources while yet remaining to a significant degree economically dependent and subject to South Africa's contradictory foreign policy can readily be seen in Allen Isaacman's discussion of the experience of Mozambique. According to Patrick O'Meara, South Africa confronts a paradoxical choice in its policy toward the region—that of whether to continue to regard it as a hinterland to exploit and cultivate or as the haven of its real and potential enemies to attack and keep off guard. Even a postapartheid South Africa will have to confront complex issues of establishing smooth economic and political relations with the other states of the region who through SADCC have attempted to rid their own economies of South African domination.

Conclusions

That the apartheid order is clearly unraveling is evident in this volume as well as in other studies.[3] Despite having resorted for decades to increasingly draconian security laws, the state has proven unable to hold the opposition in check. Faced with this realization, it has dramatically reversed course under the leadership of President F.W. de Klerk. At the opening of Parliament in 1990, for instance, de Klerk announced the lifting of bans on opposition political organizations and his intention to free Nelson Mandela, an event the world watched on 11 February. At the start of the 1991 parliamentary session, the state president noted his government's intention to dismantle much of the rest of the formal apartheid system. Specifically, legislation would soon be introduced to repeal "the cornerstones of apartheid"—the 1913 Land Act, the 1966 Group Areas Act, the 1984 Black Communities Act, and, most surprising and significant, the 1950 Population Registration Act. Africans, however, still remain without the vote.

Already badly split, the government's outright renunciation of apartheid has caused white politics to fracture even further. Increasing numbers of whites (largely English-speaking) were already pulling away from apartheid and seeking some vaguely defined, more democratic alternative. Some have now even begun to look to the ANC for leadership. Moreover, the National party, already split between a *verligte* element that sought to reform apartheid and a *verkrampte* element that sought to maintain the status quo, has been further weakened by its leadership's abandonment of apartheid. Some of its more hardline *verkrampte* elements have split off and moved into the right-wing opposition camp. In turn, the right wing is increasingly vocal and militant: Conservative party members of parliament walked out on de Klerk as he addressed the opening of the 1991 session. The liberal element, mostly white and English-speaking, argues for "classic" Western-style democracy. Squeezed by militants on both sides, however, this group is failing to attract sufficient support from those in the middle who opt for neither of the militant camps yet are unwilling to commit themselves to a liberal future.

The "African voice" is increasingly asserting itself in South African politics, thereby contributing significantly to the progressive collapse of the apartheid order. But which African voice? Is it the radicalized young, who have fallen under the sway of Black Consciousness and conduct their politics accordingly? Their political arguments are persuasive, but their organizational skills are less so. Is it the Charterists, based in the UDF from its founding in 1983 until it disbanded in 1991, whose vision is that of a democratic South Africa? Organizationally they seem to be in the ascendancy, especially with the unbanning of the ANC (the UDF had served as its surrogate within South Africa while it was outlawed and in exile) and the release of its long-imprisoned leader, Nelson Mandela. As the Charterists begin to operate fully aboveground, however, will they be able to meet current demands and expectations? The continued PAC opposition to any negotiation with the government in Pretoria, reiterated at its December 1990 party congress, suggests difficulties ahead for those who adhere to the Freedom Charter as the blueprint for South Africa. Or is it the voice of Inkatha and its leader, Chief Gatsha Buthelezi? While he may be "the man you can't ignore" (Tygesen, 1991), it is difficult to view him as more than a Zulu voice, let alone *the* Zulu voice, or a voice for the aspirations of Africans in general.

Or is the African voice that of black labor, the once slumbering giant now awakening? It has the economic base and the organizational strength to give force to its latent militancy and hostility to the apartheid order that has so ruthlessly exploited it. Yet, though it has considerable solidarity, black labor remains incomplete and divided by internal fissures and external pressures such as the rivalry between Charterists and Pan-Africanists and between Inkatha and the ANC. Finally, what of the African voice (or voices) from elsewhere in the region? Will the other Southern African states continue to maintain SADCC as a bulwark against the South African giant, invite a democratic South Africa to join them, or disband SADCC and pursue national-based strategies that might include seeking to become incorporated into South Africa itself?

In short, the African voice is not singular in nature but plural. In the past, this fact has helped to weaken the antiapartheid opposition and allowed the state to play off one faction against another. It still provides potential for those in power to enhance their position by building on divisions among its opponents. De Klerk's bold moves (in the context of the past half century of South African political history) seemingly constitute an effort to carve out a new base for continued National party rule. Much of the Inkatha-based violence in the townships may also stem from such an effort. Even as the apartheid state is unraveling, elements of the old order (e.g., large-scale capital) will try to find among the antiapartheid forces sufficient allies to enable them to retain power and privilege. At the same time the antiapartheid ranks are seeking ways to overcome their differences so as to gain power (the Mandela-Buthelezi meeting in January 1991 is a case in point). An excellent place, then, to begin assessing the strengths and weaknesses of the forces in play in South Africa is in the contributions to this volume. They provide a sound vantage point for understanding southern Africa today and from which to peer into its future.

NOTES

1. For a discussion of the policy of forced removals, numbering more than 3.5 million between 1960 and 1983, see Roger Ormond (1986:131–38). Ormond in turn was relying on the research carried out by a team of researchers known as the Surplus Peoples Project.

2. This epithet is taken from the subtitle of Les de Villiers's *South Africa: A Skunk among Nations* (1975). Ironically, de Villiers, who served as a South African diplomat in North America for ten years, intended his title to underscore what he viewed as the hypocrisy and double standards of the international community when it came to dealing with South Africa.

3. For a sampling of some of the best studies, see Davis (1987), Greenberg (1987), James (1987), Libby (1987), and Lonsdale (1988).

REFERENCES

Adam, Heribert, and Kogila Moodley. 1986. *South Africa Without Apartheid.* Berkeley: University of California Press.

Davenport, T. R. H. 1978. *South Africa: A Modern History.* Toronto: University of Toronto Press.

Davis, Stephen M. 1987. *Apartheid's Rebels.* New Haven: Yale University Press.

de Villiers, Les. 1975. *South Africa: A Skunk among Nations.* London: Tandem.

Greenberg, Stanley B. 1987. *Legitimating the Illegitimate.* Berkeley: University of California Press.

James, Wilmot G., ed. 1987. *The State of Apartheid.* Boulder: Lynne Rienner.

Johnson, R.W. 1977. *How Long Will South Africa Survive?* New York: Oxford University Press.

Libby, Ronald T. 1987. *The Politics of Economic Power in Southern Africa*. Princeton: Princeton University Press.

Lipton, Merle. 1988. "Capitalism and Apartheid." In *South Africa in Question*, ed. John Lonsdale, 52–63. Portsmouth, NH: Heinemann.

Lonsdale, John, ed. 1988. *South Africa in Question*. Portsmouth, NH: Heinemann.

Marcum, John A. 1982. *Education, Race, and Social Change in South Africa*. Berkeley: University of California Press.

Murray, Colin. 1988. "Displaced Urbanization." In *South Africa in Question*, ed. John Lonsdale, 110–33. Portsmouth, NH: Heinemann.

New York Times. 1990. 12 February.

Ormond, Roger. 1986. *The Apartheid Handbook*. Harmondsworth, U.K.: Penguin Books.

Robinson, Anthony. 1988. *The African Review*. Saffron Waldron, Essex, U.K.: World of Information.

Schlemmer, Lawrence. 1980. "Change in South Africa: Opportunities and Constraints." In *The Apartheid Regime: Political Power and Racial Domination*, ed. Robert M. Price and Carl G. Rosberg, 236–80. Berkeley: University of California Press.

Sparks, Allister H. 1990. *The Mind of South Africa*. London: Heineman.

Tygesen, Peter. 1991. "The Man You Can't Ignore." *Africa Report* (January–February): 50–53.

Wilson, Francis, and Mamphela Ramphele. 1989. *Uprooting Poverty: The South African Challenge*. New York: W.W. Norton and Company.

1

South African Security Law and the Growth of Local and Regional Violence

A. S. MATHEWS

The root cause of internal and cross-border violence in South Africa is the imposition on the black people of the country of the policy of apartheid—a policy that its nonconsenting victims correctly perceive to be inhuman, discriminatory, and unjust. Apartheid as recently as the late 1980s was neither dead nor dying, notwithstanding the final benedictions pronounced over it by the licensed comedians of the state such as Minister of Cooperation and Development Piet Koornhof. The transformation of apartheid from theory into fact has been recorded by Joseph Lelyveld (1986), whose documentation of the impact of forced removals and geographical segregation of blacks is the most telling and heartrending account yet published. This physical segregation constitutes one of the basic essentials of apartheid that remain entrenched, the others being race classification and white monopoly of power and wealth. Violence arises directly from the maintenance of these basics through state-sanctioned or "structural" violence.

Two features of government policy in particular have heightened the prospects of a violent outcome to South Africa's political conflict. The first is the ruling party's obsession with ethnicity and the resultant ordering of society into ethnic camps. Nothing could be more explosive than the channeling of political conflict along ethnic lines. The second feature of official policy that exacerbates violence is the denial (implicit in apartheid) of meaningful political rights to the newly mobilized black work force in South Africa. When the masses are drawn into a process of rapid modernization, the failure or refusal to develop institutions of political participation through which awakened aspirations can be expressed is, as Samuel P. Huntington (1968:47) has observed, a direct and major cause of violence in the modern state.

One could legitimately ask whether it is not precisely the function of a security system, and in particular of the South African security system, to deal with and eliminate the violence of which we have been speaking. The response to that question is clear. Even if the security system is an acceptable one, in the sense that it is directed specifically at violence or nondemocratic efforts to subvert the institutions of the state, its employment might still be criticized and even condemned on the grounds that the system is overburdened with responsibilities beyond its capacity. There are many tasks that can be effectively undertaken only in the political sphere and which, if they are not resolved there, place an impossible burden on the security system. Clearly, one of the reasons for the current disorder in South Africa is that the authorities have been seeking to solve by security action social problems that should be addressed politically though recently they have at least initiated efforts at finding political solutions. But the South African security system is not an acceptable one, and its focus is by no means confined to violence or subversive attacks upon the state. It is true that the security laws are framed in such a way that violent acts against the state can be punished and persons and groups practicing subversion can be restricted by detentions, bannings, and the like. But the reach of the laws, both on paper and in practice, is far wider than that. The security laws are also directed and used against those who oppose the government and its policies.

Black opponents of the government, whether in education, the media, trade unions, or community work, are bound, sooner or later, to come into conflict with the security system, which has become one of the chief props of apartheid. It may be argued that its main function is to control extraparliamentary opposition to apartheid. The system represents, according to Tapia-Valdés's typology of national security policies, "a permanent policy of exercising stricter socio-political control by granting to the national security establishment a degree of power formerly applicable only during a state of emergency." This author's characterization of the "national security state" is fully applicable to contemporary South Africa: "This enlarged security structure represents a 'militaristic' view of the political conflict which requires control of dissidence. Civilian, military and police roles are blended in order to 'manipulate' national security as a pretense to justify the use of the police and armed forces in backing a determined civilian political project and status quo." (Tapia-Valdés 1982:9–10). An almost perfect expression of this tendency is to be found in the secretly developed National Security Management System—a system of local administration in which the security forces are playing a shadowy and sinister role in the repression of community dissidence.[1]

The managers of the South African security system present themselves, not altogether surprisingly, as the operators of a true law-and-order enterprise and deny that they are in the business of sociopolitical control. It is worth a momentary diversion to analyze the techniques by which this spurious, but not totally unsuccessful, claim to legitimacy has been developed. It has taken in the bulk of the white population (including some of its more discriminating members such as judges), some black South Africans (of which Charles Sebe, former head of the Ciskeian security force, is a prime example),[2] and a substantial number of outsiders. The legitimating philosophy of the security system has been that of resistance to total onslaught. In this context, total onslaught is defined as a Communist-inspired and Communist-directed attack against South Africa conducted by all available means, including military, spiritual, and psychological assaults on the South African population. Because the attack is conceived as multidimensional, the resistance to it must be conducted at all levels, and what would be described in a democracy as an intrusion into the freedoms of thought, conscience, and expression has been represented in South Africa as a defensive action against the all-pervasive and destructive influences of Communist subversion in Africa.

The philosophy of resistance to the total onslaught has depended for its persuasiveness on a number of deliberately engineered confusions. In particular, it involves the confusion between black nationalist resistance and Communist subversion and between the liberation war and the worldwide phenomenon of terrorism.[3] The use of a number of legitimizing techniques in which South African legal technicians are quite skilled has artfully veiled these confusions and the real objectives of the security system. South Africa still declares states of emergencies, thereby preserving the illusion that "ordinary" law prevails in normal times. In fact, the ordinary law goes well beyond what most Western societies enact as emergency law, while emergency law is almost comparable to the worst examples of totalitarian excess. An imposing cloak of legality consisting of elaborate (but generally ineffective) procedures and safeguards, detailed (but generally inoperative) criteria for official action,[4] and extensive court participation (without, however, any real power of control) have skillfully covered over the basic aims of the security system. (South African ministers are fond of saying that the victims of security action are free to approach the courts, forgetting to add that the courts that are so approached are usually powerless to help.) The skillful manipulation of the theory of total onslaught and the obsessive legalism of the internal security program have concealed with considerable success the real objective of national security in South Africa—political control. The containment of violence, although it is undoubtedly sought by the managers of the system, is of secondary importance. Expressed differently, faced with the choice between reduced political control accompanied by less violence on the one hand and full political control accompanied by greater violence on the other, South Africa's rulers have consistently opted for the latter as indicated by the security program they have adopted. Although the de Klerk government has now conceded the need to share political power, the state's security apparatus remains in place.

Since security legislation has been framed broadly enough to inhibit the articulation of grievances and the development of nonviolent pressures for reform by disenfranchised South Africans, the growth of violence can hardly be a surprising phenomenon to those who have imposed the security clamps on the South African people. There is no better recipe for revolutionary resistance than that of blocking the channels of grievance articulation and redress available to a voteless, seriously disadvantaged section of society. This is especially true when that section is a majority whose political servitude is a consequence of the imposed and irrational criterion of race. The legislative blocking of these channels has been carried out with an open-eyed deliberation. The principal organizations through which black grievances and demands could be articulated were either banned or neutralized by individual bannings, detentions, and other forms of legal or extralegal reprisals until President de Klerk rescinded these measures in February 1990. The case of the United Democratic Front (UDF) is instructive in this regard. Even though it was not banned until February 1988 (when the government used its emergency powers to ban it, along with sixteen other organizations, for the duration of the declared state of emergency), its leadership suffered grievously under a wide range of legal actions (as defined by security legislation) brought to bear on it. Furthermore, the state had declared the organization itself an affected organization under the provisions of the law, thereby depriving it of funds from abroad.

Under security legislation the right to hold public meetings and processions is practically nonexistent—all outdoor meetings (except sports gatherings) are illegal without prior government approval. Indeed, the mass public demonstrations in Cape Town, Johannesburg, Pretoria, and other cities in the week following the September 1989 elections were the first such gatherings that the government had approved. Yet within a week or so afterward police arrested more than 150 demonstrators who attempted to hold a meeting after having refused to seek a permit (on the same day, right-wing white extremists held a meeting that had received government approval and at which there were calls for the execution of Nelson Mandela). The government regularly prohibits indoor meetings of opposition groups, either specifically or on a blanket basis. The press, especially the black press, is subject to extensive security law controls that include bannings (such as of the *World*, the Soweto daily newspaper), the requirement of a forfeitable deposit of up to R40,000 as a condition of the registration of a newspaper, and extensive restrictions on what may be published. Arbitrary restrictions on freedom of movement, assembly, association, and expression regularly violate the individual rights of black leaders and activists.

The surprise and outrage expressed by the ruling elite at the violent explosion that has followed this process of screwing down the lid on South Africa's seething social cauldron is largely feigned. The outcome was entirely predictable. The dissembling nature of the rulers' reaction is sometimes evident in the ill-contained glee with which government authorities attribute the latest atrocities to the opposition movements. However inexcusable and unjustifiable, acts of violence thus bear a direct relationship to the government policy of holding down the lid and simultaneously sealing all outlets and safety valves.

The South African internal security system may be condemned today as one that has manifestly failed to contain violence and disorder. The first of the draconian laws of the era of National party rule, the Suppression of Communism Act in 1950, was enacted at a time when the country was in a state of peace. The *Survey of Race Relations* (South African Institute of Race Relations 1950–51:21) of that year records only two activities demonstrating unrest—a one-day work stoppage and a peaceful protest meeting against apartheid legislation. In 1985, after three and a half decades of tough law-and-order medicine, unrest accounted for 824 deaths and 2,615 injured persons. In the same year there were 136 so-called guerrilla incidents (South African Institute of Race Relations 1985:533, 541). These data do not read like the success story that the managers of the security system claim for their operations. Deaths, property destruction, and acts of insurgency did ultimately decline under the state of emergency declared in 1986. The pattern of ever-increasing violence after each campaign of repression does not appear to have been broken, however, if the violence in Natal and the Transvaal townships is any indicator. It is difficult to see how it can be until reform touches the essentials of inequality and security law measures are directed at real subversives rather than opponents of the system.

With the foregoing remark about the political victims of the security system we come to the nub of the problem of so-called national security in South Africa—the grotesque overreach of security legislation. From the perspective of social stability, the problem with the security laws is that they are excessively broad and indiscriminate and that they tend to create more enemies than they can eliminate. The security crackdown after the 1976 disturbances drove thousands of young blacks across the borders of South Africa and into ANC training camps. Several years later there was a dramatic increase in guerrilla attacks in the country. The crackdown of the mid-1980s, which was far fiercer than the actions taken in 1976, would no doubt in time have produced its own counterreaction of insurgency violence if it had not been forestalled by the events of February 1990. It is not enough, therefore, to criticize the security system for its failure to contain violence. The system must also be condemned as a begetter of violence in South Africa and across its borders. This is a serious charge that calls for extended analysis and justification.

Trends in South African Security Legislation

The security system's capacity for generating violence is due principally to two trends in security legislation of the past four decades. The first is the progressive tendency of freeing the security authorities from legal accountability for their actions. The second tendency is more recent but overlaps with the first and consists of the steady reduction, to the point of elimination, of the political or public accountability of the security authorities. Both trends have a direct bearing on the growth of violence. A separate examination of each is necessary to assess their import.

Diminished legal accountability for security actions has been a feature of South Africa's security system from the outset. Reduced accountability to the law has always been implicit in any emergency government, but this has generally been tolerated because emergencies are usually short-term affairs in the nature of intervals between periods of full accountability for official action. The permanent nonaccountability of security authorities is a totally different matter and cannot be acceptable in a society that puts any value upon individual freedom and democracy. This is more strongly the case where accountability is not merely reduced but actually eliminated. So-called ordinary security legislation in South Africa (nonemergency legislation) provides examples of partial, substantial, and total exemption from accountability to the law. Some examples of each will be helpful in measuring the South African security system's conformity to the rule of law.

Partial Nonaccountability

Persons charged with security law violations (terrorism, subversion, sabotage, intimidation, furthering the aims of communism or of a banned organization, and so forth) are brought before the ordinary courts, which in the main apply basic fair-trial procedures. With respect to security crimes, therefore, the authorities remain responsible to the law, and in contrast to the Soviet Union, for example, there are frequent acquittals in South African political trials. But the accountability in the sphere of security crime is limited by a number of factors. First, some security crime charges are excessively broad or vague (or both). Thus, once the decision to charge is taken, conviction may be a predictable outcome. This is disturbing where the crime encompasses acts of extraparliamentary opposition, such as passive resistance or strikes. Second, the extended interrogation of state witnesses held incommunicado provides the police with the opportunity of manipulating the prosecution case, and convictions based on coerced evidence and confessions carry no conviction, to make a poor pun. Third, the imbalance between the mighty resources of the state in political trials and the vulnerability of the accused (who is frequently held incommunicado until the trial) can be so severe as to jeopardize the fairness of the trial.

Substantial Nonaccountability

When the security authorities take extrajudicial action against persons perceived to be security threats, they operate substantially outside the constraints of the law. This has generally been achieved by making the power to take such action conditional on "the opinion" of the authority concerned. The banning of individuals and organizations is conditional upon the opinion or state of satisfaction of the designated authority that a threat to state security exists. According to the courts, if this opinion or state of satisfaction is apparently genuine the restriction cannot be challenged as being unsupported by objectively present reasons or facts. Most forms of detention in South Africa may be ordered if the empowered official believes that incarceration is justified.

Detention orders, then, are generally proof against legal challenge. An exception to this is section 29 detention, which depends upon the official in question having "reason to believe" that the detention is justified.[5] This phrase, the appeal court recently held in the *Hurley* case, means that the official must act upon proven grounds for detaining the suspect.[6] While this judgment introduced a welcome measure of court control, it is not applicable to other forms of detention (such as indefinite preventive detention under section 28). Furthermore, a new form of detention (section 50A detention), introduced in a bill published (significantly, perhaps) on the same day that the *Hurley* judgment was delivered, nullified the court's decision. It follows that that form of detention is still effectively beyond court supervision. This applies also to detentions under emergency law.

Total Nonaccountability

The clearest example of a security power that falls into the realm of nonlaw (or Lon Fuller's "patternless exercises of power") is the ministerial power to ban meetings.[7] This power is challengeable only on the mythical ground of proof of bad faith or improper purpose on the minister's part. In effect, the minister has an absolute power to control assemblies of two or more persons in public or private places in South Africa.[8]

When we turn our attention to emergency legislation, as distinct from the supposedly ordinary legislation discussed above, the powers all fall into the substantially or totally nonaccountable categories. Emergency detention, for example, may be ordered without any prior hearing, without the control of review committees, and according to the subjective discretion of the detaining authorities. In the few cases where the courts have released emergency detainees, the arresting authority has been guilty of so blatant a misuse of power that its bad faith or reliance on improper considerations has proclaimed itself (as in the case of the arrest and detention of a nun who had objected to a police assault on a young township dweller during unrest operations). Where the authorities do not act with obvious impropriety, the detention is practically beyond the control of the courts and therefore not subject to legal controls. There are three instances, in particular, of powers that appear to fall into the absolute category (total nonaccountability) and are a cause of grave concern to those who hope for a peaceful resolution of conflict in South Africa. Each requires separate discussion.

The Indemnity Clause

Acts of indemnity are usually passed after the conclusion of an emergency to exempt those responsible for restoring law and order from legal liability for bona fide but illegal actions taken during the crisis. In all three emergencies declared in South Africa under the Public Safety Act of 1953, the security forces have been exempted in advance from civil and criminal responsibility for actions taken under the emergency regulations which the authority in question genuinely believed to be necessary. This prior licensing of illegal conduct virtually frees the authorities from the restraints of law so long as they believe their emergency actions to be necessary to terminate unrest. What the security forces believe to be necessary can be gauged from incidents such as the notorious 1985 "Trojan horse" ambush in which several young persons (including a boy twelve years old) were shot dead after being trapped into stoning a police vehicle. Another telling piece of evidence is the instruction sent to divisional commissioners of police before the shootings at Uitenhage that those who threw petrol bombs should be eliminated.

The Search and Seizure Clause

The security forces have power under the emergency regulations to enter premises for purposes of search and seizure at any time and without the requirement of a warrant. Once on the premises they are authorized to take such steps as they deem necessary for the maintenance of law and order or the safety of the public. Blacks in South Africa have never enjoyed security of hearth and home. Even the remnants of that security were swept away by the emergency search and seizure power.

The Use of Force Clause

If the presence or conduct of any person is deemed by a commissioned, warrant, or noncommissioned officer of the security forces to be a threat to public safety or order, the officer concerned may order such persons to disperse or desist from such conduct and, if they do not do so immediately, may employ such force (including lethal force) *as he deems necessary* to secure compliance. The effect of this emergency provision is to free the security forces almost entirely from legal controls in dispersing groups or preventing unwelcome conduct. The criteria for the use of any force used, including lethal weapons, are expressed in terms of official belief and are therefore subjective in nature.

Though these powers are emergency powers that should lapse with the lifting in 1990 of the 1986 state of emergency, they can be reintroduced on an area basis under a new provision of the Public Safety Act of 1953.[9] This provision, introduced in 1986, permits the minister of law and order to declare areas of the republic to be unrest areas and to exercise for these areas the same powers of legislation as the state president may exercise in times of national emergencies. The provision in effect provides for a "no hassle" localized emergency. When these micro-emergencies are introduced, we can be fairly certain that the lawless powers conferred by the three provisions just discussed will be brought into effect. Official lawlessness has possibly been perpetuated for South Africa even when a government representing the majority of the population takes power.

The second major feature of recent security legislation is that of steadily diminishing public accountability for security force actions and conduct. The Official Secrets Act, one of the dubious blessings that imperial Great Britain conferred upon commonwealth countries, has always facilitated secret military and security operations and seriously limited the democratic accountability of the martial power in the state. In 1975, South Africa invaded Angola. The ensuing war was successfully maintained as a state secret for several months by the threatened use of official secrets and defense legislation. Subsequently, the government used the Official Secrets Act of 1956[10] to block publication of a book that almost certainly contained information about South Africa's military adventures across the borders of Angola and Mozambique.[11] Defense and official secrets legislation also blocked disclosure of the extent of government involvement in the abortive Seychelles coup, and the relevant parts of the trial of the mercenaries that followed were held in camera.[12] Operating behind the screen of secrecy laws, the ruling party managed to turn the sanctified policy of noninterference in the affairs of nearby countries into its opposite without any political accountability for this drastic reversal. Military strikes, assassinations in neighboring states, and possibly even parcel bombs—the full repertoire of "dirty tricks"—thereby became the new norms of conduct of the security/military arm of government as it was progressively freed from public accountability.

Secrecy and the Growth of Official Lawlessness

Until quite recently South Africa's security authorities remained accountable to the public for internal operations. Though there were exceptions, such as legislation protecting the police and prison authorities from "untrue" disclosures and the secrecy surrounding the treatment of detainees, by and large the nature and extent of internal-security operations could be published and were made known by the media. This changed dramatically and perhaps permanently with the promulgation of nationwide emergency regulations on 12 June 1986 when a number of repressive controls on the media were introduced. Though some of these regulations were quickly struck down by the courts, they were amended and reenacted and had these main effects: (1) the exclusion of all journalists, cameramen, and reporters from places where unrest is taking place; (2) a prohibition on news or comment on unrest or on security force actions in unrest areas; (3) a ban on pictures, sound recordings, or films of any kind of unrest activity or security force action to counter it; (4) the imposition of prepublication censorship with the power to ban a publication for periods of three months for violating censorship provisions. These controls limited news and comment about unrest and security force activities to official releases from, or reports approved by, the Bureau of Information or other government departments. In short, a "Ministry of Truth" told the public what it should believe as long as the state of emergency was in force.

It is significant that the impenetrable screen enveloped security force conduct after the expression of internal and external outrage about the frequently brutal manner in which not only unrest but also peaceful demonstrations and protests were being put down. The South African government sought to have us believe that the main reason for the growth of violence and disorder in South Africa was that such matters were reported in the media. This was a farcical claim that was meant to divert attention from the prime causes of violence and to give the security forces a free hand in dealing with alleged troublemakers. After legal accountability for security operations had been virtually eliminated, only public accountability remained as an obstacle to complete freedom of action. The 1986 emergency measures removed the final obstacle and gave the security authorities, both legally and politically, a free hand in dealing with opponents of the government. With this development, the locus of power shifted decisively to the military-security alliance.

The security enactments briefly reviewed here had the effect of establishing the security forces as a substantially lawless power in the state. In addition, the security authorities positioned themselves beyond effective political control, allowing them to act with little sense of accountability to the public. A major result of these developments was a massive increase in official violence against the opponents of the government both within South Africa and across its borders. The extent of official internal violence clearly emerges from a comparison with Northern Ireland. In seventeen years of civil strife in Northern Ireland, the security forces were responsible for 265 deaths. In 1985 alone, South African security forces killed approximately 400 persons. The percentage of persons killed by the security forces in Northern Ireland has been 10.8 percent of those dying in the violence, while in South Africa the security forces were responsible, at the time of writing, for more than 50 percent of unrest deaths. Moreover, the figure of 50 percent actually represents a decline, since in earlier years, before the phenomenon of so-called black-on-black violence had appeared, the ratio of official to other killings must have been considerably higher.[13]

The South African government would no doubt explain the growth of official violence simply as a state response to the increasingly violent attacks upon itself and those who support its policies. It also has sought to justify this violence by distinguishing between state-sanctioned force (which is morally acceptable if not actually good) and antistate violence (which is not just unacceptable but actually evil). Both explanations are simplistic and self-serving. I leave aside the moral argument except to say that the earlier part of this paper has sufficiently illustrated the poverty of the ruling party's claim to legitimate use of violence. Turning to the argument that official violence is no more than a reaction to antistate violence, several points need to be stressed.

First, the use of force by the authorities has become increasingly undiscriminating and ferocious. Nothing illustrates this better than the extent to which young children are becoming the victims of security force action, including torture.[14] Such repression produces its own harvest of hatred and counterviolence. Some very moderate voices in South Africa have given expression to this lesson. Speaking from his chair in an Afrikaans university, Professor Lourens M. du Plessis (1985:233, 236) has warned that "coercion from above...tends to give rise to chaos from below." Sometime earlier, advocate D.P. de Villiers (1983:393, 415), speaking from within the ranks of the ruling party, said that drastic measures are likely to be ineffective and counterproductive in the longer term. The counsel of these quieter voices was scarcely heard during the 1980s in the din of growing conflict in South Africa.

The second point to note is that in the entire history of resistance to apartheid, the most fateful decision taken by the ruling party was to suspend the legal and political controls applicable to the security forces. The implications of this step have been well expressed by Paul Wilkinson (1977:42, 124) as "the creation of a power-hungry security apparatus" and the growth of general chaos in which "private armies and vigilante groups will spring up like a jungle of weeds." These words are disturbingly appropriate to the South African situation. As official lawlessness has increased, violence and terror have become commonplace in many communities. Vigilante killings and property destruction, political assassinations, Mafia-style gunning down of enemies, and public executions (usually by necklacing) became everyday occurrences. There is growing evidence that the security forces are involved in some of this violence and that they do little to prevent it when directed against antigovernment elements. Lawlessness at the center—within the very agencies that are responsible for law and order—is like a corrosive acid that is bound to spread through the whole system. Though the security forces have not, as a rule, created violence, their lawless interventions have provided a powerful impetus to its growth in the society. The situation has become even more volatile with the growth of right-wing resistance to de Klerk's efforts at reaching an accommodation with the anti-apartheid forces.

Finally, due to the inadequate and sometimes nonexistent rule-of-law controls over the security authorities, they have been able to neutralize and indeed eliminate black leaders even when these leaders have been moderate and nonviolent. One result of the war on black leaders has been the steady replacement of moderate leaders with more militant ones who are not infrequently committed to violence as "the only language that the white man understands." Another significant result has been the creation of leaderless mobs and the growth of anarchic or unstructured violence in the country. Once again, the contribution of the security laws to these developments is both direct and significant.

The increasing resort to force, the suspension of political and legal controls over the security forces, and lack of adherence of the security authorities to the rule of law all served to make it impossible to accept official violence in South Africa as a simple and natural response to antistate subversion and terror. Freed from the constraints of law and political accountability, the security forces pushed conflict resolution decisively in the direction of a military (and therefore nondemocratic) resolution. Secrecy laws ensured that this process took place by stealth and without adequate evaluation or public debate of its frightening consequences.

When we turn from the internal to the cross-border situation, the same phenomenon of an exponential growth of violent incidents is evident. Guerrilla raids into South Africa and defense force strikes across the border until recently regularly took place and were publicized and widely known. There is, however, a darker side to regional conflict in Southern Africa of which knowledge, within South Africa at least, is rather shadowy. The reference here is to defense force involvement in regional conflicts such as the RENAMO/FRELIMO conflict in Mozambique, the toppling of Chief Jonathan in Lesotho, and the Angolan civil war. In all these situations there has clearly been a South African involvement, but the use of official secrets and defense legislation has effectively concealed its exact nature and extent. Occasionally, the statutory veil is lifted when unavoidable publicity follows the more blatant acts of aggression, such as the seizure and abduction of two Swiss nationals from Swaziland. In the main, however, security legislation has ensured that the full facts cannot be made known. More importantly, it has made impossible adequate public debate and evaluation of the repercussions on regional peace and stability of what appear to be the imperialist/military ambitions of a regional superpower. Depending on the degree of success de Klerk enjoys in adhering to the course he has charted for his government, the portents could still promise growing regional conflict and continued public ignorance in South Africa as to where policy would be leading. It would be well if Andrei Sakharov's words could be heeded in South Africa before it is too late. In an interview (*Observer*, 11 January 1987) given just after his release from exile, he said "A state is bound to be more dangerous if it is governed not openly by the people, but secretly by political forces that are not widely known or understood."

NOTES

1. See, for example, Sparks (1986). The de Klerk government has reportedly dissolved the NSMS.

2. See Lelyveld (1986), chapter 6, for a discussion of Sebe.

3. Part of the persuasiveness of the total onslaught philosophy is that it rests upon partial truths of a mainly self-fulfilling kind. The ANC has resorted to armed struggle, which some termed terrorism, and has had contacts with other liberation movements, which again have been charged with terrorism, and its cooperation with Communists and the support it has received from Communist regimes are well known. These are developments for which government policy must accept a large share of the blame.

4. The criteria for official action, despite being detailed and specific, are in reality determined largely by official whim.

5. Section 29 of the Internal Security Act 74 of 1982.

6. *Minister of Law and Order* v. *Hurley* 1986 (3) SA 568 (A).

7. Section 46(3) of the Internal Security Act 74 of 1982.

8. *Metal and Allied Workers Union* v. *Castell N.O.* 1985 (2) SA 280 (D).

9. Section 5A of the Public Safety Act 3 of 1953. Since the withdrawal of the national emergency, a number of areas have been under emergency rules as "unrest areas."

10. Now replaced by the Protection of Information Act 84 of 1982.

11. *S* v. *du Plessis* 1981 (3) SA 382 (A).

12. *S* v. *Hoare* 1982 (4) SA 865 (N).

13. For a brief discussion of these figures, see Mathews (1986:278).

14. Affidavits claiming the torture of young children were read out in Parliament by Helen Suzman at the beginning of the 1987 session (*Sunday Tribune*, 8 February 1987). Official figures released by the minister of law and order indicated that 91 children under fourteen years of age and 167 children under age fifteen were being detained.

REFERENCES

de Villiers, D. P. 1983. "Change in Respect of Security Legislation." In *Change in South Africa*, ed. D.J. van Vuuren et al. Pretoria: Butterworths.

du Plessis, Lourens M. 1985. "Thoughts on Law, Order and State Security." *Tydskrif vir die Suid-Afrikaanse Reg.*

Huntington, Samuel P. 1968. *Political Order in Changing Societies*. New Haven: Yale University Press.

Lelyveld, Joseph. 1986. *Move Your Shadow: South Africa, Black and White.* Johannesburg: Jonathan Bell.

Mathews, Anthony. 1986. *Freedom, State Security, and the Rule of Law: Dilemmas of the Apartheid Society*. Cape Town: Juta and Co.

South African Institute of Race Relations. 1950–51. *Survey of Race Relations in South Africa.* Johannesburg: South African Institute of Race Relations.

———. 1985. *Race Relations Survey*. Johannesburg: South African Institute of Race Relations.

Sparks, Allister. 1986. "Botha's Secret Army." *Observer*, 28 December.

Tapia-Valdës, I.A. 1982. "A Typology of National Security Policies." *Yale Journal of World Public Order* 10, no. 22.

Wilkinson, Paul. 1977. *Terrorism and the Liberal State*. London: Macmillan.

2

White Politics in Transition: Multidimensional Uncertainty

KENNETH W. GRUNDY

It is possible to discern two simultaneous trends in white South African politics today. On the one hand, we can see discord, division, bitter hostility, and internecine struggle for control of the government and for the conscience of the white nation. Hopes have been raised by domestic and regional accommodations. Yet at the same time, there is a growing polarization of the polity along racial lines. Because of white efforts to gain black allies, to divide blacks, and to set black on black, middle-of-the-road politicians of all races are in danger of being isolated and rendered ineffectual. Both the fragmentation and the polarization are reflected over the past fifteen years in the mounting militarization by the parties to the struggle and, in particular, by the government. South Africa's militarization is partly a set of policy responses to what many regard as an increasingly hostile world and to the internal challenge to white rule. It also reflects a change of mood, a pernicious drift into a war mentality.

These trends and processes have already been well described and documented (Cock and Nathan 1989; Dean 1986; Frankel 1984; Grundy 1987, 1988). They span a number of social dimensions—from religious doctrine and the churches to the economy, education, and daily routine. They affect all racial groups, all age levels, and all regions—rural and urban areas, the homelands, the so-called "national states," and neighboring states. It will not be easy to transform a mind-set that for years has shaped interracial politics.

In this regard the struggle of the 1980s and 1990s is, to borrow a much-criticized appellation, a "total onslaught." It is total, not in the sense that the strategic planners and National party politicians use the term to depict a structured, externally fomented and orchestrated attack on every component of the white state, but total in the dynamic sense of a tidal wave rising up and enveloping all in its bore.

In most respects we are dealing with a social issue that involves all population groups. Normally it would be unwise to chop up the study of South African politics into neat racial compartments. There is no question that the turmoil among whites represents disagreement over how best to deal with the tide of black rage. Yet as Stanley Uys (1986) so presciently wrote: "The single, inescapable fact of life in SA today is that nothing is going to change in the white-black conflict until the mould of white politics is broken, because that is where the guns and the power are. This is the starting point. And there is abundant evidence that the mould one day will crack." Blacks may someday acquire the means to smash that mold, but at present most are still struggling to survive. White politics is important chiefly insofar as it addresses or fails to address the questions of black power and majority rule.

The symptoms of the breakdown in the white polity could be seen in the ideological and policy confusions, the ferment, the heightened tensions, the lack of confidence and trust in all quarters, the pattern of constitutional experimentation (within, for blacks, unacceptable parameters), the preparations for a violent showdown, and the retreat by some into rigidity. The impending crisis in white politics is real, yet the struggle with black nationalism is deadlocked. It could remain so for years. It is a costly stalemate—especially for the insecure black community—but it has not hurt the dominant white citizenry enough to force all of them to entertain radical restructuring of the regime. We are witnessing a transitional politics that changes a lot and yet seems to move at a snail's pace.

Because of the presence of a competitive and often critical white press, there is an element of wishful thinking in the coverage. Journalists seem to want to see changes on a scale they can comprehend. They want to spin controversy and portent out of each disclosure. In South Africa's white political arena (mainstream media really do not or are not allowed to follow carefully black politics), subtle shifts, defections, criticisms, and rumors are amplified into trends, and every trend is seen as having profound implications for the future. Still, I do not hold with those who maintain that white politics is irrelevant. In fact, what happens in the white polity quite directly affects the nature, the means, the pace, and the eventual outcome of the black struggle for power. But bear in mind that a measure of balance is required to find meaning and direction in the parade of events. Like the critical intelligence analyst, we must filter out the "noise." In this paper I try to fit the more recent developments in white politics into the total South African picture.

The Fraying of the White Polity

In three distinct areas of white politics, the fabric of order and control is unraveling. First, in the arena of electoral and partisan politics, deep divisions have emerged that are leading to a realignment of partisan identities. Second, in a related public and high-profile arena, parliamentary politics seems to be less and less relevant. Not only is the sequence and pattern of parliamentary affairs new and unclear, but Parliament's lack of leadership and power has led to shifts among white politicians toward extraparliamentary efforts to move the system. Third, in the less open give-and-take of politics within government and within the administrative structures of the state, we can see the emergence of power centers no longer fully obedient to the dictates of government and increasingly developing their own agendas. In short, fragmentation is leading to a restructuring of white politics in ways less familiar to some long-standing South Africa observers.

Electoral/Partisan Politics

In the twenty-one years from the time the National party (NP) gained control of government until the Herstigte Nasionale party (HNP) was formed in 1969, there was no serious challenge to the NP from within the party or the Afrikaner nation. The NP was the voice of the *volk*, and all efforts were made to preserve that exclusive claim. During the 1969 parliamentary session a former cabinet minister, Dr. Albert Hertzog, accused the NP of deviating from its original principles. In his view, only Calvinist Afrikaners could be entrusted with rule in South Africa. Prime Minister B.J. Vorster called an election to weed out the "rebels." This precipitated the resignations of Hertzog and three other M.P.s, who then formed the HNP. But the crude threat from the right posed by the HNP had little immediate electoral impact. HNP candidates usually lost their deposits. At its peak in 1981, the HNP garnered only 11 percent of the vote. No HNP candidate won a seat in a general election, and not until a 1985 by-election was the HNP able to focus its resources and thereby gain a seat. Today the HNP is virtually dead. In the 1989 election, it totaled only 5,501 votes nationally.

A far more serious threat from the NP's right was posed in March 1982, when Dr. Andries Treurnicht, a member of the cabinet and leader of the NP in the Transvaal, along with several other NP members was expelled from the party. Others resigned party membership. There had been speculation that Treurnicht and his followers might join the HNP. But Jaap Marais, then the leader of the HNP, had never forgiven Treurnicht for failing to join the HNP back in 1969. The alliance on the right never came about. Instead, Treurnicht and his fifteen supporters founded the Conservative party (CP), and they were joined by Dr. Connie Mulder and his National Conservative party, a feeble 1979 creation.

With the formation of the CP, the HNP lost much of its support. A 1982 survey showed that HNP support had fallen to 2.7 percent of the electorate (from 6 percent three months earlier), and the CP received the support of 18.3 percent (South Africa Institute of Race Relations 1983:13). Still, the CP's entry into the partisan picture held out the promise of a consolidation of right-wing politics. The CP has a considerable following among lower- and middle-class Afrikaners and among the lower ranks of the civil service, the police, and the defense force. Prior to the May 1987 election, the CP held eighteen seats in the House of Assembly, only two of which they had won at the polls under the CP banner (in by-elections). In the 1987 election the CP won twenty-two seats and became the official opposition. Had the HNP and the CP not split the right-wing votes, the CP might have gained thirty seats. In fact, right-wing appeal is even greater. If South Africa used some form of proportional representation the CP-HNP following would have rendered at least forty-nine seats.

The October 1988 elections for local and municipal councils further marked the CP as a growing force in white politics, but they also demonstrated the boundaries of that power. The CP did especially well in the Transvaal, carrying sixty of the ninety-five municipalities (including Pretoria, where it failed to win a single constituency in the 1987 parliamentary election). In Natal and the Cape Province, the CP made virtually no impact. The vigor with which some CP-controlled councils went about resegregating public facilities and central business districts showed how fanatic is their commitment to old-fashioned apartheid. But it also showed how impractical they were as politicians. This was borne out in the 1989 general election when the CP did poorly in constituencies where their local governmental policies had been enacted.

The CP and other right-wing political elements are a vocal and ominous reality that have served notice on the NP that it has moved too quickly to the left and that the falloff in popular, mostly Afrikaner, support will end its hold on the white citizenry. This is no hollow threat, as the now discontinued Progressive Federal Party (PFP) contended. The ultraright is not a paper tiger. An unsure NP jumped at the right's every move. In that respect, the right's presence was used to justify the government's resistance to demands for significant political reform. Now President de Klerk seems determined to reconfigure the NP base.

In fact, that very lack of serious movement toward reform under P. W. Botha accounted for the emergence of a group of maverick M.P.s, the so-called New Nats, on the NP's left (van Heerden 1986). Most stayed in the NP and had an especially vocal role in the 1989 election campaign. Albert Nothnagel, for example, had written that no lasting peace in South Africa can be achieved without the African National Congress (ANC). Although he had been forced to recant, nowadays people at the heart of NP power utter similar views and act on them. Others, such as Wynand Malan (M.P.-Randburg) and Dr. Denis Worrall (until early 1987 the ambassador in London) resigned the party and ran as independents in the 1987 election. Malan was victorious while the other independents were defeated, Worrall by only thirty-nine votes. The NP easily captured Parliament, holding 123 out of 166 elected seats, yet the government was pinioned between two wings of the party, forced to reconcile incompatible positions.

Other political parties were also in disarray. The New Republic party (NRP), which had held five seats in Parliament and had been reduced to one in 1987, was wracked with defection. Beginning in 1984, some of its leaders joined the NP and others retired. Other senior members announced their resignations because of an NRP election pact with the PFP. Many in the NRP regarded the PFP as "soft" on security issues and on the ANC. Considering that just four years earlier the NRP had campaigned in support of the NP's endorsement of the constitutional referendum, the switch in alliances was surprising. But it did nothing to save the NRP, which today is defunct.

The PFP had been the official opposition for years prior to the 1984 election. Its representation fell from twenty-seven to nineteen seats and its majorities were reduced in several other constituencies. Still, a proportional representation system would have inflated the support for a PFP-NRP-independent coalition to around twenty-nine seats. In keeping with the unsettled tenor of politics, the PFP also faced dissatisfaction on both its right and left fringes. In February 1986 PFP leader Dr. Frederick van Zyl Slabbert and the chairman of the party's federal council, Dr. Alec Boraine, surprised the country when they resigned from the party and from Parliament just a few days into the parliamentary session. Slabbert (1986) claimed that his presence in the Parliament left him with an "overwhelming feeling of absurdity" when measured against what was really happening in South Africa. He vowed to work for an end to apartheid, but outside of the disillusioning parliamentary scene. Longtime PFP parliamentarian Helen Suzman (1986) expressed a more conventional PFP view, determined to use her parliamentary voice for liberal change. (In 1989, however, she announced that she would not stand for reelection in the September elections due to "personal reasons.") On the right Horace van Rensburg had been criticizing his party, and eventually he was forced to resign. He was defeated as an independent in his bid for reelection to Parliament. Further postelection defections on the left, including the PFP national chairman and a second M.P., left the party with only sixteen elected seats and the feeling that it was unable to expand its influence beyond white parliamentary politics. The three

October defectors promptly enrolled in the National Democratic Movement, but they were subsequently reunited with their PFP colleagues when the Democratic party was formed in 1989.

The PFP had constantly grappled with the dilemma of moral rectitude versus pragmatic politics. Should it be true to its nonracial principles and thereby risk becoming a perpetual and ineffective gadfly and opposition party, or should it seek to win elections, appeal to the white center, challenge the NP for power, but in so doing water down its nonracial message? The 1987 electoral results and the events since 1989, however, have led many progressives to question whether they have any serious national appeal to an all-white electorate. Issues such as defense, national military service, dealing with the ANC, constitutional compromises and even legislative reform, and police excesses played on divisions in the PFP. These divisions and the prospect of a purge of the PFP right hovered about for some years, in fact, since the Progressives absorbed members of the disbanded Reform party in 1974 and the United party in 1977.

After months of behind-the-scenes and sometimes public jockeying for advantage, in February 1989 a new party was launched, seeking to bring together those to the left of the NP in Parliament. The Democratic party (DP) stands for universal suffrage and the rule of law in a nonracial South Africa. It sees itself as a bridge, participating in the white House of Assembly and yet open to links with extra-parliamentary organizations, including the ANC even when it was still banned. Initially it unified the PFP, the National Democratic Movement, and the Independent party, together holding twenty-two seats in Parliament. More impressive was the national appeal of two of its leaders, Denis Worrall and Wynand Malan, plus the national electoral base of the PFP, led by Zach de Beer. Yet personality, tactical, and policy differences sap the DP on its fringes. The problem for a party on the left is simple: can it inspire those who have lost confidence in propelling reform from within the parliamentary system? Whether the unification (which may be too strong a word) of the parliamentary parties of the left will reinvigorate what passes for liberalism in South Africa is open to question. The 1989 election helped to provide a partial answer.

The formation of the DP was designed to rectify the absence of any viable, largely white parties to the left. By its very nature the liberal tradition in South Africa had difficulty remaining united. The PFP was rooted in the capitalist economic order. So insignificant were the PFP and the NRP that Adam and Moodley (1986) did not even accord them a section of their own in the chapter titled "Conflicts in White Politics." American journalist Joseph Lelyveld, despite his close acquaintance with PFP members such as Helen Suzman, made little of the PFP impact in his Pulitzer Prize winning book *Move Your Shadow* (1985).

President de Klerk's initiatives may have stolen the march on the DP. The NP has won over many English speakers and Afrikaners who had followed Wynand Malan into the DP coalition. Malan himself subsequently quit Parliament and stepped down as DP co-leader in 1990. The NP has also made serious overtures toward the ANC and by so doing virtually seized the DP's own agenda. Now there is deep debate in the DP as to whether it should continue as the opposition on the left within Parliament, combine with the NP against the right-wing threat, or identify with the ANC and thereby try to position itself for a central role in the "new" South Africa.

In sum, all the major parties show signs of disunity. One can sense, since the 1981 election, a drift toward what in effect is a three-party system. The 1981 election, everywhere but in Natal, amounted to a two-party contest—liberals (PFP) against the ruling conservatives (NP). That sort of analysis, although fundamentally correct then, would be terribly simplistic today. The brooding omnipresence of the reactionary right, so long in the wings, materialized in the form of the CP and the militant, quasi-Nazi movement, the Afrikaner Weer-standsbeweging (AWB). Together the CP and the HNP captured 29.3 percent of the 3.1 million white votes in 1987. The NRP and the HNP fluttered about the sidelines and, except in selected constituencies, had little overall impact on the outcome. By 1989 opposition on the right had registered 31 percent of the white votes. Twenty HNP candidates, however, lost their deposits. The NRP had gone out of existence.

This view of a three party system is not shared by all analysts. Professor Willem Kleynhans (*Financial Mail*, 26 September 1986, 59–60) sees South Africa drifting again toward "two real camps" in white politics: a broadly based grouping of "progressives" centered in the reform-minded NP against conservatives sharing the philosophy of Verwoerd and the old NP. Thus, he regards the NP and the PFP as a natural coalition arrayed against a CP-HNP alliance. The great issue is "color." The right wants to preserve racism, and the reformists favor varying degrees of movement away from racial discrimination. From various by-election results, Kleynhans discerned considerable progressive support for NP candidates. But the petulant behavior of State President P.W. Botha toward reform made one wonder how far the NP was prepared to bend in order not to break.

The alignments within and between parties are still too fluid to group them into two camps. But it is possible to see the emergence of a three-cornered partisan alignment. The dominant force is the center and moderate left of the NP, joined by a few former NRP and PFP conservatives. This combination stands for shared power provided whites exercise a disproportionate role. It is prepared to entertain serious change to deflect external pressures and to mollify and co-opt moderate black opinion. This element still perceives of race politics in group terms. Power sharing with whites retaining dominance seems to be this faction's unstated marching song.

To the right is a vocal and uncompromising constellation of forces led by the CP. Some on the right of the NP feel comfortable with CP views if not the CP's fellow travelers. They are complemented and kept militant by the AWB and other extraparliamentary fanatics. The rightist factions favor racial separation, the old Verwoerdian order. They would like to return to the days when blacks were firmly and ruthlessly suppressed, without apology or guilt.

The leftmost white grouping in Parliament could be called reformist. As presently organized, the Democratic party is prepared to work toward power sharing, but one suspects that its underlying mentality (often unstated) is also that white power must be afforded a disproportionate share of influence and protection through constitutional or legal means. The first electoral test in 1989 demonstrated that the DP is more than a convenient cluster of those to the left of the Nats. Because of the direction in which white politics is heading, the nature of resistance and change in South Africa is such that the reformist coalition seized the opportunity to jell.

The 1987 Election

On the surface, the election of May 6, 1987, was an empty and pointless exercise. Eighty to 85 percent of the adult citizenry were not eligible to vote. As a test of the workings of the new constitution the election was worthless, since neither of the two other racial groups involved in Parliament were permitted to vote.

As the first general election since dissident M.P.s broke away from the NP in February 1982 to form the CP, it served as a general barometer of CP strength nationally and of white resistance to reform. Yet as a test of white opinion, the election was suspect. The positions of the parties were unclear and the white fears expressed at the polls were fairly predictable. State President P.W. Botha claimed that he held the election early because he wanted to learn what white voters would say about "reform." But NP reformist intentions had never been clearly articulated. Delay had been very much a part of the Botha agenda. He made reference to the two centuries that it took the United States to achieve real political rights for blacks. He hinted that the Swiss historical model—it took from 1291 to 1848—is more appropriate for South Africa. The fact is that Botha had nothing to offer black South Africans, at least on his own defined terms. His offers to negotiate with blacks who unconditionally renounce violence went a-begging. The gap was wide and those who were trying to build bridges were unable to demonstrate strong foundations on either bank of the divide.

In short, under Botha there was no evidence that "reform" remotely achieved its goals. On the contrary, the insecurities of change, the inequities of apartheid, and the repression of the state precipitated a black uprising and defiance that smoldered out of control. Moreover, no one in the ruling party seemed prepared to lead South Africa out of the hurting stalemate (Grundy 1990; Zartman 1988).

Another feature of the 1987 election was that the threat to government itself at the polls was almost negligible. No ruling party in South Africa has ever lost an election to a rival on its left. To be sure, the NP was not in the best of health. The threat of defection from New Nats was real. Some 24 percent of NP members expressed dissatisfaction with the pace of reform (*South Africa Digest*, 6 March 1987, 3; *Weekly Mail*, 13 February 1987, 5). NP supporters (52.6 percent of the 1987 electorate) were divided nearly equally on the issue of racial integration (limited though they may envision it). About one-third said "yes," one-third "no," and one-third "don't know." Twenty-four Nat M.P.s, a fifth of the parliamentary caucus, did not stand for reelection. Natural attrition and a desire to avoid a bloodletting in the *volk* explained this unusually high number. But bloodletting occurred, for this election and that of 1989 and the subsequent mobilization of the hidebound right were public manifestations of a continuing *broeder-twis* (brothers' quarrel) among the Afrikaner people.

In fact, a great deal of this generalized dissatisfaction again broke surface after P.W. Botha's "mild" stroke in January 1989. Within two weeks he resigned the party leadership and was promptly replaced by F.W. de Klerk, the NP leader in the Transvaal. With leadership split between an NP chief and a state president, Botha prepared to return to work. To his dismay, the NP caucus and the federal council called for him to step down as president in favor of de Klerk. A crisis was averted when Botha bowed to the near-unanimous pressure and indicated that he would resign as president after a general election, later scheduled for September 1989.

Although the NP was easily returned to power in 1987, it had suffered some embarrassments, too. The NP fell steadily in popularity (from 57 percent of the total vote in 1981 to 52.6 percent in 1987 and 48 percent in 1989). But in light of the weakened state of the other parties, the NP did not suffer the loss of many seats in 1987. But 1989 was different.

The 1989 Election

The parliamentary elections of September 1989 took place in an atmosphere of ferment and confusion. Chief among the issues was the leadership of the National party. Many in the party were anxious to get on with consolidating forces behind the new party leader, de Klerk. But Botha not only felt personally slighted by being forced to step down as party leader but was also determined to stay on as state president until after the election. The rivalry came to a head in August when de Klerk announced that he would visit President Kenneth Kaunda of Zambia before the election; Botha publicly criticized this policy and complained that he had been excluded from the decision. Within days he was forced to resign the presidency, and he did so bitterly on national television.

The DP, however, had its own leadership problems. As a merger of various groupings on the center-left, the party ended up with three leaders (Worrall, de Beer, and Malan). The NP media campaign focused on what it called the Three Blind Mice. Still, enthusiasm ran high in DP and CP circles. They gained added hope from the performance and exposure of opposition candidates in the debates on state television and from the fact that in 1987 many of the seats were decided by very narrow majorities. A small shift of votes might bring about a significant shift of seats. Some analysts were predicting a hung Parliament in which no single party would gain an absolute majority of seats. Then government would be forced to call a second election or to search for coalition partners, either the DP, the CP, or defectors from these groups.

This turned out to be wishful thinking. The NP was returned to power with ninety-three seats. It lost seventeen seats to the CP and twelve to the DP. One seat ended in a CP-NP tie. The DP won thirty-three seats, not quite the combined PFP-NRP total from 1981. But it did manage to win back voters it had lost in its 1987 debacle. Its 20 percent of the electorate still tends to concentrate among English-speakers in Cape Town, Johannesburg, and Natal. The CP took thirty-nine seats and 31 percent of the vote. It managed to break out of its Transvaal heartland, gaining seats in the Free State and Cape Province for the first time. So many NP seats were carried by thin majorities (under 1,000 votes) that a hung Parliament might soon be within reach.

Although the NP lost to the right and left combined only 30,000 votes from its 1987 result, it won only 48 percent of the white votes. So it formed a government with the votes of only 6 percent of the adult population of South Africa—hardly the mandate the NP boasted. The NP seemed lucky in a way: it managed to convince many that its vague vision of change will work while at the same time others believe that the NP is the best hope for avoiding change. The "mandate" is muddied at best and hardly adequate to justify the major shifts necessary to sustain the status quo.

Apartheid was firmly in command, if not in name, at least in effect. Fully 81.6 percent of those who voted in 1987 decided that apartheid in some form is the solution to South Africa's problems. The combined CP, HNP, and NP vote in 1989 was 80 percent, and given de Klerk's continued insistence on "group"-based law, apartheid in some guise is likely to be preferred and maintained.

Given the NP victory and the rise of de Klerk, it would be helpful to discuss the policy direction of the NP. Certainly the balance of forces within the NP is as crucial as the relative strength of other parties. On the surface there were few ideological/policy differences between Botha and de Klerk. If anything, de Klerk's past record indicated an even more conservative leaning than Botha's. De Klerk had been Botha's loyal lieutenant, leading the move to oust Treurnicht from the NP in 1982. Their differences might be characterized as stylistic and managerial. Botha was often irascible, vindictive, and belligerent with his colleagues and even his close associates. He sought, on occasion, to humiliate those who disagreed with him, even though he needed their cooperation. De Klerk, on the other hand, has emerged with a reputation for patience, compromise, and tolerance of criticism in party ranks. He promised a major reformist thrust (but so did Botha make such promises from time to time). Currently, most Nats are prepared to take de Klerk at his word. The NP might well return to the reformist path lost sight of (and scorned by the black leadership) in the last few years. Cooperation among those on the right wing might have reduced the NP majority. But significantly, the CP successes in 1987 and in the 1988 municipal elections had for a while a chilling effect on NP winners in marginal constituencies.

The 1987 and 1989 elections, then, can be regarded as transitional or positioning elections. The issue was not who won—that was a foregone conclusion—but who came in second and what the outcome and the campaign itself demonstrated with regard to Afrikaner cohesion and to the English speakers' proclivities. Which party is best positioned to replace the Nats, or, if it is to be the Nats in the future, who will set the ideological tone for the party? The elections were, at best, an imprecise barometer of an increasingly fragmented yet still dangerous white minority.

In a fashion, many of these questions have been answered and others have been deferred. It seems clear that the NP, although not well organized and generally without enthusiasm, emerged from the voting in command of the government and its vital institutions. The

NP succession issue, barring a major stumble, seems to have been resolved. De Klerk went into the election with a reservoir of popularity that Botha had never achieved.

On the other hand, a number of questions remain unanswered. The status of the opposition, to the right and to the left of the Nats, is uncertain. The CP is active, yet it is periodically embarrassed by the antics of its right-wing fellow travelers, who it is often reluctant to criticize. Its geographical appeal is bounded, and hence it risks being regarded largely as a provincial phenomenon. On the left, the DP responded well in the 1989 election, and yet its diverse composition hints of possible disintegration should the major political questions be posed in a divisive fashion. In fact, de Klerk's dynamic approach to negotiations may have rendered the DP irrelevant. In that regard, the 1989 election again serves as an indicator of future trends.

Parliamentary/Extraparliamentary Politics

Since the institution of the tricameral Parliament in 1984, legislative politics has been somewhat experimental. Procedures are sometimes worked out in process. Trial and error is common and the parties and structures seem to operate in the dark. Particularly unsure of themselves are the Colored and Indian chambers and their members. The NP government and the drafters of the constitution carefully assured that NP predominance would be maintained over all (Boulle 1984). Although members of the House of Delegates (Indian) and House of Representatives (Colored) and the white opposition party members outnumber the NP, in the aggregate and on the standing committees, the Colored, white, and Indian members vote separately, in "blocs," and are required to consult their caucuses before voting. There is no commitment to consensus government.

If, by chance, the NP should be unable to get its way in Parliament, government has a backup in the sixty-member President's Council, two-thirds of whom are white. The council has both decision-making and advisory functions. It examines selected problems at the request of the state president (e.g., the Group Areas Act and the Reservation of Separate Amenities Act), and its specialist committees may look at the more general issues (economic, social, or constitutional affairs). Its primary function is to offer advice to Parliament.

When disagreements arise among the three houses of Parliament, and even when the white House of Assembly is opposed by the other two chambers, the state president decides on his own whether to submit the disagreement to the President's Council. When the Houses of Representatives and Delegates refused to pass two controversial security bills put before them in 1986, President Botha used the

President's Council with its NP majority to override them. Only the NP and the CP voted for the bills. All the Colored and Indian parties and the PFP opposed them. Opponents objected both to the procedures used to present the bills and to the substance of the bills. Yet the bills were enacted into law. Of course, the government could also declare a state of emergency under the Public Safety Act, as it did in June 1986, to assert its will over parliamentary objections.

The case of the 1986 security bills is unusual because it involves members of Parliament opposing government initiatives and support- ing a more active defense of political and civil liberties. Far more common criticisms of Parliament are that it lacks courage and imagi- nation and that it serves merely to legislate government policy deci- sions. The real reason for the inadequacy of Parliament has been the growing concentration of power in the hands of the executive. Since P.W. Botha became prime minister in 1978, the Parliament (until 1984 only a white House of Assembly) has declined in importance, as has the parliamentary caucus of the NP. How ironic it is that outsiders demanded that the South African government negotiate with genuine black leaders, when the government under Botha did not even con- sult seriously its own party caucus.

Parliament today is little more than the public phase of a decisional process controlled by the cabinet. As a public institution that is sup- posed to embody the principles of open debate and deliberation, Parliament is unwieldy. The tricameral legislature does not work as smoothly as the NP had hoped. It has not deflected outside world pres- sure, nor has it convinced South Africans that it is inclusive and "multiracial." Parliament has compounded managerial awkwardness, especially in those rare instances when it refuses to rubber-stamp gov- ernment's decisions arrived at in camera.

The DP and the CP realize the impossibility of bending Parliament to their legislative purposes. Nonetheless, they attempt to use ques- tion time and the debates to force government to reveal more and more information regarding government corruption, emergency con- ditions, budget, and the security situation. Although Parliament remained the only quasi-reliable official source of information under the state of emergency, the fact is that under Botha government dis- closed less and less information under the generalized excuse that dis- closure would not be in the country's interests. Particularly on the issue of security, questions were dodged. The sort of data that were compiled on blacks in the security forces back in the late 1970s and early 1980s would not have been made public in the final Botha years (Grundy 1983). Parliament might also be used, as it had been by the PFP, to make public what it had independently come to learn about the emergency. But even these practices were severely curtailed, and especially the media's right to report them, when government contended that parliamentary reports must not promote the cause of "undemocratic organizations." The official opposition is no longer to the left of government, but even before the 1987 election centrist-left parties appeared to be rethinking their role as publicists on apartheid and civil liberties (*Star*, 20 December 1986; *Financial Mail*, 2 January 1987, 21 and 24).

Institutionally, since Botha came to power, and even more markedly since the 1983 constitution came into force, white politics evolved from a constitutional parliamentary limited democracy into a de facto bureaucratic/security autocracy. The 1983 Republic of South Africa Constitution Act vested vast powers in the executive arm of government, powers that, to a large extent, the Botha government had already exercised before the new constitution was in place. Other than the occasional but necessary legislative authorization (especially regarding the expenditure of state funds), government was conducted largely without parliamentary cooperation.

Even if, under the new constitution, the executive is unable to obtain the legislation it proposes, it can resort to extraparliamentary powers. In addition, the state president now enjoys greater security of tenure vis-à-vis Parliament than did prime ministers under the 1961 republican constitution. Even a majority of parliamentary members or chambers cannot force his removal. Built-in "fail-safe" provisions prevent politicians in the Colored and Indian chambers from removing the state president. The State Security Council under Botha served as an "inner cabinet," further removing the executive from moderate black influence and from parliamentary oversight, indecision, and recalcitrance (Grundy 1988).

The de Klerk style is still in flux, especially in light of the fluid agenda of negotiation with the black majority. The sensitive and delicate nature of his position vis-à-vis the black majority and the ANC and his growing unpopularity among his Afrikaner constituents mean that he must feel free to move swiftly as challenges arise. The powers centralized under Botha serve de Klerk well, but as he exercises them, he further alienates the most uncompromising white voters, many of whom seem determined to act against black militants, independent of government policy.

In sum, power in the white polity comes from the top down, and decisions are arrived at in camera, not in public (Dean 1986). Even the white chamber of Parliament is increasingly powerless. The NP caucus in the House of Assembly listens to the state president, not the other way around. This secretive style of government came to blanket politics at the local and regional as well as national levels. The pervasive National Security Management System (NSMS) and its web of committees and subcommittees hardly encouraged representative government, as A.S. Mathews has so clearly shown in the previous chapter, unless we are speaking of representing the security and civil services rather than the citizenry. Since the NSMS was Botha's instrument, however, not de Klerk's, de Klerk in late 1989 took steps to downgrade it and to remove it from defense force influence. Government uses Parliament when it can and avoids Parliament when it must. Often it is rule by administrative fiat. If there is to be a fundamental change in South Africa, even among white South Africans, it will likely take place outside of Parliament, not within it.

Blacks have always been excluded from the centers of power. More recently whites have come to realize the implications of this and have formed groups that reflect the bankruptcy of parliamentary politics. The Slabbert and Boraine resignations speak directly to the powerlessness of the legislature, not just for progressives but for all parties.

A plethora of new white groups, on the right and on the left, have emerged to try to encourage extraparliamentary change. It would not be possible at this juncture to describe the politics of all of these groups. On the left, the End Conscription Campaign (banned in August 1988), Slabbert's Institute for a Democratic Alternative for South Africa, and the Johannesburg Democratic Action Committee, to name just three, seek to educate and move the white citizenry toward nonracial, unitary, and democratic governmental forms. Some largely white organizations are affiliated with the United Democratic Front. They also seek to close the racial divisions in society and to create nonviolent and national means to end apartheid and the insensitive and exploitative capitalist structures. Their members sense that Parliament, as presently constituted and chosen, is an inadequate instrument for radical change.

The right has not given up entirely on Parliament. Indeed, the CP as the official opposition intends to use Parliament to broadcast its views and hopes eventually to form a government. Many other right-wingers are prepared to abandon Parliament altogether if middle-of-the-road Nats should be pushed to concede too much (which, to the right, means virtually any concession) to black sensibilities. Within the long-established Afrikaner organizations are vocal and uncompromising fringes. The Broederbond, the Ruiterwag, the Dutch Reformed churches, the press, diverse professional and cultural associations, student and sports groups, and trade unions have all faced revolt and dissent.

More importantly, more militant right-wing groups have been formed and have grown in strength. They include the Blanke Bevrijdingsbeweging (White Liberation Movement, banned in November 1988 and unbanned in February 1990), the openly violent

Wit Wolwe (White Wolves), the separatists of the Vereniging van Oranjewerkers (Society of Orange Workers) and the Boerestaatparty, the Afrikaner Volkswag (a "nonpolitical" cultural organization that seeks to offset "liberal influences"), and the Afrikaner Weerstands-beweging (AWB), a paramilitary neo-Nazi organization with its own "Blitzkommando." There are dozens of smaller right-wing fringe factions. Some of these groups have allied with reactionary parties. Some seem ready to take up arms, to launch a new Boer war. Most seem to abide by the maxim "Dominate or be dominated." Most work exclusively outside the formal institutions of electoral polititcs. But as a growing phenomenon they testify to the right wing's disenchantment with even modest, conservatorial changes forced upon the NP. Although formally extraparliamentary, these groups have an impact on the ruling party, on the CP, and on their members in Parliament and at local and provincial governmental levels.

The search for alternative political models goes on constantly in South Africa and not just on the fringes of electoral/parliamentary politics. Conservative bridge building, it might be called. The essential purpose is to hit upon formulas to conserve, as much as possible, the semblance of order and Western (read "white") power and influence in a perceived ominous, Third World (read "black") sea. Many of the schemes so devised fasten on providing inducements for whites to stay on (bills of rights, weighted voting, parity in legislative bodies, territorial juggling, and federal divisions) at the same time that they experiment with ideas of "power sharing," group- or race-based cooperation and consultation, and even limited majority rule. At base, however, what most have in common is a group-based framework in which the franchise, the distribution of seats, or the weight of political influence at the central, provincial, and local levels is founded on group identity rather than on numerical, majoritarian, or nonracial considerations.

Perhaps the most publicized but probably stillborn experiment to bridge the impasse was played out in Natal province. There, after months of hard bargaining, an agreement was reached in November 1986 by twenty-four of thirty-seven delegations that participated in an *indaba*, or high-level conference. The *indaba* participants sought a multiracial regional government for Natal and for the black bantustan of KwaZulu. Theirs was an innovative set of proposals that encompassed a bicameral legislature and an executive that included majority and minority parties. The proposed legislature was to consist of a one-hundred-seat lower chamber elected on the basis of one-person, one-vote by proportional representation, and a fifty-seat upper chamber with ten seats each for Africans, Indians, Afrikaners, and English speakers, and ten additional seats for people who do not wish to be classified racially or culturally. Another crucial issue involved the proposed division of authority between the central government in Pretoria and the proposed government of "KwaNatal." But the group basis of so many of its provisions rendered the proposal unsatisfactory to black progressives.

Experimentation may be necessary to save South Africa. Many liberals in South Africa and some conservatives in the West hope that cooperative provincial and regional plans can be implemented that, if they should work, would have a demonstration effect on the populace and on the central government and might lead South Africa out of its current violent stalemate. No sooner was the KwaNatal plan announced, however, than it was rejected by the Natal leader of the NP (*Weekly Mail*, 5 December 1986, 12–13). The proposal did not, he said, provide for "effective and equal powersharing." Later, at the opening of Parliament in 1987, P.W. Botha offered a more definitive rejection of the plan. In addition, many political candidates who advocated an *indaba*-like solution fared badly in the parliamentary election.

The indaba was doomed from the start. The two major forces in the South African struggle, Afrikaner nationalism and radical black nationalism, were not party to the agreement. They refused to participate, although the NP opted for observer status. A constellation of radical popular black organizations—the ANC, UDF, PAC, and Black Consciousness groups—declined invitations from the outset. Inkatha, the Zulu "cultural" organization, was the only major black body to sign the agreement. Black nationalists regard the indaba as a ruse to prolong white control by using black "collaborators," such as Chief Mangosuthu Buthelezi's Inkatha and the Indian parties. The Afrikaner cultural and commercial organizations that participated in the deliberations either refused to sign or abstained. They reflect, presumably, the long-standing Afrikaner fear that English-speaking whites might enfranchise blacks and then ally with them to end Afrikaner political domination.

Divisions within the Executive Branch

A further evidence of the fragmentation of white politics is the growth of divisions within the executive branch itself. Simply put, even if a firm direction for change should be decided upon by government, by Parliament, by the NP, and in concert with the ANC, it is not altogether clear that the policies would or could be implemented.

Within the executive are pockets of resistance, offices and agencies and departments less committed, indeed, downright resistant, to change and reform. The civil service, in particular, has a reputation for dragging its feet on reform. High-court rulings such as the *Rikhoto* judgment of 1983 regarding residence rights under the Blacks (Urban

Areas) Consolidation Act have been slow to be enforced. The repeal of the Prohibition of Mixed Marriages Act of 1949 has changed little, and applications for waiver of the Group Areas Act for mixed-race couples are denied more often than not. The active cooperation of the massive state bureaucracy is imperative if reform or, more important, radical change is to move at a pace necessary to deflect the masses. That cooperation is not likely.

Competition for influence, especially regarding foreign policy and security policy, is intense. To appreciate why, it is necessary to address the impact of the rise of the security establishment and the growing militarization of the country. Suffice it to say here that while the white government pleads frustration because it claims not to know who speaks for black South Africans, it is not clear, on some issues, who speaks for white South Africa. Either the government has used this fragmentation as an effective dodge or excuse for its inaction, or, in fact, there is a struggle at the top for determination and control of policy.

The government under Botha developed no coherent program. Given the present distribution of power, the content of reform is confusing. Nationalist control of the polity is assured, yet Afrikanerdom is split. As Adam and Moodley (1986:69) contend, the reform process may develop its own dynamic, but for now, under de Klerk it faces profound resistance. Neither power bloc is unified and able to assure compliance. Energies for too long were centered on control and repression of the black populace and on resistance to external sanctions. The collective morale of the white establishment is more divided and disorganized than it has ever been since the Nats took power, and de Klerk has only slightly improved that picture. Most whites realize that the old order cannot be restored, that some change is imperative to preserve white interests even if the white oligopoly of legitimate power cannot be justified or held.

In restructuring white politics, ad hoc conservative politics has led to a shift in the arena of white politics from the parties and Parliament to the executive, the bureaucracy, and the security establishment. The regime until Mandela's release was in retreat—economically, ideologically, diplomatically, and politically, but not militarily. The retreat was toward the ultimate base of white power, the instruments of force.

Militarization

Perhaps the most dominant feature of life in South Africa these days is the increased prospect of negotiation and significant restructuring, with their conflicting meanings to the various parties, alongside the continued militarization of diverse aspects of politics and society (Grundy 1987, 1988). Certainly for someone who has been victimized by the South African authorities, it would be fair to say that the regime has all along possessed militaristic tendencies. Violence, coercion, and repression have been and still are the handmaidens of the racist order.

Nonetheless, one can discern since the Soweto uprising in 1976 and especially after P.W. Botha took over as prime minister in 1978, a pernicious militarization of the South African polity. Although de Klerk has made efforts to downgrade the "securocrats," the evidence is still unclear that this has occurred. And because of Botha's official orientation, many segments of society have taken up the theme. By militarization is meant the process of imbuing individuals and hence institutions and groups with a belief that their lives and fortunes are most obviously a product of coercion and violence. As a result they perceive their problems at base as issues of power, which they narrowly define in coercive terms. For wide segments of the populace, life becomes a series of circumstances associated with asserting dominance and protecting, in physical terms, life, space, rights, privileges, and possessions.

Central to this trend has been the rise of what might be called the security establishment. Diverse public and some private institutions and agencies charged with the management of security, strategy, and defense have grown in size and importance in national life. Many of these bodies compete with one another for influence and budgetary favor. But taken as a group, they stand as an effective force proclaiming a consistent if not uniform militaristic perspective on state policy. Their sometimes insecure, often pugnacious *weltanschauung* sees public issues primarily in terms of defense of the South African regime. From that perspective they have demanded and have been given a greater voice in policy issues not normally regarded as defense or security issues.

A form of Gresham's law of militarism has applied, by which the cooperative, negotiable, and compromisable have been driven out by the violent and assertive. The heavy-handed wielding of power has been rationalized. Moderation, tolerance, and cooperation have retreated. The military metaphor has replaced the diplomatic and the conciliatory. There have been occasions and even longer periods when negotiation appeared to be popular in government circles, but invariably the government has returned to the ultimate foundation of the racist state, coercion.

The establishment of the Conservative party as official opposition in 1987 only added to this trend. In the words of its leader, Andries Treurnicht, "Minority rights cannot be protected democratically. A minority must have military power so that it can assert itself" (*Financial Mail,* 10 April 1987, 57).

It is not necessary to document the increased levels of violence, including civil unrest, detentions, protests that become violent, and bombings; the spread of weaponry, beatings, and political intimidation; the frequent deployment of the South African Police (SAP), the South African Defense Force (SADF), and special auxiliary forces; and the rise in vigilantism and free-lance banditry. The spiraling effects of this heightened insecurity under the guise of reestablishing stability were pervasive. What emerged in South Africa is what Richard A. Falk (1971) has called, when looking at the larger global context, a "self-help War system": a set of social and political relationships in which activists assumed and expected that violence was likely to be used to settle conflicts with other groups and among hostile factions in their midst, and even if negotiation is in process, the ability to demonstrate coercive power provides the effective leverage in "peaceful" talks.

How many times had P.W. Botha or Magnus Malan or Adriaan Vlok justified the use of force and warned of their intentions to use more? The SADF threatened that it had "not even started to use [its] muscle and capabilities" against neighboring states. Opponents of South Africa were told that they were safe nowhere. But the government was not alone in threatening violence. Eugene TerreBlanche of the AWB postures for the extreme right with characteristic bravado: "I want to tell the world out there and the ANC: Touch the Boer nation and we'll blast you until you are level with the ground!" (*Star,* 2 June 1986, 15) For members of the South African right, *kragdadigheid* is a way of thought and of life. Their newfound popularity and militancy have precipitated a need for counterorganization among blacks, in self-defense.

Overall, however, the mood of white South Africa is less pessimistic than it was under Botha. An early 1988 survey (du Pisani 1988:5–6) indicated that 55.8 percent of whites think that a Namibian-type guerrilla war will eventually develop in South Africa. A similar 1986 survey reported that 71.1 percent of whites held that opinion. Partisans of left and right white parties were even more convinced of war's unavoidability. However, more and more whites are convinced that the SAP and SADF can control the domestic unrest. Some three-quarters of those interviewed felt some confidence in the security forces. A mark of the division among communities was that only 26.5 percent of the white respondents felt that "South Africa's blacks have a good reason to take up arms against the government." De Klerk's unbanning of antiapartheid groups, his release of Mandela, the end to the state of emergency, and the launching of talks, seem to have opened white eyes to the seriousness of black grievances even as they have further polarized the white citizenry.

The primary impact of militarization was modal, atmospheric, and paradigmatic. It remains to be seen if the more positive attitude toward talks has similar ramifications. When segments of society behave as if confrontation and armed struggle are inevitable, the tension escalates.

If the white ruling elite is not unified, its members share what has been called a survival ideology, the lowest common denominator of a divided ruling class under siege. All whites did not share the view that they faced a "total onslaught," and even some who perceived an onslaught contend that the way to deal with it is to remove the causes for discontent and protest. For them, if the regime were to revert to a full-scale police state, this would precipitate deep ideological cleavages among the white elite. It would test the bonds of racial cohesion. It would leave the vaguely united white front further fractured. Today, the idea of "total onslaught" has been widely discredited.

Militarization was also manifest in a variety of policies, most openly in the deployment of SADF troops in the townships and the homelands deep inside South Africa. Several current strategic themes indicate that defense force planners are increasingly concerned with the domestic scene. What in the past had been the responsibility of the departments of police, justice, Bantu affairs, internal affairs, community development, and law and order, for example, now includes and in some instances has become a major responsibility of defense. And since the independence of Namibia and the pressure for a cease-fire on Angola, the redeployment of these forces in South Africa is more likely.

An important development in the shifting security situation and one with wide political ramifications was the increased insinuation of military and security considerations into South African policy making. Indeed, there had been a growing, direct involvement of security personnel in the decision-making process at all levels of government. This was manifest chiefly in the National Security Management System, whose rise to prominence had been called by the *Weekly Mail* (3 October 1986, 1 and 12–13) "the army's quiet coup." While this may be an exaggeration, it does draw attention to a neglected feature of South African politics. Most of the attention has heretofore been paid to the State Security Council (SSC) (Dean 1986; Geldenhuys and Seiler 1984). The SSC was at the pinnacle of the NSMS. Formally it was a cabinet committee that met twice a week and "advised" the cabinet on security matters. In reality its conception of security was all-inclusive.

The SSC, its work committee, and the interdepartmental committees beneath them were just the tip of the iceberg. What was revealed was an elaborate network of operative bodies fleshing out the NSMS.

There were 9 joint management centers (JMCs) operating at the regional level, 82 sub-JMCs, and 320 mini-JMCs at local levels. Virtually the entire country, to one degree or another, was drawn into the security network. It was a parallel administration, one not subject to the ordinary constraints of elective politics. It touched all manner of public issues. The provision of water or housing, for example, may not normally be regarded as a security question, but if a local mini-JMC sensed that lack of these services might lead to a riot or a protest, then it became a security matter (Boraine 1989). The NSMS reflected the "total strategy" against the "total onslaught." Furthermore, should ordinary civil government falter or break down, the JMCs were in place to provide an alternate administrative structure. The civilian and military arms of government were locked together, often under military direction. The resistance and resulting instability since 1984 speeded up this process. De Klerk's effort to gain control of this alternative administration was as much an element of intrawhite politics as an approach to black protest.

Aware that it would be costly, if not impossible, to fight both an external and an internal war simultaneously, some SADF thinkers urged domestic political, economic, and social reforms to defuse the tense conditions in the townships and a firm demonstration of power to assert their control. The proposed strategy was one of using the carrot and the stick in tandem, of keeping the "enemy" off balance.

To establish domestic order, SADF personnel were increasingly deployed throughout the country. The Civic Action program ostensibly provided the carrots. The armed troops were the stick. But in the end, the purpose was singular—to tamp down and contain the revolution and to keep control in the hands of the NP government. The policy of coercion, the stick, was most evident and commanded the attention of the citizens and policymakers. A succession of executive orders, regulations, and legislation gave the security forces greater latitude in suppressing resistance. The two states of emergency, from June 1985 to March 1986 in selected magisterial districts, and nationwide from June 12, 1986, until October 1990, were the most comprehensive.

SADF personnel received authority (formerly reserved to the police) to search for and seize articles and, in some instances, to detain people and disperse crowds. Government regulations are still enforced with zeal beyond reason. Much of this is legally beyond the scrutiny of the media and the courts. No single issue seems to have focused black anger and opposition to the government more than the presence of the army in the townships. Among whites, a "Troops Out" campaign was launched by the End Conscription Campaign, but it achieved little more than sensitizing some white national service recruits and their families to their own collaboration with repression.

In the overall domestic context, we saw the regime trying to foster a defensive and security perspective among leaders in a variety of civilian institutions. The authorities tried to engage the industrial and financial elite in advisory roles. They sought to establish civil defense programs at various economic installations (state and private). The National Key Points Acts seek to provide for the defense of important facilities. Commandos are required to be organized throughout the economic community. All facets of business have been made security conscious. In South Africa's current economic doldrums, security is one of the few growth industries. Most important, a viable defense industry was created to counter sanctions, boycotts, and embargoes and to assure domestic supplies of strategic matériel. A number of decisions regarding domestic production of nonstrategic products have been shaped by government pressures relating to the NP perception of onslaught.

In education, the media, research, and constitutional revision, security is still a key consideration. Certainly many whites resist this tendency. Parents, for example, counter efforts by government to propagandize their youngsters at schools. Many criticize school cadets, veld schools, visits by SADF representatives to schools, recruitment in the schools, and field trips to military installations. Militarization has grown but is not uniformly accepted.

The militarization has been internationalized as well. In the face of a mobilizing black resistance, the already militarized state apparatus has engaged in diverse policies that threatened and weakened other governments in the Southern African region (Grundy 1987). The state did this under the pretense of striking at ANC and South West African People's Organization (SWAPO) operatives in exile. But this, of course, was only part of the picture. Much has been undertaken in clandestine actions directly involving SADF and related units or else by proxy forces either created or aided by the South African government.

Conclusion

The tendencies discussed above—greater pressure for white unity in the face of the "revolutionary onslaught," growing militarization of large sectors of the citizenry and the polity, and the further fragmentation of the white elite—were to be expected. The white polity never has been fully unified. It was almost inevitable that when confronted by a serious and of necessity violent challenge from the black majority, already existing cleavages would widen over how best to address the dissatisfaction, protest, and threat.

Despite the economic and political advantages of their skin color, many white South Africans do not accept the ideological baggage associated with apartheid. Others who do are not prepared to risk all to defend what they know to be morally unacceptable. Still others see this as a time of opportunity—a chance to address problems definitively, a chance to restructure society along more equitable lines that might lead to an inherently more stable order. Tensions, in short, bring out the best in some people, the worst in others. But common problems do not inevitably mean solidarity—unless they are allowed to destroy entirely the openness and vitality of white society. That, of course, is very much a possibility. Today the regime is not sure where it is heading, but at least it seems open to participation by all population groups.

Oh, for those crystalline days when Professor Gwendolen M. Carter (1959) drafted her pathfinding study, *The Politics of Inequality* (1958; rev. ed. 1959). The Nats knew what they wanted and where they were going. The Liberals likewise saw a preferred future with clarity. The United party, more muddleheaded and disputatious, still had some cohesion and direction. Today there are as many constitutional schemes and political proposals as there are politicians—and more still, for the continuous social changes lead to continuous modifications, adaptations, and emendations. The South Africa of thirty years ago and the South Africa of today could hardly be more different. In that bygone era, those in power saw their land ostensibly as a tabula rasa on which white dreams and aspirations could be etched. At that time, Professor Carter was correct when she wrote: "Throughout much of the discussion of South African affairs in this book non-Europeans have been virtually disregarded. This is because, in practice, they have relatively little to say about the political, economic or social policies which affect their lives" (1959:417).

Yet Professor Carter also appreciated that it would never stay that way. Blacks would, in the end, become "the most important factor of all" in South Africa's future. Blacks would eventually speak out, assert themselves, and act on those demands. Therein lies the apparent confusion and chaos of the present white political scene. A large part of the white political contest is caught up in responding to black initiatives and in trying to anticipate black reactions to white initiatives.

REFERENCES

Adam, Heribert, and Kogila Moodley. 1986. *South Africa Without Apartheid: Dismantling Racial Domination*. Berkeley: University of California Press.
Boraine, Andrew. 1989. "Security Management Upgrading in Black Townships." *Transformation* 8:47–63.

Boulle, L. J. 1984. *Constitutional Reform and the Apartheid State: Legitimacy, Consociationalism and Control in South Africa*. New York: St. Martin's Press.

Carter, Gwendolen M. 1959. *The Politics of Inequality: South Africa since 1948*. 2d ed. London: Thames and Hudson.

Cock, Jacklyn, and Laurie Nathan. 1989. *War and Society: The Militarisation of South Africa*. Cape Town: David Philip.

Dean, Barry. 1986. "Control by Cabal." *Leadership* 5(4): 58–62.

du Pisani, André. 1988. *What Do We Think? A Survey of White Opinion on Foreign Policy Issues*. No. 4. Johannesburg: South Africa Institute of International Affairs.

Falk, Richard A. 1971. *This Endangered Planet: Prospects and Proposals for Human Survival*. New York: Random House.

Financial Mail. (Johannesburg). 1986 and 1987.

Frankel, Philip H. 1984. *Pretoria's Praetorians: Civil-Military Relations in South Africa*. Cambridge: Cambridge University Press.

Geldenhuys, Deon, and John Seiler. 1984. "South Africa's Evolving State Security System." Paper presented at the International Political Science Association meeting, West Berlin, September 15.

Grundy, Kenneth W. 1983. *Soldiers Without Politics: Blacks in the South African Armed Forces*. Berkeley: University of California Press.

———. 1987. "Regional Coercion for Domestic Domination: South Africa's Militarization at Home and Abroad." Paper presented at a conference on "Militarisation in the Third World" at Queen's University, Kingston, Ontario, January.

———. 1988. *The Militarization of South African Politics*. Rev. ed. Oxford: Oxford University Press.

———. 1990. "Some Thoughts on the Demilitarization of South and Southern Africa." In *Toward Peace and Security in Southern Africa*, ed. Harvey Glickman. New York: Gordon and Breach.

Lelyveld, Joseph. 1985. *Move Your Shadow: South Africa, Black and White*. New York: Random House.

Slabbert, Frederick van Zyl. 1986. "Into the Wilderness." *Leadership* 5(1): 50–53.

South Africa, House of Assembly. 1986 and 1987. *Debates (Hansard)*.

South African Digest. 1987. 6 March, 3.

South African Institute of Race Relations. 1983. *Survey of Race Relations in South Africa, 1982*. Johannesburg: South African Institute of Race Relations.

Star (Johannesburg). 1985–1986. Weekly air edition.

Suzman, Helen. 1986. "Interview." *Leadership* 5(1): 34–41.

Uys, Stanley. 1986. "It's Incomprehensible." *Financial Mail*, 21 February, 60.

van Heerden, Dries. 1986. "The New Nats." *Frontline*, March, 35–37.

Weekly Mail (Johannesburg). 1986 and 1987.

Zartman, I. William. 1988. "Negotiations in South Africa." *Washington Quarterly*. 11(4)(Autumn):141–58.

3

Between the Hammer and the Anvil: The Quandary of Liberalism in South Africa

C. J. DRIVER

Because this essay constitutes a personal view of the future of South African liberalism in the context of the escalating violence and instability of the region, I must begin with various disclaimers. First, I am not a scholar; I am a headmaster—what North Americans would call a high school principal—and, in my not very spare time, a writer, mainly of fiction. More than seventy years ago, Ian Hay noted that "a Headmaster is too busy a personage to keep his own scholarship tuned up to concert pitch; and if he devotes adequate time to this object— and a scholar must practise almost as diligently as a pianist or an acrobat if he is to remain in the first flight—he will have little leisure left for less intellectual but equally vital duties" (Hay 1915:5).

Furthermore, I have, to a large extent, been excluded from the future of South Africa; this is partly by my own choice—I chose to leave South Africa in 1964 after serving two years as president of the National Union of South African Students (NUSAS) and four weeks in police detention and solitary confinement under the old Ninety Day Detention Act. I did not choose to have my South African passport taken away from me in 1965, nor to have my citizenship revoked, nor to become the prohibited immigrant in that country which I still am— though I have twice in recent years been allowed to visit briefly a brother who has since died of cancer. I did not choose to have my first two novels banned in South Africa. One has recently been unbanned and republished, but one has been rebanned (*Send War in Our Time, O Lord* [1970]); the South African authorities are not strong on irony. However, I did choose to disengage myself physically from South Africa, and, in a sense, that disqualifies me from talking about its future. In self-defense, I would say I am not of the right stature for quietly subversive work, and I did not relish the idea of spending most of my life in and out of jail, which I suspected would be a main consequence of a commitment to South African politics. I was also fairly sure then—as now—that it is not the proper role of white liberals to be sacrificial lambs; yet for a white liberal to keep out of jail is all too easy. Lacking the faith of the political martyr and the selfless ambition of the scholar, I confess I also lack the chutzpah of the genuine journalist; I retreat from revolutions, takeovers, intrusions, and telephone calls. So, when I am not a headmaster, I am a writer of what purports to be more truth than actuality; and perhaps there is inevitably an element of imaginative fiction in this essay, since I am describing what has not yet happened.

In disclaiming scholarship, I must also refer to my biography (1980) of the South African radical politician Patrick Duncan. Though I suppose it must be counted as a work of scholarship, its motivating force was not scholarship but a desire to understand and explain a complicated man—a novelist's purpose rather than a scholar's. May I also inform those who do not know the book (I fear, judging by its lack of sales, a large majority of any audience) that much of the scholarship was provided by my research assistant for the book, Tom Lodge, a genuine scholar by any reckoning, as a study of his book, *Black Politics in South Africa since 1945* (1983), will surely reveal. One may not delegate scholarship, but one may make good use of scholarly friends, as I have done in this essay and elsewhere.

Definitions

Before I say what I think is happening in South Africa and then extrapolate some of what I think may happen, I must explain something about the meaning of the term *liberal* in South Africa.[1] There are problems in any discussion involving this term; like the word *romantic*, it has come to mean so many things that it may have ceased to serve any useful function as a verbal sign. In South Africa whites often use *liberal* to mean "nonracial," and some joined the now disbanded Liberal party only because they and it were nonracial. Since Communists also claimed to be nonracial, *Communist* and *liberal* became synonymous, though not to Communists, liberals, or Liberals. There were, for instance, some in the Congress of Democrats who called themselves liberal, though never "liberals": that is, on the white left, the adjective *liberal* was less pejorative than the substantive *liberal* or the designation Liberal. There were some who joined the Liberal party who would, in most other societies, have called themselves socialists, and some who would have called themselves conservatives. The extent of one's liberalism in the Liberal party could sometimes be defined in terms of the lengths to which one was prepared to go in opposing racialism and the government; thus Patrick Duncan was very liberal, a "left-wing liberal." Sometimes one's left-wing-ness in the Liberal party could be defined in terms of one's commitment to socialism; in those terms Patrick Duncan was not very liberal, or he was a "right-wing liberal." Sometimes liberal was defined in relation to the Congress movement, the alliance of anti-apartheid organizations in the 1950s headed by the African National Congress (ANC). As Brian Bunting wrote: "There is no ideological unity in the Liberal Party, there are only Liberals and Liberals. One wing of the Liberal Party can almost be described as reactionary; but another wing is moving ever closer to the Congress point of view, and already works closely with the Congresses in some centres" (Bunting 1957:18). In those terms, Duncan was very liberal in his desire to cooperate with the Congresses but reactionary in his attitude to communism. Yet another complication is that whereas many whites used *liberal* or *liberalistic* in a pejorative sense of "nonracial" (also "impolitic," "impractical," "dangerous," and "wicked"), many blacks (not only in Southern Africa) used liberal in a sense of "halfhearted," "condescending," or, occasionally, as a synonym of "bourgeois," or "not in favor of complete equality of white and black."

Yet for all the problems of the term and for all the lack of ideological unity in the Liberal party, there were ways in which most members of the Liberal party were liberal, in more familiar and positive senses of the word. They were reformists rather than revolutionaries (some Liberal party members became revolutionaries after 1960 but, when discovered, were expelled from the party). Most, if not all, would have accepted the adjective *liberal* in front of their substantive nomenclature: liberal socialist, liberal capitalist, liberal conservative, and so on. Many, though not all, were gradualists. They thought social change disrupted fewer lives if it did not occur without warning and preparation. Most disliked thinking of people in groups and preferred to think of them as individuals; while by no means all were egalitarian, nearly all preferred moral and political judgments based on individual worth rather than on race or class. Most had some notion of democracy, if not all were democrats. Many thought there was a connection between morality and politics.

I need to complicate the problem still further by saying that in South Africa white liberals, white socialists, and white Communists tended to live rather similar kinds of lives, though their backgrounds were often very different. They tended to be intellectuals—that is, they cared about ideas, books, and the arts. Because they were in opposition to the government and (at least) to the most easily visible parts of the social system, and because they were in a small minority within their own class and race, they were generally nonconformist and even those who accepted ideology tended to be antiauthoritarian. They tended to look outwards from South Africa, to have links abroad. Many were able to choose to leave South Africa, temporarily or permanently, and were able to lead satisfactory lives elsewhere (it has always been much more difficult for black exiles to find this kind of home abroad). It is worth noting that we are discussing no more than a few thousand people; the Liberal party never had more than five thousand members (and of these only a proportion were white), the Congress of Democrats (COD) about five hundred. That is, for all their ideological differences, they had sociological links and, in that sociological sense, there is a certain "liberality" linking them.

Let me define *liberalism* in a more imaginative way. The first great antiliberal was Procrustes, the tidy-minded host of Greek mythology, who welcomed visitors, wined and dined them, and then put them to sleep in his peculiar bed. He liked things to fit neatly, however, so if the guests were too short for his bed he stretched them, and if they were too long he cut off the excess. This is a characteristic of all those who wish to force reality to conform to their theories; and it is an uncomfortable distinction between (most) natural scientists and (some) social scientists that the former, faced with a fact that does not fit a hypothesis, assume that the hypothesis is probably wrong; while the latter, faced with a similarly inconvenient fact, assume that the fact is inappropriate, irrelevant, biased—or merely just wrong. (This information would fit the bed very well if it were a foot longer; we would make better sense of things if human beings behaved better.) The strength of the liberal is that he or she is more akin to the natural scientist: uncomfortable facts are not put aside; rather, the theory is put aside, or at any rate seen as very partial, capable of dealing with only a narrow range of reality. For some, that strength overrides all else.

However, the liberal does have manifold weaknesses, and it would be illiberal not to recognize this fact. First, there is passivity: because there is always more reality to discover, no theory can ever be complete, and because nothing is ever complete, it is very difficult to act. The watchword of the liberal is "Festina lente," or, more vulgarly, "Hang on a moment." Sometimes that comes very close to the great motto of the conservative: "If something isn't broken, why mend it?" Liberals, however, are usually more prepared than conservatives to believe that something is broken before it actually falls to pieces in their hands. Liberals are, almost by definition, relativist: while they see the attraction of Utopia, they will not easily agree that ends justify means. If their strength is a sense of irony, their weakness is to suppose that in everything there is an element of truth, just as in every man and woman there is an element of the godhead; but if everything is true, nothing has value, and if everyone is God, then there is no God. You spend so much time seeing the other person's point of view you forget your own. You spend so much time respecting the autonomy of others that you fail to notice that your own autonomy has been circumscribed.

Those characteristics taken together have made it an article of faith in South Africa that blacks hate liberals. Liberals always want to wait; they never act. Liberals are always too willing to listen to the views of anyone, even the views of a racialist. In the early days of the Liberal party it was a crucial disqualification from serious treatment by blacks that party policy did not call for universal adult suffrage as a necessity of political freedom. Because liberals know that one could have a vote and still be oppressed, they argued that having a vote was not a necessary part of escaping from oppression (though perhaps what they really meant was that they did not trust illiterate and landless blacks to vote wisely). Though it is a digression, may I note in passing that it is actually much less important for me to have the vote than it is for the garbageman who visits my backyard once a week: I have the power of position, education, wealth, and privilege; the poor and needy require votes much more than I do if they are to be protected by and against politicians. Finally, liberals lacked conviction, or maybe they merely lacked convictions, because they were not ready to go to jail—though I must make honorable exception of men like Eddie Daniels, who served fifteen years without remission on Robben Island for the part he played in the African Resistance Movement (ARM) and who was (I have discovered recently) treated there with honor and respect by the leaders of that much larger organization, the African National Congress. Which exception is, I think you will have realized, a splendid example of the way liberals love exceptions and are always seeking to qualify their generalizations by finding bits that do not fit rather than lopping them off or stretching them. "In my father's house are many mansions": even if not everything is true, humankind is plural.

Visions of the Future

To understand better the possible role of South African liberalism in the coming years, it will be helpful first to distinguish five main views from the spectrum of opinions regarding the likely future of South Africa.

The Verkrampte View

First, there is the *verkrampte* vision: the extreme right-wing view (history with rifles) which states that whites won South Africa by force of arms and will keep it by force of arms. God intended them to have this country, and He will make sure they keep it. It is difficult for educated and sensible Westerners to grasp the full force—or even the simplistic attractiveness—of this view. Everyone negotiates in the end, does he not? You and I know, do we not, that life is a compromise? One gives a little, one takes a little, things work out in the end…and actually, we are inclined to think that this eventual settling of the balance is good. The notion of the Aristotelian mean lies deep in the dominant political culture of the West. Not so for the verkramptes. The verkrampte vision is embedded in Afrikaner consciousness, and it has surfaced before. At the end of the Boer War, the group of Boers who would not accept the terms of the Peace of Vereeniging but wished to continue fighting were known as the *bittereinders* (bitter-enders). The son of one of them, P.W. Botha, served as prime minister and then president of South Africa between 1978 and 1989.

We must go further than that: the triumph of Afrikaner nationalism depends on a theory of political as well as racial purity. Compromise is a specter that terrifies Afrikaner politicians; part of F.W. de Klerk's bravery in talking to Mandela and the ANC lies in his facing the inevitable cries of "Compromise!"—not as praise but as an allegation of weakness. One of the constraints on any Afrikaner politician is the knowledge of the whispering campaign that destroyed General Hertzog after the formation of the United party and was the precursor of the triumph of the purified Afrikaner Nationalist party in 1948. The Afrikaners of the Western Cape are still liable to the taunts of *ware Afrikaners, ware Boereseuns* (true sons of the Boers). Their ancestors stayed at home in the comfortable Cape while the truly committed trekked into the supposedly empty interior to escape the British—and there is no doubt but that the verkramptes harness the immense psychological force of the Great Trek to pull their latter-day wagons. They could have enjoyed economic progress, comfort, and a position in the world if they had stayed in the beautiful Cape, but that meant compromise, and so they went into the fastnesses on the other side of the mountains. Add to these images the Old Testament images of a chosen race carving out from the wilderness a new Zion promised by God, and you may understand why I say these people will not be bought off, nor are they going to be frightened by economic boycott. Indeed, the puritanical basis of much of their belief makes economic boycott attractive to them because it promotes self-sufficiency, and they can fall back on images of belt-tightening, dispensing with luxuries and living on water, salt, dried meat, and rusks (biltong and biscuit).

One must not think of the verkramptes as simply a group— TerreBlanche and the rest. There are, of course, actual verkrampte individuals; they have a party and some seats in the House of Assembly, and they are totally and publicly committed. However, the verkramp is part of the character of the Afrikaner people. To ask why an Afrikaner politician, purportedly a *verligte* (enlightened), is behaving in a verkrampte way is to misunderstand. In the middle of enlightenment, like a stone in a peach, is the verkramp—though I shall shortly explain why the fruit of enlightenment seems rather worm-eaten, despite its apparent freshness.

The Ultrarevolutionary View

The polarity of the verkrampte is the unrelievedly violent revolutionary. One would think that no one in his or her right mind would assert that violence is ever anything but a last resort. It is possible, however, to argue that because the verkrampte or bittereinder is so deeply a part of the Afrikaner character, true liberation will never take place until the wars that were lost are fought again and won. What whites used to call the Kaffir Wars are known by black South Africans as the Wars of Dispossession; if blacks are to possess their country again, they must fight for it. Just as the Afrikaner says, "We fought for this country, and we won," so the black ultrarevolutionary says, "This country will not be ours again until we have spilled our blood for it." It may too easily be seen as a kind of Roman despair: there is nothing left for black South Africans but to die in battle or fall on their own swords. Some commentators claim that is what the Sowetan schoolchildren feel; what little I have been able to discover of their motives and behavior makes me feel that the defiant courage of those who throw stones at armored personnel carriers is not despair but something closer to what the Algerian theorist of violence, Frantz Fanon, described:

> For the colonized people this violence, because it constitutes their only work, invests their characters with positive and creative qualities. The practice of violence binds them together as a whole, since each individual forms a violent link in the great chain, a part of the great organism of violence...The mobilization of the masses...introduces into each man's consciousness the ideas of a common cause, of a national destiny and of a collective history. At the level of individuals, violence is a cleansing force. It frees the native from his inferiority complex and from his despair and inac-

tion; it makes him fearless and restores his self-respect."
(Fanon 1965:73–74)

The Verligte View

Between these polarities I wish to isolate three other visions of South
Africa's future. The first is that of the verligte, the so-called enlightened Nationalist. There is no doubt that in the twenty-one years I was
absent from South Africa (1964–85), there was a noticeable change in
the surface appearance of apartheid. In my very first moments back in
my country, I was delighted to find that I no longer had to check
whether the lavatory or bench or public entrance was for whites or
nonwhites. There is no doubt that, along with the removal of the signs
of apartheid has come greater integration in, for instance, restaurants,
hotels, and shops. I would not think the change deeply significant,
though it would be silly not to welcome it. Much more significant, to
my mind, was that the old open-doored houses of my childhood were
now locked, barred, and burglar-alarmed, protected by high fences
and often patrolled by large dogs.

Yet the verligte is an element in Afrikanerdom that must be taken
into account. It was characterized, with startling force and simplicity
in June 1986 by Donald Masson, retiring president of the Afrikaner
Institute of Commerce: "If we really want to lose everything, then we
must hang on to everything now" (Sampson 1987:11). A black radical, hearing that remark, would quite properly say, "What you mean
is that you want to concede, not as much as you should, but as little as
you can safely get away with; your concern is not justice or equality,
but your own skin." In other words, enlightenment is concessionary;
and (I speak as a headmaster now) concessions rarely produce the
expected effects. This does not mean one should never make concessions, but one must do so in conscious humility that they may have
surprising results. Indeed, I would suggest that is one of the themes of
this essay: too often in talking of the future of South Africa there has
been a simplistic analysis of likely consequences of any particular
action or set of events. This is as true now in the euphoric aftermath of
Nelson Mandela's release as it was beforehand.

The Ameliorist View

A step further than enlightenment is the ameliorist vision of the
future, sometimes called the Oppenheimer thesis. More accurately, it
is the O'Dowd thesis because its original author was Michael O'Dowd,
a president of NUSAS in the early 1950s and now a senior official in

the Anglo-American Corporation (see O'Dowd 1974). The thesis (wildly oversimplified, because for all one's reservations one must acknowledge O'Dowd's considerable scholarship) argues that the concessionary position is inevitable and the revolutionary view nonsensical: there has never been a successful revolution in an industrial state—indeed, one might even argue that industrial states cannot have revolutions, and South Africa is, in broad terms, industrial to at least a European level. That being the case, the truest analogy to South Africa's situation would be Europe in the nineteenth century, where increasing industrialization produced not only urban misery but also an emergent middle class and then a gradual process of the extension of political rights to follow in the train of economic advancement. In other words, one really needs to do nothing in South Africa except to create wealth, because economics will do everything else.

I first heard this theory in 1961 from O'Dowd himself, three years before his thesis appeared in printed form, and the inchoate objections I felt then are now more firmly rooted in my mind.[2] First, it seems to me an inhuman thesis because it removes from consideration all aspects of life other than the economic; indeed, it reminds me of the sillier versions of Marxism in which the importance of anything other than economic forces is denied. There are times when, in the words of less intelligent people than O'Dowd, the ameliorist position seems similarly asinine. Second, in giving due weight to economics, the O'Dowd thesis ignores the actuality of racialism. The argument is that economic advancement and economic necessity will render racialism first obsolete and then inconceivable. To that point of view all I can say is that my own version of South Africa understands racialism as an intransigent and deeply powerful element in the culture of white South Africans and particularly in Afrikanerdom.

Allow me to digress from the discussion of the five views of the future to suggest that one of the reasons the phenomenon of Black Consciousness was treated more seriously by South African liberals than by South African Marxists is that Marxists tend to assume that once the economic causes of racialism are removed, racialism itself will cease to exist. The liberal view would see racialism as caused by more complex circumstances than economic forces alone, and so Black Consciousness, which is rooted in a psychological analysis of the effects of oppression, found much more intellectual favor among liberals than among Marxists. I would argue similarly against the O'Dowd thesis; it is a kind of upside-down Marxism, and I would in fact claim, ironically, that one of the positive effects of the O'Dowd thesis has been to force Marxists in the Congress movement to be a little less simplistic in their analyses than they used to be. In disputing that O'Dowd's thesis is big enough to fill the whole bed, however, I would not wish to underestimate the importance of the economic forces at work in South Africa. Obviously, they are hugely important: the use of black purchasing power as a political lever; the growth of black trade unions; the new urban black middle class, caught between radical youth in the townships and the repressive machinery of Afrikanerdom, but itself an active force, not a passive recipient of change. The international moves toward divestment and economic sanctions are still very much Congress policy, though it is an interesting illustration of the gap between expectation and effect that some black unions now regret that they are no longer negotiating with mainly liberal overseas directors and multinational officials but with white South Africans less prone to accept pressure for change. It is equally ironic that in terms of the O'Dowd thesis, the use by blacks of their economic power internally is seen as a positive step forward, whereas external economic sanctions are seen as retrogressive interference with supposedly natural economic forces. Even if one does not accept O'Dowd's thesis in all its aspects, the idea that economic reform will happen inevitably and so prevent violent political upheaval with widespread bloodshed and economic chaos is attractive both to the liberal and the conservative. If wishes were horses, beggars would ride.

The View of the Congress Movement

The last vision of the future I propose to outline is the more conventional revolutionary one; I call it the Congress view for obvious reasons. Briefly, the outlook developed as follows: For years and years—for more than half a century, in fact—the Congress movement tried peaceful means to resist oppression and to persuade their rulers to nonviolent change. The tactic failed. According to the Marxist wing of the Congress movement, the strategy did not work because it could not work: it was romantic resistance, an early phase in the struggle, based on an incorrect analysis of the class structure of Southern Africa. According to the other wing—the Gandhian wing, to use a convenient shorthand—it failed because the Afrikaners were so utterly intransigent. The proper Gandhian theory of passive resistance is *satyagraha* (soul-force), by which the soul of the oppressed triumphs over the soul of the oppressor because it is prepared to suffer more than the other is prepared to inflict suffering—even to suffer death. But peaceful resistance did not change the Afrikaners because they were incapable of change. So, reluctantly rather than joyfully, the Congress movement and its allies turned to violence against objects, rather than against people. More recently, however, there have been two developments, the first being the realization that one may hardly destroy a gun without harming the hand that holds it, and second, the recognition that the innocent have to suffer sometimes in the cause of a wider necessity.

Now I have referred to "the Congress movement and its allies," but actually one of the first groups involved in the sabotage of public installations (railway lines, power pylons, and so on) was not a Congress group at all but a group of young liberals in the African Resistance Movement (ARM). I am tempted to write more about ARM, although I have already written a heavily fictionalized account (Driver 1969) of its origins, ambitions, and downfall and of the subsequent bombing of the Johannesburg railway station by John Harris, a minor and a peripheral member of ARM, though the only one to be executed—and he died, incidentally, with far greater heroism than the way one or two leading figures in the ARM managed to find themselves in police detention. No one, however, has written a scholarly account of the group. (The only nonfiction book that has been written about ARM is so appallingly inaccurate and ignorant that I cannot bring myself to advertise it even by mentioning the title.) But the point I need to make here is that ARM was essentially a group of liberals—primarily members of the Liberal party of South Africa, though they were ultimately expelled from this group. In the South African context, to be a liberal (in a broad sense) did not necessarily preclude the view that to achieve change violence would, regrettably, be necessary. To assume that the violence could be limited to objects and not harm the innocent was unwisely romantic, such as the sad case of Harris's unheeded warning to the police that he had planted a bomb demonstrates.

Organized guerrilla activity in South Africa now appears to be largely in the hands of the military wing of the ANC, *Umkhonto we Sizwe* (Spear of the Nation). The beating of blacks by white youths is hardly a new phenomenon, nor is the violence of the police. The so-called suicides in police custody, the shooting of prisoners "because they tried to escape," and random murders are endemic. There appears to be a great deal of unorganized violence by blacks, much of it directed against the easiest targets: other blacks—police informers, government servants, and no doubt the occasional social parasite or innocent bystander falsely accused. The latest and most hideous version is necklacing, by which a tire is placed over a victim's head and arms so he is immobilized, petrol is poured inside the tire, and then the petrol is set afire. "Instant" it possibly is, though rather slowly instant, but "justice" it certainly is not, because there has been no due process of law, not even in a revolutionary sense, and liberals believe in the law, for all its imperfections! "Slow murder" might be a better description, and one notes with relief that more people are condemning the practice and that fewer are apologizing for it. I mention it mainly because I would not want anyone to suppose that I talk about revolutionary violence without recognizing what may actually happen in revolutionary violence. Bombs in shopping arcades chop off the legs of children as well as the arms of policemen.

The Complexities of Pluralism in South Africa

Let me summarize these five views of South Africa's future:

1. *The verkrampte version,* an Afrikaner future very much like the Afrikaner past, with the blacks safely subservient in their own provinces or fleeing from brilliantly accurate riflefire.

2. *The ultrarevolutionary version,* which says, "We won't own this land again until we have won it with our blood."

3. *The verligte version,* in which the Afrikaners, having recruited the bulk of the English speakers to their side, also persuade the Indians and especially the Coloreds to join federal forces against the world. Whether their world includes the black states in which black South Africans have gained their national citizenship and the independent black states within or on the South African borders depends on how quiescent those states are; if they are not, South Africa has many means at its disposal to destabilize them or to impose a puppet government. Careful but gradual concessions, along with international diplomacy and, now, careful negotiation with the ANC—especially an ANC as it exists after the collapse of Soviet hegemony—would produce a slow change within South Africa, so slow as possibly to be imperceptible but enough to persuade the Western world that change is happening. The light in enlightenment has very low amperage.

4. *The ameliorist version,* by which a judicious sharing of economic wealth and a gradual creation of a black middle class would prevent a revolution and promote a less-than-perfect but still not offensively undemocratic society: a second-best society, perhaps, but not ravaged by violent revolution. Again, negotiation will be crucial.

5. *The revolutionary version,* which sees blacks and their allies winning an urban guerrilla war after a long, dreadful, and necessary but ultimately successful struggle. The ANC still

> has not entirely abandoned this possibility and will not
> until it sees real evidence that the government is converted
> to real democracy. How long will it wait? That is a critical
> question!

No doubt you are waiting for me to commit myself to one view: that is
exactly what I am not going to do, though I trust I have presented
each view persuasively enough to make some readers think each is
likely. Though I risk the weakness I mentioned before, that liberals
may sometimes think the truth is so multifarious that everything is
true, I wish to assert that all these futures are going to happen, indeed
may already be happening.

Each scenario is not discrete but rather is part of a spectrum.
Indeed, in Anthony Sampson's brilliantly informed study *Black and
Gold: Tycoons, Revolutionaries and Apartheid* (1987), the argument is
taken a step further. First, "it is absurd for western governments or
companies to expect Pretoria to make reforms by itself, to dismantle
the structure of apartheid." Revolution of some kind is inevitable;
however, judicious use of Western resources, especially in the bordering states, would help ensure that the revolution would be "as blood-
less and manageable as possible." "The longer the west refuses to face
up to a future black majority, the more anti-western it is likely to
be"—and the prime power of the West is in the hands of the tycoons,
the managers of the multinational companies (Sampson 1987:
263–265). If one wanted to place Sampson's position in the spectrum
of the five visions of South Africa's future, it would fit somewhere
between the ameliorist and the conventional revolutionary perspectives. The heart is ameliorist, but the head is revolutionary.

The moral repulsion one feels for institutionalized racialism has
made one think of South Africa as much more monolithic than in fact
it is. It is a very diverse and pluralistic country. To make this claim is
risky, because it is so often heard as a prelude to an argument in favor
of apartheid or as an argument in favor of gradualism. I want to use it
in a much more complicated way, however, because I want to include
all aspects of the pluralism—historical, cultural, racial, regional, linguistic, economic, local and psychological. What is going to happen in
South Africa is all the futures mentioned and more. Of course, in an
absolute sense, the future of South Africa is very certain indeed.
Anthony Trollope, who visited the Cape in 1876, put it clearly and
starkly: "South Africa is a country of black men—and not of white
men. It has been so; it is so; and it will continue to be so. In this
respect it is altogether unlike Australia, unlike the Canadas, and
unlike New Zealand . . . the important person in South Africa is the
Kafir and the Zulu, the Bechuana and the Hottentot,—not the
Dutchman or the Englishman" (Trollope 1968: 332–333).

The processes by which that certain future will happen, as well as the times and the places, are very uncertain indeed—and much more complex than anyone has yet (as far as I know)'said. The argument is always between scenarios: nonviolent or violent, revolutionary or ameliorist, long and nasty violence or short and sharp. My position is that the arguments "between" are absurd. Nonviolent change is happening; so is violent change. Violent opposition to change is happening; concessions are also being made. Violent opposition to change is, in some instances, masquerading as violent change—the hand grenade may be thrown into the cinema by a PAC man or by a hireling of the Afrikaner Weerstandsbeweging (AWB, the Afrikaner resistance movement), which wants the PAC and the ANC to be regarded as indiscriminately murderous. In the same town, the ANC may be organizing a boycott of a chain of white-owned shops that is causing a reexamination of financial policy in the area. It is not one scenario or another that is true; all are true, though they may not happen in the same sequence, or the same place, or at the same time.

One partly appropriate word is *balkanization,* but even that is too superficial. From the time of the formation of the Union of South Africa in 1910, there have been regional variations of a major kind. The partial implementation of geographical apartheid, the independence of the former British and Portuguese colonies, and the United Nations' supervision of Namibia's transition to independence in 1990 have accelerated that process. It is a fact that in some areas of South Africa there has been what amounts to a tacit and temporary balkanization. A great deal of political theorizing in South Africa is based on the large urban example. The small town is a less familiar notion, but it needs to be taken into account in the sociology of revolution. So think of a small town in South Africa where black purchasing power is such that if it is withdrawn almost totally, a great many white businesses may be pushed into bankruptcy. In two such areas (I have it on good but unattributable authority) an accommodation has been reached between the white town council and white chamber of commerce on the one side and the black township on the other, which effectively leaves the white town ruled by whites and the black town ruled by blacks. The power of the police is tamed and discipline is maintained by black vigilantes. I have not done any research on this situation, but I have been told that there is one small town where there is not merely a tacit agreement but an actual signed written accord between the local chamber of commerce and a committee representing the black township. Local political concessions would result in a discontinuation of a very effective boycott of white businesses by black consumers.

While I cannot state authoritatively that this is true, I would not be surprised if it is. Given the talks going on between ANC delegations and state government and between Mandela and de Klerk about the future of South Africa, one would presumably find similar dialogue occurring at a local level. Of course any agreement is dependent on a quiescent local police force. All it takes for a precarious—and illegal—modus vivendi to be toppled is for a vigorous and rigorous new chief of police to take over or for a guerrilla group to begin operations in the area.

I should also report that I have heard—and again, it is hearsay evidence—that in some areas there has been considerable conflict between the police and the army. In the account I was given the conflict was between a local police force psychopathically determined to enforce the letter of the law and a local army group anxious to try to keep the black population moderately cooperative. Again, I cannot quote my source without endangering it, but I can say that one could expect this kind of conflict. Within the police force itself local South Africans recognize distinctions of discipline and professionalism: the "greens," the "browns," and the "blues." A white South African I know, who regularly enters a particularly nasty black township in a particularly nasty town, goes into the black township under armed guard. Because he is in these circumstances a volunteer, he can demand certain safeguards. One of them is that he will not go into the township with policemen of the locally recruited variety, because he is much more afraid of them than he is of the local population. He is less unhappy with the professional police and least unhappy with the army units attached to the police locally. They have a limited job to do and they do it and nothing else. Given that the army has behaved with indiscriminate brutality along the border areas, this internal distinction is particularly noteworthy.

Let me continue to complicate the scenarios. For instance, one that is occasionally mentioned is the possibility of an army coup. There are already areas in South Africa where the army rules, as evidenced by the localized state of emergency, and this pattern is bound to continue. The influence of the army on government is considerable, and surely there will be times when the army takes over the government. However, it will not happen as a stage in a process. It will happen incidentally and out of any order.

Another scenario often mentioned is that of partition. In a sense, that has already happened in the creation of the bantustans, and the fact that they are nominally under black rule should not prevent one from acknowledging that they show even less respect for individual rights and personal liberty than does the central state. In other words, partition need not result in one democratic and another undemocratic state but may result in two undemocratic states. It is possible to have two small towns within fifty miles of each other where in one town there is racial cooperation of a kind that makes one hopeful for the future of South Africa and in the other there is racial confrontation of cataclysmic horror, where a young white visitor from overseas addressing any civil word to a black resident is hissed at with bitter loathing as a matter of course.

A scenario we have not yet seen—as far as I know—is a communal explosion in which a large element of the black community sets out to kill as many whites as possible. South Africa came close to this situation at the time of the Pan-Africanist Congress when in the early 1960s it inspired the insurrectionary movement called Poqo (see Lodge 1983:241–55), and the more recent Soweto rising demonstrates that there is a capacity for reckless self-sacrifice in the thrall of racial anger. The localized and indiscriminate uprising of blacks against whites will, however, surely happen sooner or later, and it will be horrible. The reverse has certainly happened, and I doubt if we can begin to know the full extent of the carnage. However, when a government is prepared to settle out of court a case for damages after police have opened fire on a black funeral procession, then communal violence is at least two-sided.

Let me continue the complications. South Africa today is in a phase when the emergence of legal and semilegal black trade unions seems of enormous importance. As I was first drafting this essay, the miners were on strike: the 170,000 striking members of the official union were joined by either 60,000 workers (if you believe the Chamber of Mines) or 160,000 (if you believe the miners' leaders). We have been waiting for such developments for twenty years. Why has it taken so long? The black workers did not have the muscle beforehand; their employers would simply sack them and bring in new hands—from Mozambique, from the Rhodesias, from Bechuanaland. Things have certainly changed, but will it last? Is this the beginning of the end? I hope so, but I doubt it—we have had too many beginnings of the end for me to believe in them anymore. I think it is very significant that blacks are beginning to assert their economic power not just as producers but as consumers as well. However, strikes can be broken. What I wish I knew more about is deliberate inefficiency—industrial sabotage, to give it a grand title. In *Schindler's List* (Keneally 1982), the Jews whom Schindler has rescued from the concentration camps make armaments, but nothing ever quite fits.

Yet on a Karoo farm run by a deeply conservative white farmer, I saw in 1986 an example of worker participation I would be surprised to find anywhere on a farm in Western Europe. Each laborer there owns a proportion of the main herd of Angora goats, and his goats run with the whole herd. So the better the herd does the better the laborer does. In terms of the Karoo farms of my childhood, that seems close to a revolution in attitude, even if not in ownership of the land.

There is one other certainty I would add to my assessment of the eventual outcome and of the complexity of the processes that are occurring and will occur in South Africa, and that concerns the time scale. The processes, some of which have already begun though not in any hierarchical or temporal order, will take a very long time to reach a conclusion. Violence of one kind may be succeeded not by revolutionary change but by nonviolent reform; concessions may result in communal uprisings; apparently successful sanctions may result not in a weaker ᵒouth Africa but a stronger one; and so on. The cry "How long, O Lord, how long?" will be met, I fear, with a steady gaze and a shake of the head by all except the foolish optimist or the sanguine revolutionary. The release of political prisoners and the return of the exiles are events devoutly to be welcomed and cheered; but there is much work still to be done, and premature optimism is the parent of despair.

What Is to Be Done?

What is the function of liberalism in this complexity? Has it a function, or a future, at all? Should it declare itself an outmoded creed and seek to convert to one of the revolutionary radicalisms? Or should it take refuge in ameliorization, or fit a breathing device in a coffin and bury itself for a generation or two? The Procrustean view sees the liberal crushed between the hammer and the anvil, the hammer of the Congress movement and the anvil of Afrikanerdom. On this bed may lie only the true revolutionary. The first problem is that the bed of the true revolutionary tends to have rather a movable shape. Last year's orthodoxy is next year's heresy, and great guerrilla leaders often end up jailed in their liberated country. The hammer has been known to miss the anvil entirely.

Moreover, the Congress movement is by no means ideologically single-minded, even in its international and exiled form, where the influence of the Soviet Union has been very strong. Its leadership is by no means entirely illiberal. It is not just an historical oddity that one of the former officers of the ANC was the chaplain-general and its president, Oliver Tambo, is avowedly a Christian, as are a great many other black South Africans. Within South Africa, the United Democratic Front (UDF) constituted by all accounts a heterogeneous movement containing many disparate forces. For instance, the old Africanist side of the Congress movement, some of which formed itself into the Pan-Africanist Congress (PAC), appears to have returned to the larger fold.

The splits and expulsions that characterized an earlier phase of the ANC and the PAC in exile do not seem to have happened in the UDF—nor, indeed, in the ANC anymore, thanks largely to the generous leadership of Oliver Tambo.

In other words, it is simply not enough to say that the liberal will have no place. Ask almost any black South African how he or she regards the Black Sash—run by white women of a generally conservative liberal kind—and one will hear evidence of the complexity which I have asserted. Mandela himself spoke most generously of the Black Sash and of NUSAS upon his release from prison, the latter particularly because of its role in the Education Scheme it ran for political prisoners. At the same time, one has to accept the limitations of the place of the liberal, particularly if one is white. Though I have many admirable friends who were left almost totally bereft politically by Frederick van Zyl Slabbert's startling decision to abandon parliamentary politics, one must, I think, applaud his decision. His Institute for a Democratic Alternative for South Africa (IDASA) is likely to prove a more useful vehicle for liberalizing the inevitable change in South Africa than will quasi-parliamentary opposition. Of course, part of the result of what some called his desertion was the apparent "move to the right" in the most recent whites-only election. I cannot see that as very significant, however, because there is no evidence that a move to the left would have produced any more concessions than would a move to the right, and in any case, concessions rarely produce their intended effects.

What, then, do the white liberals do? They talk, they listen, they argue, they write, they speak out—but they do not pretend to be black, nor do they pretend that their moral suffering is a patch on the actual suffering of the black opposition. They are prepared to go to jail, but they probably no longer take the Gandhian view that their going to jail may soften the hearts of their jailers. They are perhaps even prepared to die for the cause, though they do not pretend that dying will increase their virtue or necessarily advance social and political change. They see that the true leaders are the black leaders, and they will take proper account of this leadership, even when they reserve the right (as all good liberals must) to dissent. They long for the restoration of the rule of decent law.[3] They hope, by their witness, to keep alive some of the ideas that will inform the society they hope will eventually allow people to live decent and orderly lives in South Africa. And, they are probably not optimists.

None of these ideas is original. More than half my lifetime ago, when I was president of NUSAS, I presented a paper to a seminar at a Methodist youth camp called Bothashill. It earned NUSAS, and me personally, considerable opprobrium from most white South Africans;

but among the black members of NUSAS—and other South African blacks—it earned a certain respect that is still not entirely forgotten. What I said then is still true, and it makes more sense now than when I said it in 1964. I think the same may possibly be true of this essay, in twenty years' time.

NOTES

1. This paragraph, and the two that follow, are substantially a quotation from Driver (1980:128–30). For further discussion of the meaning of *liberalism* in its main global context, see Bramstead and Melhuish (1978) and Raz (1986).

2. Although O'Dowd did not publish the paper containing his thesis until 1974, his ideas had already become well known since his paper had been circulated widely in its original unpublished form from its initial appearance in 1964.<EP>

3. For a detailed definition and defense of a liberal theory of law, see Dworkin (1981).

REFERENCES

Bramstead, E.K., and R.J. Melhuish, eds. 1978. *Western Liberalism*. London: Longman.

Bunting, Brian. 1957. "Multi-Racial Conference." *Liberation* (Johannesburg).

Driver, C. J. 1969. *Elegy for a Revolutionary*. London: Faber.

———. 1970. *Send War in Our Time, O Lord*. London: Faber.

———. 1980. *Patrick Duncan: South African and Pan-African*. London: Heineman.

Dworkin, Ronald. 1981. *Taking Rights Seriously*. New impression with a "Reply to Critics." London: Duckworth.

Fanon, Frantz. 1965. *The Wretched of the Earth*. New York: Grove Press.

Hay, Ian. 1915. *The Lighter Side of School Life*. London: T.N. Foulis.

Keneally, Thomas. 1982. *Schindler's List*. New York: Simon and Schuster.

Lodge, Tom. 1983. *Black Politics in South Africa since 1945*. London: Longmans.

O'Dowd, Michael. 1974. "South Africa in the Light of the Stages of Economic Growth." In *South Africa: Economic Growth and Political Change*, ed. A. Leftwich, 29–44. London: Allison and Busby.

Raz, Joseph. 1986. *The Morality of Freedom*. Oxford: Clarendon Press.

Sampson, Anthony. 1987. *Black and Gold: Tycoons, Revolutionaries and Apartheid*. London: Hodder and Stoughton.

Trollope, Anthony. 1968. *South Africa*. Volume 2. Reprint of 1878 edition. London: Dawsons of Pall Mall.

4

Racial Proletarianization and Some Contemporary Dimensions of Black Consciousness Thought

C. R. D. HALISI

During the 1970s, with the established South African liberation movements still in exile, three distinct social forces found new expression in black politics. These were neo-ethnicity (as exemplified by Inkatha, the organization headed by Chief Gatsha Buthelezi ostensibly to promote Zulu cultural and political interests, and Bantustan leadership), radicalized youth (Black Consciousness and student movements), and the black working class (independent trade unions).

Ethnic leaders drew their strength from long-standing ethnic identities. These politicians sought to forge new political constituencies from old ethnic loyalties in the hopes of wielding power in both rural and urban communities and of gaining greater government patronage. In this respect, these were neo-ethnic, rather than ethnic, leaders who most often campaigned with government support. For many black South Africans, however, the political legitimacy of bantustan leaders was compromised by their close association with the policies of the government. The South African state manipulates ethnic divisions as a counterweight to racial and class solidarity and seeks to link class formation to "traditional" institutional residues in the hope of encouraging the formation of a more conservative and state-aligned black segment of the bourgeoisie. The pernicious reification of ethnicity in South Africa is well known. Apartheid ideology can be usefully viewed as a racist "anthropology," one which categorizes Africans as perpetual "tribesmen" (Crapranzano 1987).[1] Perverted ethnic institutions have been incorporated into capitalist and state structures. Whether signified by the *induna* (boss boy) in the mines or the chief in the homelands, a degraded version of African culture "legitimates" both segregation and apartheid.

On the other hand, ethnic-based resistance has contributed to contemporary nationalist movements. The memory of resistance by chiefs serves to remind black Africans that their plight as a conquered people is not in all instances the result of complicity. Ethnic and racial consciousness can be at one and the same time mutually supportive and antagonistic forms of consciousness. Well into this century, "chiefs still had considerable power over the daily lives of their subjects, and it is this, in part, that explains the retention among migrants of the ideology of precapitalist social formations" (Marks 1986:110).

The social engineering of ethnicity has been the organizational cornerstone of South African state strategy; ethnic-based incorporation has allowed for minor restructuring from above and for a distinctive form of class formation. Scholars who stress its colonial character argue that the South African state as presently structured is incapable of accommodating the basic African demands for full citizenship and common political institutions; nor is it in a position to accommodate any significant segment of the African population: hence its continued reliance on repression.

An opposing view contends that the state has a strategy of accommodation that owes a great deal to its incorporation of ethnic structures.[2] The fact that black state auxiliaries inherit the legitimation crisis of the regime should not be confused with an absence of power or influence. As a result of Pretoria-style social engineering, a substantial number of politicized urban Africans deeply resent ethnic-group politicians and all that they have come to represent. The aspirations of urban Africans have been thwarted by the government's institutionalization of tribal identity. Still, ethnicity cannot be dismissed as a mere chimera, and ethnic leaders often represent politically important constituencies.

Obviously, ethnic politics will not be the foundation for a "postapartheid" South Africa—that would contravene the very meaning of the term. Arend Lijphart (1987), the major consociationalist theorist, has continued to insist that ethnicity need not be inconsistent with postapartheid planning and may indeed be compatible with democratic constitutional reform. If the European, Soviet, and American experiences are any indication, ethnic influences on a postapartheid democratic process will not totally disappear. The centrality of ethnic divisions to apartheid ideology, as well as the state's divisive ethnic-based "reform" agenda, has discouraged radical movements from articulating a realistic policy on ethnicity. The role of ethnicity in a postapartheid South Africa remains a controversial question both in academic and political discussions. Should the process of reform initiated by President F. W. de Klerk and Nelson Mandela in 1990 result in the establishment of a credible electoral system, and should liberation movements be converted into full-fledged political parties, the interplay of ethnic, racial, and class constituencies will form the basis of a new real politique.

Even as ethnic-based resistance gathered strength, radical black students and youth, the second of the social forces mentioned above, rejected the ethnicization of black politics. In many respects, the Black Consciousness Movement (BCM) evolved as a counterethnicity movement; its young members were the victims of government experimentation with retribalization policies. They were compelled to speak their ethnic languages in elementary school while having their academic futures determined by proficiency in the two official European languages. If sociolinguists are correct in their contention that language provides the primary medium for consciousness formation, it is not surprising that the Soweto rebellion of June 1976 began over the government's language policy. The preoccupation of apartheid ideologues with ethnicity has prompted Neville Alexander, the articulate theorist-activist from the Cape Action League (CAL), to conclude that "ethnicity is a substitute in modern social theory for the concept of 'race'" (1985:36).

The largely mission-educated older generation of leaders, while rejecting the homelands policy, were never as uncompromising on the issue of ethnicity as was the Soweto generation, which suffered more directly from the policies of Bantu education. In the face of government-imposed ethnic nationalism, the BCM was prompted to reconstruct black nationalism as a theory of antiethnicity. The term *Black* was an explicit rejection of the primacy of Colored-ness, Indian-ness, Zulu-ness, Xhosa-ness, and so forth. Some of the most well known Indian members of the BCM refused to join specifically Indian organizations on the grounds that they fostered ethnic division.

The BCM criticized even antiapartheid groups affiliated with the United Democratic Front (UDF) for their refusal to reject the name *Indian* or *Colored*—not to mention the despised Zulu nationalism of Inkatha. The attempt by the most de-ethnicized part of the black population to transcend ethnicity—to construct black unity as a new culture of resistance—constituted simultaneously the most utopian and radical dimension of the Black Consciousness platform. The rejection of neo-ethnic politics led the BCM to formulate Black Consciousness as the nemesis of ethnic identity. The question of how Black Consciousness theory should interpret ethnicity as well as how the movement should relate to ethnic-based politicians and movements and indeed to the ethnic sentiments of the black masses remains a recurring theoretical problem, even though the official antiethnicity stance of the BCM has been uncompromising.

Nonetheless, the limitations of many of the ideological constructs of the period became obvious with the growth of the independent working-class movement, the third of the social forces to find new expression in black politics of the 1970s. Beginning with the landmark

Durban strikes of 1973, black trade unions organized hundreds of thousands of black workers within an incredibly short span of time. The existence of black independent trade unions challenged all varieties of non-working-class leadership to consider the needs of the large, complex, and diverse black working-class majority. The new working-class politics, however, also confronted older ideological cleavages.

By the 1980s, a variety of new community and labor federations sought to reconcile these social forces ideologically and organizationally. Black exclusivism of the radicalized youth (and previously of the Pan-Africanist Congress [PAC]) and nonracialism, represented in its radical variant by the African National Congress (ANC) and the UDF and in its moderate form by Inkatha, have retained their currency as competing ideological/organizational strategies. The legacy of racial proletarianization,[3] the development of class relations under the auspices of racial domination, makes the tension between nonracial and Black Consciousness perspectives an integral part of black political discourse in South Africa. Racial nationalism and nonracial democracy contain two distinct but entwined visions of black liberation. As core values, both racial autonomy and racial equality will continue to shape black political thought.

The Political Reconciliation of New Social Forces

During the 1980s, violent internecine confrontations have erupted between the two wings of an ideologically divided nascent black bourgeoisie in alliance with, or in competition for, the allegiance of black youth and the middle and working classes. The black working class is divided along the lines of migrant and urbanized workers—this includes the unemployed and gangster elements, each of which has been recruited on both sides. The working class taken as a whole includes a substantial number of Colored and Indian workers as well. The political content of contemporary township violence differs from that surrounding the Soweto rebellion in that there is today a greater degree of internecine violence. The reconciliation of established political movements and the new plethora of social forces has required ideological reconstruction from major political groupings.

Inspired by the ANC and its document on a postapartheid South Africa, the Freedom Charter, the UDF leads a racially inclusive political movement. Its vision of the future is of an essentially social-democratic polity where neither ethnicity nor race is the basis of power. Upon his release from prison, ANC veteran Walter Sisulu, when asked by reporters if he anticipated a black head of state in his lifetime, reiterated his organization's view of a nonracial democracy: "We don't judge people in terms of color. We are talking about a democratic method whereby a black man can be president or a white man can be president" (*New York Times*, 16 October 1989).

Alternatively, at talks initiated in March 1987, KwaZulu Chief Minister Gatsha Buthelezi, the Natal provincial government, and other civic leaders discussed the possibility of regional power sharing between blacks and whites (O'Meara and Winchester 1987). Advocates of nonracialism in South Africa, while receptive to white participation, are still forced by circumstance to organize on a primarily racial basis. Yet attempts to implement the Freedom Charter's principles, more than any other democratic manifesto, have inspired new democratic thought both within and outside of the nonracial framework.

Duncan Innes and Stephen Gelb (1987:558) divide the demands of the Freedom Charter into four categories: (1) security of employment and adequate wages; (2) increased provisions of goods and services, such as food, clothing, housing, transport, and social services; (3) full democratic rights including democratic organs of self-government; and (4) nationalization of mines and industry and redistribution of land. A heated debate between advocates of nonracial and Black Consciousness interpretations has resurfaced with the adoption of the Freedom Charter by the UDF. Africanist and Black Consciousness thinkers continue to reject what they would consider the multiracialism (as opposed to genuine nonracialism) contained in the Freedom Charter.

In opposition to the Freedom Charter, Black Consciousness groupings have promulgated the Azanian Manifesto approved at the Azanian People's Organization (AZAPO) conference in Hammanskraal in June 1983. Implicit in this statement is a more direct correlation of racial domination with capitalist exploitation. As an alternative to nonracial strategies, the BCM advocates an exclusively black multiclass coalition as a means of assuring black leadership within the opposition.

Not unlike other black movements, the black trade unions include a mainstream committed to nonracial democracy, in the form of the Congress of South African Trade Unions (COSATU), while the National Council of Trade Unions (NACTU) functions as a vocal Black Consciousness opposition. On 1 May 1986, Inkatha formed the United Workers Union of South Africa (UWUSA), which espouses a pro-free-enterprise and antidisinvestment program. The Federation of South African Trade Unions (FOSATU), before it disbanded to join COSATU, recognized that migrant labor was Inkatha's Achilles' heel. FOSATU therefore adopted a strategy of vigorously organizing Zulu workers and representing their interest as workers without directly challenging Inkatha's political hegemony in Natal. In hindsight, FOSATU's approach proved sagacious. In the late 1980s and continuing into 1990, Natal would experience the most extreme manifestations of internecine warfare between Inkatha and UDF loyalists. Some township moderates and ethnic politicians have recruited—often with the assistance of the South African police—vigilantes to contest the challenge of radicalized youth, popularly known as *comrades*. Inkatha also organized its own Youth Brigade as a counterforce to ANC/UDF youth movements.

Racial Politics and the Transfiguration of Class Analysis

Racial privilege has been the linchpin of apartheid and therefore state power rests on psychological as well as political foundations. In practice, "white democracy" and "white welfare capitalism" are the result of an intraracial coalition of white classes that transcends ethnic distinctions. The racial coalitions that have sustained apartheid have begun to disintegrate; segments of the capitalist class favor a liberal-democratic alternative to apartheid. In a liberal democracy, economic elites would depend on political institutions to reduce the intensities of social conflict and discontent. The great dilemma faced by the white minority regime has been how to permit even limited economic redistribution without a fundamental expansion of democractic participation. Hence, the political reform of the organization of white power has proven more difficult than racial reform within industrial capitalism. Thus the National party, with increasing difficulty, has worn two hats—the party of capitalist development and that of white supremacy.

Clearly, the distorted political economy of apartheid operates in conjunction with a racist social psychology. Racism is a personal imperative of white rule. The internalization of racial norms is a requirement for white mobilization on behalf of racial privilege. Despite their different approaches to racism, both nonracial and Black Consciousness thinkers challenge the negation of black subjectivity. An ethnographic study of a small white South African community reveals an almost total inability on the part of respondents to comprehend the feelings of black people without resorting to racial massification—the inability to view black South Africans as distinct and feeling individuals (Crapranzano 1987).

While racial domination remains the fulcrum of politics in South Africa, the relationship between state racial policies and capitalist development constitutes the central problem that underlies much of the scholarship on South Africa. Similar concerns influence debates within the black movement. All groups within the antiapartheid movement must address the question of black solidarity. Nonetheless, anticapitalist black thinkers have been most concerned with the relationship between socialism and black struggle—a project that has generated a variety of analyses. AZAPO, the contemporary manifestation of the BCM, has gravitated toward the view that race is class. This is the core assumption of those political thinkers who seek to reconcile exclusivist black nationalism with Marxism. Conversely, multiracial Marxists believe that class alliances across racial lines are both possible and desirable. In either case, black political thinkers in South Africa have to deal with the internal relationship of race and class. During the past ten years, the emphasis on racial domination has been supplanted by more class-based interpretations of black struggle.

For the purposes of this analysis a central question is, might not racial proletarianization transfigure a class understanding of black politics? The use of class concepts in explanations of racial domination represents an attempt by black radicals to indigenize class analysis; it should therefore be investigated as a dimension of black political thought. This interconnection is also important for empirically based studies of contemporary Marxist thought. For, as Ernesto Laclau (1979:12) has observed, the attempt to extend Marxism beyond the Eurocentrism of the Second and Third Internationals has contributed to its maturation. Afro-Asian nationalism and socialism greatly contributed to the revolutionary fervor of the Third International and racial struggles were accorded greater revolutionary significance. So strong was the myth of Afro-Asian solidarity as a political/psychological force that it produced an attempt to create a Third World International at Bandung in 1955.

With respect to racial issues, however, mainstream Marxism has been primarily nonracial in persuasion. Thus, analytical categories crucial to the Black Consciousness tradition are not easily conceptualized within an orthodox Marxist framework. In both South Africa and the United States nonracialist/integrationist and black republican/ Black Power approaches provide black activists with competing conceptual frameworks and organizational strategies. At issue is whether racial domination is merely an instance of class exploitation. By applying Marxism to questions of racial liberation, left-wing Black Consciousness thinkers transfigure many of the fundamental tenets of Marxist thought.

In-depth studies of black nationalist movements suggest that Marxism has appealed to black radicals as a guide to racial as well as class politics. Peter Walshe (1971) and Gail Gerhart (1978) have found that the African National Congress Youth League was far more concerned with the multiracial implications of Marxism than with standard disputes over the nature of class struggle. As Neville Alexander observes with respect to black radicals in the Western Cape after World War II, "The Westernising aspects of Marxism automatically appealed to a youth being threatened with a retrogressive policy of tribalization" (1986:9).

In both South Africa and the United States, left-wing black nationalists have experimented with "Black Marxism" as a result of the nonracial propensity of orthodox versions of Marxism. AZAPO has taken this theoretical path and its theoreticians argue that true freedom can only come with South African socialism—with the abolition of both racism and capitalism.

Since 1978, the main Black Consciousness organizations have been AZAPO and later the National Forum Committee (NFC), a federation of community organizations with which AZAPO is affiliated. Just as there has been a realignment of the nonracial tradition through the UDF, so too with the black republican tradition—that strand of black nationalism which argues uncompromisingly that a liberated South Africa (Azania) must be under black rule. Opposition to the ANC and the South African Communist party (SACP), with which the ANC has developed a fraternal relationship from the 1940s onwards, has always been expressed by black nationalist organizations such as the PAC and black Marxist groups like the Non-European Unity Movement (NEUM). The PAC opposed the ANC's relationship with the Communists on primarily racial grounds, while NEUM combined both racial and class issues in their objection.

In response to the UDF's nonracialism, the NFC has forged a loose alliance of black nationalists and black Marxists. This has been dramatized by the fact that both AZAPO, with its origins in the BCM, and CAL, with its origins in NEUM Marxism, function within the NFC. Lybon Mabasa, a member of the AZAPO executive, provides a telling list of intellectual influences that include both racial and socialist, civil rights and Black Power thinkers—Kwame Nkrumah, Frantz Fanon, Lenin, Marx, and Rosa Luxemburg (Gastrow 1985:144). On the other hand, Neville Alexander, the CAL theoretician who was expelled from NEUM in July 1961, insists that "race is not only irrelevant, from a scientific point of view it is a non-entity; it simply does not exist" (1985:36). The basic tenets that unite adherents to the otherwise eclectic NFC are (1) the rejection of whites in black liberation politics, (2) opposition to the Freedom Charter, and (3) a critique of the two-stage theory of the struggle for socialism (Lodge 1985:18). Disagreements, however, have surfaced within the NFC regarding the role of whites in the liberation struggle.

Where race and class are combined, a more radical, if not consistent, brand of Marxism is possible since the black race and the working class are taken to be virtually the same. By the 1930s, the leadership of NEUM and its chief theoretician, I.B. Tabata, were attempting to reconcile class and race within a black Trotskyist analysis. Nonracial Marxists were no less aware of the challenge of the race-class issue. In a famous letter written in 1934, Moses Kotane, a respected black South African Communist, called for the Africanization (and by this he also meant the Bolshevization) of the SACP. Kotane noted that in Europe class consciousness had developed immensely but that in South Africa national and racial consciousness still predominated. He readily confessed that it was difficult to convince black workers that they shared a common plight with their counterparts across the racial divide (Kotane 1981:119–20).

This perception was readily understood by the Africanists, who broke with the multiracial ANC in 1959 to form the uniracial PAC. In exile after 1962, the PAC was attracted to Maoist versions of racial militancy but failed to formulate a coherent theory of racial revolution. Instead, the PAC virtually adopted the position of Tabata and the NEUM. Critical of the ANC/SACP alliance, both organizations contend that in the South African context multiracial Marxism is by definition reformist. Both the PAC and the NEUM considered the Soviet-aligned SACP to be dominated by a clique of white left liberals and charged that the Communist party, fearing true black power, would cling to multiracialism and a reformist political agenda (Jordaan 1968:12–20). Even when rival black nationalist groups have adopted aspects of Marxian analysis, as have the ANC, PAC, and NEUM, they remain divided over how to interpret the relationship between socialism and black nationalism. George Padmore remarked that on such questions South African radicals are the "best hairsplitters in Africa" (1972:339). Therefore, whatever may be the immediate political rationale, the alliance between AZAPO and CAL has deep historical roots in the tradition of black revolutionary thought.

The Soviet Union, which has always favored the ANC, continues to view the immediate struggle in South Africa as one for democracy (not socialism) and nonracialism, although socialism may result from a later stage of popular and working-class struggle against capitalism. Soviet-oriented Marxists have favored multiracial coalitions; more radical black nationalists, when they have embraced Marxism, tend to favor anti-Soviet approaches. With China's withdrawal of financial support from Southern African liberation movements, factions more oriented toward a theory of racial struggle were forced into extinction or compromise and even collaboration with South Africa. In a cogent and lasting analysis of Southern African liberation movements in exile, John Marcum (1972:267–68) observed that Moscow has tended to support movements led by the well-educated, multiracial, urbanized elite with some grasp of Marxism-Leninism. Beijing, on the other hand, leaned toward uniracial or nonwhite, less well educated (except for the top leadership) groups, and it preferred peasants or manual workers rather than intellectuals. Hindsight has allowed many analysts to conclude simplistically that "liberation losers" have always been racial reactionaries and bearers of an "incorrect line."

In racially divided South Africa, black-movement theorists have been forced to comprehend both race and class and to assert the possibility of either intraclass/interracial solidarity (black and white unite and fight) or intraracial/interclass solidarity (working or middle class leadership of a multiclass exclusively black movement). Under the conditions of racial proletarianization, as racially divided working and bourgeois classes develop, two forms of populist ideology are possible: a nationalist populism that dissolves class differences into assertions of national or racial solidarity and a socialist populism that asserts that the termination of capitalism will automatically resolve racial inequality. Socialist populism can be of either a Black Consciousness or multiracial variety. These two forms of populist thought differ on the question of what constitutes national consciousness—is it black (racial) or multiracial (all South Africa's people minus apartheid)? In this analysis, populism is conceived as an alternative to both socialist and liberal thought. It may be the most prevalent theory of democracy in the non-Western world. Like socialist and liberal democracy, populist democracy has failed to eliminate class rule. Although populism shares an affinity with the socialist critique of capitalist society, it ultimately stresses national, racial, or ethnic rather than class consciousness.

As was true of its European counterparts, the emergence of the working class as an independent center of political activity in South Africa has forced black revolutionary thinkers to examine black politics in light of mass democratic principles. By the mid-1970s, both Black Consciousness and nonracial-oriented groups had come to recognize that neither approach resolved the problem of intraracial class distinctions. This recognition, encouraged by the growth of the independent trade union movement, prompted much reconsideration of the relationship between community-based antiapartheid and trade union movements. Trade union federations, protective of the interests of workers, have on occasion accused the antiapartheid leadership of a policy bias toward the emergent black bourgeoisie. In order to protect the interests of workers, unionists have demanded worker control of trade unions. Both Black Consciousness and nonracial organizations now agree that the principle of working-class leadership should be respected within the antiapartheid movement.

But while COSATU defines working-class leadership in the broadest possible terms and would welcome white workers, for NACTU working-class leadership means in practical terms the leadership of the black working class. Since the overwhelming majority of workers are black, the question is moot, except for the role of white intellectuals in the trade union movement. Black Consciousness organizations demand black leadership and control of the labor and community opposition to apartheid. Soon after its formation in 1985, COSATU's leadership agreed to adopt the Freedom Charter. This was done with the apparent understanding that the document will be interpreted so as to encompass the specific interests of workers. Some activists view the Charter as a blueprint for a socialist rather than a nonracial democratic society.

The ANC has gradually sought to distance itself from a purely racial or socialist analysis of South African politics. In exile it expelled both its radical black nationalist and Marxist factions but now confronts complicated theoretical (and organizational) problems as it attempts to stake out a credible centrist position as a legal opposition inside the country. As early as 1984, Thabo Mbeki, a leading member of the ANC, emphasized that the ANC is not a socialist party, although many of its members are committed to a socialist future for South Africa.[4]

Black Consciousness and New Left Thought

In South Africa and in the United States, the politics and thought of the New Left, together with the Black Consciousness and the Black Power movements respectively, constitute distinct variations of a generational theme. White and black intellectuals of the same generation have rarely been members of the same organizational cadres and have not shared a common political perspective on the experiences of their generation. Black Consciousness thought, as a critical reconstruction of the black South African political tradition, is distinguishable from traditional black nationalism. When this is not appreciated, the subtleties of the relationship between Black Consciousness and New Left radicalism is missed.

Looking back, "Terror" Lekota, national publicity secretary of the UDF, contends that the political writings of the BCM are vastly inferior to the Freedom Charter. His description of his own political evolution, however, captures the generational politics of the period: "The banning of the ANC in 1960 . . . plus the exiling of uncompromising opponents of apartheid opened a wide and yawning gap between the following generations and those who had gone before. . . . We were determined to discover our history. We knew that as long as we remained untutored in the history of struggle we would repeat the mistakes of the past" (Lekota, 1986:197). In its original manifestation, Black Consciousness philosophy, as a moment in the history of black political thought, was a South African contribution to the worldwide development of New Left critical theory. Dick Howard (1984:8) defines a critical theory as the paradoxical formulation of a norm that seeks to negate the conditions of its own possibility. Black Consciousness philosophy found aspects of liberalism, Marxism, and even black nationalism to be forms of noncritical theory. In other words, when these three perspectives were applied to the contemporary dimensions of racial domination, they either functioned in some manner to defend the status quo or sought to define liberation in a way that obfuscated the political and psychological dynamics of racial oppression.

During this same period, many white radicals were engaged in a similar process of rethinking the definition of class, the relationship of class struggle to politics, and the meaning of "revolutionary subject" in contemporary capitalism. New Left experimentation with revolutionary thought transcended ideological boundaries and revived concern with the issue of human emancipation as a transideological project. New Left social theory "rejects capitalist reform, socialist and communist social systems as well as the social theories that justify them. Social inequality, elitist authoritarian hierarchy and repressive manipulation are seen as the common coordinates of bureaucratic domination which lie behind ideological mystifications buttressing each of these systems. In place of such structures, New-Left social theory posits the possibility of an egalitarian society free of the alienation characteristic of contemporary society" (Hirsh, 1981:6).

Black Consciousness thought offered a critique of capitalism that was radical without being explicitly Marxist, and democratic while offering a critique of the limits of South African liberalism. A distinctly Black Consciousness approach to liberalism remains a central part of the Confederation of Unions of South Africa–Azanian Confederation of Trade Unions (CUSA-AZACTU) (which later became NACTU) demand for black leadership of the trade union movement: "Liberals have one common characteristic and that is they want to lead and direct the pace of our struggle" (CUSA/AZACTU 1987:2). Indeed, this approach to liberalism is very close to the view of both the PAC and NEUM that liberals (all white radicals) constitute a fifth column within the opposition movement. The BCM's critique of liberalism upset many white sympathizers but its major challenge was offered to the black movement itself. Simply stated, the central contention of Black Consciousness philosophy was that heightened racial awareness and solidarity had to be the primary goal of the liberation movement. The lack of racial consciousness was rooted in black self-hatred and this had major political implications: the black person's low sense of self-esteem fostered political disunity, allowed ethnic leaders and other moderates to usurp the role of spokespersons for the black masses, and encouraged a dependence on white leadership. Black Consciousness philosophy was viewed by its advocates as an alternative to psychological and ideological complicity with racial oppression.

Critics of the BCM, including some who are deeply committed to the ideas and methods of the previous generation, have not been generous in their assessments. It has often been pointed out that the BCM failed to provide vanguard leadership to the youth and worker movements (Hirson 1979; Mafeje 1978; Brooks and Brickhill 1980). Another oft-repeated criticism of the BCM is that its racially based political analysis ignored class and was therefore retrogressive, as was its practice (Fisher 1977; Hirson 1979; Alexander 1985). With a few notable exceptions, the BCM has not been evaluated as a philosophical or social movement by critics who have stressed its failure to produce a vanguard party.[5]

What may have been the most revolutionary aspect of the early BCM was its essentially nonstatist orientation. Not only did it oppose the apartheid state, but it did so without viewing itself as a "state coming into being." Consistent with its revolutionary self-perception, during its heyday the BCM refused to form another liberation movement that would make black unity more difficult, and it gradually called upon the emerging black middle class to commit "class suicide" on behalf of popular leadership. BCM strategy sought to capture the ground of spontaneity somewhere between the politics of sectarianism (the squabbles between the ANC, PAC, and NEUM) and that of reformism (the bantustan leadership).

The politics of the BCM has been shaped by the generational dynamics of the late 1960s and early 1970s. Although many analysts initially pigeonholed the BCM as an Africanist organization, thus linking it to the PAC, the movement was always ideologically eclectic, and so it remains. Some leading members of the BCM joined the ANC, others the PAC. Those who remained inside the country became members of either the UDF or the NFC as well as various trade unions. Cyril Ramaphosa, general secretary of the National Union of Mineworkers (NUM), an affiliate of COSATU, began his career as an activist in the BCM, as did many others.

The late Steve Biko sought to combine theoretical elements from ANC, PAC, and NEUM analyses. During his testimony at the South African Students Organization/Black People's Convention (SASO/BPC) trials held between February 1975 and January 1976, Biko refused to criticize any of the factions of the liberation leadership; he openly acknowledged the contributions of leaders committed to either violent overthrow of the apartheid state or communism. Biko defended the liberatory tradition in all of its manifestations. He even lamented what he considered to be the waste of able leaders, like Gatsha Buthelezi, who chose to operate from a government-sponsored platform.[6]

Presently, AZAPO functions as an opposition within the nonracial mainstream of the antiapartheid movement. While they are often accused of being sectarian themselves, the leading advocates of the Black Consciousness position contend that sectarianism (the belief that everyone who disagrees with my party's political position is an enemy) constitutes one of the most dangerous developments in the liberation struggle (Alexander 1986:13). The rhetoric of spontaneity, central to Black Consciousness thought of a decade ago, has shaped the self-perception of many contemporary activists. Noncollaboration, however, is the BCM's most consistent policy stance. Strini Moodley describes the role of AZAPO as that of a watchdog of the liberatory struggle. He believes that AZAPO must work to reinforce the doctrine of noncollaboration and to prevent any type of sell out arrangement (Gastrow 1985:199). Black politics during the present decade has been marked by both increased confrontation with the state and a far greater degree of internecine warfare between black movements. The rationale for confrontation with the police and military may be ungovernability, but the rationale for internecine warfare is the "policing" of the form negotiations will eventually assume. In this regard, AZAPO's and the NFC's staunch policy of non-collaboration may represent the most uncompromising position within the black opposition.

Eddie Webster observes that "the rise of Black Consciousness in South Africa coincided with the renewal of Marxist thought in universities in Britain, Europe and North America" (1985:45). Black and white intellectuals have addressed political issues within the confines of historically segregated societies. With specific reference to South Africa, the government's hostility to universal educational norms and its constant intervention in the educational process have turned the campus into an arena of permanent protest. The racially based unequal allocation of educational resources and the denial of black civil rights also ensure that intellectual politics will have a Black Consciousness dimension. The philosophy of Black Consciousness is distinguishable from the BCM, or any other specific organizational manifestation, and will continue to be a factor in South African politics.

Today, as in the past, the left-wing intelligentsia in South Africa is divided over the race-class question. Disputes between Black Consciousness and neo-Marxism are not only expressions of conflict among generational cadres but also expressions of power relations within a highly radicalized multiracial intelligentsia. While the NFC probably has less of a proletarian following than the UDF, both AZAPO and CAL have strong intellectual followings (Lodge 1985:18). Thus, the BCM's insistence that white liberals want to dominate the black movement articulates a deep-seated concern of the new black intelligentsia. Although neo-Marxist and Black Consciousness intellectuals castigate liberalism on different grounds, the critique of liberal politics provides them with a common point of departure; both groups of intellectuals end up advocating the centrality of the black working class. Webster is candid about the competition between black and white intellectuals: "Liberal institutions were to come under sharp attack by the Black Consciousness movement in the 1960's because of their ineffectiveness within the white power structure. The emphasis of Black Consciousness on the need for blacks to mobilize as a group left white liberals with a deep uncertainty about their role in change in South Africa. Marxism, with its bold claims of class as the motor of history, offered a new generation of white academics an intellectually coherent political alternative to Black Consciousness" (Webster 1985:45).

In a discussion of the politics of the radical intelligentsia in South Africa, Craig Charney makes the insightful observation that the BCM was "an effort to reconstitute the black middle class as an independent political force through the efforts of the black intelligentsia" (1986:12–13). He then characterizes BCM conceptions as "vague and idealist" and describes Black Consciousness thought as a species of black liberalism proffered as a response to the complacency of white liberalism. From the beginning, some members of the old left had castigated Biko as a liberal (Toussaint 1979).

Debates over the role of whites in the black opposition movement have changed ground and may reflect a growing confidence on the part of the black intelligentsia. Attitudinal surveys of educated blacks reveal that the most educated 10 percent of that population have the strongest commitment to an "ethos of equality" and that this informs their views on alliances with whites, the democratic franchise, tribal ties, and support for political change as well as for political violence (Brewer 1986:289).

A recent spate of writings attempting to formulate a general theory of intellectual activity question whether the politics of the New Left can be adequately comprehended by the term *petty-bourgeoisie*, the standard Marxist category. Several class-analytic approaches prefer either *professional managerial class* or *educated labor*. The late Alvin Gouldner goes further and identifies the intelligentsia as a New Class. Gouldner believes that *career* is the operative word even in the study of a revolutionary intelligentsia (Gouldner 1979:11). In this respect, he claims that "Lenin's call for the development of 'professional' revolutionaries as the core of the vanguard, is a rhetoric carrying the tacit promise of a career-like life which invites young members of the New Class to 'normalize' the revolutionary existence" (1979:5).

In a similar vein, John Brewer has employed the concept of educated labor in an attempt to explain why there are so many middle-class groups at the forefront of black protest in South Africa, why the protest movement is more community-based than plant-based, and why protest ideology tends to de-emphasize concrete material gains. Brewer (1986:288) notes that South Africa represents the optimal milieu for the development of black revolutionary intellectuals. South African capitalism, like capitalism in general, is becoming dependent on educated labor:

> Whites can simply no longer run the factories, produce the goods, and manage the administration without the assistance of black South Africans. Through its series of reforms, the government is opening up occupational mobility and economic rights to a privileged section of Blacks. This is reinforcing the demographic and economic trends that are behind the creation of educated labour. Together, they have produced a restructuring of the racial divisions of labour in South Africa. The enormous growth of Black education has been both the cause and effect of this occupational restructuring. Contained herein is the essential contradiction in the government's attempt to win Black compliance and support. For it is the higher educated strata of the black population, who as educated labour fill the middle management, technical and professional positions and who are the object of the state's co-option measures which is leading to black protest. (Brewer 1986:287)

Thus, the postuniversity careers of the black intelligentsia have become radicalized, and this strata is the backbone of many black protest organizations.

Unlike the demands of the previous generation of black republicans, the most radical of whom called for the total removal of all whites from South Africa, almost every strain of Black Consciousness thought today accepts the proposition that whites have a future in a nonracial South Africa. Every new theory of black politics has an implicit conception of the role of whites in a liberated South Africa, as well as in the movement to realize that goal. The very recognition of continued white involvement in politics, however, makes the question of black leadership and efforts to define its meaning all the more crucial and controversial for the BCM. Debates over "leadership" usually evoke a host of theoretical concerns regarding criteria of accountability and representativeness. Leaders are expected to embody the cultural values and social goals of their supporters. Such expectations relate questions of leadership to those of ideology.

Racial Capitalism and Black Consciousness Socialism

The Black Consciousness critique of capitalism is consistent with the long-standing view of many African revolutionaries that the individualistic and assimilationist tendencies of capitalist development impinge upon racial or communal solidarity. The belief that capitalism poses a major threat to black identity is prominent in the thought of the radical anticapitalist populism of Frantz Fanon as well as the more moderate Negritude philosophy of Leopold Sedar Senghor. Tom Lodge (1985:17–19) notes that democratic or progressive nationalism, communal socialism, and workerism are three ideological currents that influence all shades of black resistance politics in South Africa.

The roots of BCM socialism are to be found in the characterization of the South African political economy as "racial capitalism," of which apartheid is viewed as merely an expression. Thus, the NFC contends that socialism must be a prerequisite for democracy. In contrast to the BCM, the ANC and its ally the SACP advocate a "two-stage theory of revolution" that disaggregates democratic and socialist phases of struggle. No longer exclusively associated with Black Consciousness, "racial capitalism" has become a uniquely South African approach to socialist thought. From this perspective, apartheid rests equally on the twin pillars of capitalist and state power and can only be replaced by a socialist order. The racial-capitalist thesis has been fully elaborated in the Azanian Manifesto issued in June 1983. This document is based on five essential principles: (1) antiracism, (2) anti-imperialism, (3) noncollaboration with the oppressor, (4) independent working-class organization, and (5) opposition to all alliances with ruling-class parties.

The racial-capitalist conception seeks to combine a form of class analysis that does not negate the need for racial solidarity with a critique of the coalitional politics of the nonracial wings of both the trade union and liberation movements. Race-class synthesis often sacrifices a strict Marxist class perspective. Adam and Moodley sarcastically note that the black socialist position "not only overlooks all the refinements of class analysis in the last decade but also fails to take into account the autonomous role of the state" (1986:98). With reference to trade unions, Brewer (1986) estimates that there is greater support among better-educated blacks and whites for trade unionism than among black workers. He believes political unionism is a manifestation of the politics of the educated labor class in relation to alliances with the working class. Charney notes that "now university educated whites and blacks queue to become trade union organizers, the new campus idols" (1986:18).

Indeed, Brewer is quite correct in his observation that black educated labor is most acutely aware of the impact of racial restructuring within the state and the capitalist economy. The black intelligentsia recognizes that economic reforms do not automatically translate into power for the black community. The racial-capitalist critique is consistent with the social character of a class of black educated laborers who will certainly be generously represented in any postapartheid dispensation that empowers black South Africans. The continuing political challenge to this growing class of blacks is how best to manage a successful struggle against apartheid rule. Virtually all attempts to sum up the political trends of the 1970s have rightfully stressed the interaction of the trade union and community movements and the spread of anticapitalist sentiments among the intelligentsia.

The important socialist scholar John Saul, who empathizes with aspects of the racial-capitalist critique—if not specific Black Consciousness groupings—warns that South African capitalism has breathed new life into racial hierarchy in the past (Saul 1986). He therefore considers it essential that the transition to socialism be kept on the agenda of the democratic opposition. Saul clearly shows the differences between the Black Consciousness racial-capitalist analysis and the ANC's two-stage revolution analysis. The ANC believes that South African struggle is characterized by (1) a colonialism of a special type, (2) a two-stage revolution with a national democratic stage being the first and a socialist stage following, and (3) the possibility of a genuine revolutionary alliance between proletarian and nonproletarian as well as anticapitalist and antiracist forces. On the other hand, the racial-capitalist analysis assumes that (1) colonialism is moot given the level of capitalist development, (2) socialism is the only way to terminate apartheid, and (3) democracy is only possible under socialist conditions.

Over the last decade, important advances in democratic thought and practice have resulted from the need for non-working-class leaders to relate to the demands of the far larger working-class majority. The impact of educated labor on the trade union movement has not been a unidirectional development. Numerous analysts argue that the independent trade union movement has had a tremendous democratizing impact on those intellectuals who have been involved. The argument of COSATU member Alec Erwin (1985) to the effect that the workers' movement has helped to push the politics of liberation toward a politics of transformation is compelling. Before the growth of the independent trade union movement, liberation politics tended toward a reified orthodoxy with respect to the relationship between reform and revolution. Both the ANC and PAC considered the Sharpeville massacre the turning point beyond which anything but armed struggle was sheer folly. As Dennis Davis and Robert Fine point out, "A tendency was born which equated armed struggle with revolution and legal struggle with reformism" (1985:39).

The explosion of trade union and community organizations has overwhelmed the ability of any national leadership to control the democratic demand for accountability and has served to reintroduce the possibility of what Andre Gorz (1973) refers to as a revolutionary strategy of democratic reform. The trade unions, of course, call for worker control and in some places migrant workers have begun to demand democratic behavior even in their hostels (Sitas 1985:32–43). There are instances as with the Alexandra Action Committee where Johann Maree reports that "since most of the people were workers so the structures were based along the lines of trade union structures—accountability, elections every year and so on" (1986:81).

Steven Friedman finds that union democracy is contagious in a society where few blacks have any experience of democracy and most are workers. Local leaders now have to be more responsive to grass-roots initiatives, particularly in predominantly working-class townships. Thus, beneath the heavy-handed state repression of the last decade a deepening of democratic politics has occurred. According to Friedman, "Disturbances have prompted the first attempts by both the authorities and black activists to resolve conflicts outside the factories by negotiation. This trend has been most noticeable in smaller townships which seems to suggest that the potential for local negotiation politics is stronger if residents are organized into smaller units whose leaders can retain firmer links with their constituents and are less subject to pressures from high-profile national leaders hostile to local negotiations" (1986:7).

Although it was ruthlessly battered by the Botha regime, the reemergence of a multiclass black opposition inside the country has necessitated a reconsideration of the characteristics of a nonracial and democratic society. In South Africa, formulation of an effective strategy for change is complicated by the interconnections between race and class. Determination of the actual relationship between racial domination and capitalism is no less complicated. The South African left has generally associated the contention that capitalism corrodes the racial state with liberal ideology. Likewise, political analyses that stress the autonomy of racial struggle from class struggle have also been discarded by leading theorists of the BCM.

The initial critical imperative of the BCM was its refusal to allow the demand for black solidarity to be subsumed by liberal or socialist perspectives. Given the long history of racial oppression in South Africa, a transition to a nonracial democracy will not preclude a role for organizations that are primarily concerned with racial upliftment and progress. Political organizers will still have to build coalitions on the basis of previously existing social divisions even as they attempt to construct social welfare policies designed to transcend the long history of racial domination and injustice. Irrespective of the successes or failures of its particular organizational manifestations, Black Consciousness perspectives will not immediately disappear even in a postapartheid South Africa. And while Black Consciousness thought may remain a distinctly minority tendency when compared with nonracialism, the complexity of black political thought cannot be appreciated without considering both approaches to the negation of white supremacy.

NOTES

1. See also Crapranzano (1985).

2. For a discussion of these two approaches to the dynamics of the South African state, see James (1986), in which he revises his harsher view of Nolutshungu contained in his paper presented at the Conference on Economic Development and Racial Domination in Bellville, South Africa (8–10 October 1984). Cf. Nolutshungu (1982).

3. While white settlement in South Africa was linked to early forms of international capitalism, racial domination produced its own class counterpart—racial proletarianization. Thus, the relationship of racism and captialism can be understood as a particular phenomenology within which numerous research projects are possible. Racial proletarianization defines a field of events that are not self-evident but can be made meaningful within the boundary categories of race and class. Furthermore, the plethora of recent historical writings on South Africa can be read in light of their ability to comprehend racial politics within the framework of the emergence of South African capitalism. "Racial proletarianization" is not necessarily an argument for "racial capitalism" as that conception is propounded by the left wing of the contemporary Black Consciousness Movement. We need not assume that in all instances racism serves the interests of capitalism or that there can be no reorganization of power without a concurrent abolition of capitalist production. In other words, liberal-democratic and social-democratic options need not be dismissed solely on logical grounds. The manner in which capitalist relations of production are consummated or terminated should be the subject of inquiry.

4. Mbeki (1984) was responding to Fatton's (1984) accusation that the ANC has abandoned socialism.

5. For critical appraisals of the BCM, see Baruch Hirson (1979); Archie Mafeje (1978); Alan Brooks and Jeremy Brickhill (1980); and Fozia Fisher (1977). For more positive assessments, see Nolutshungu (1982) and Tom Lodge (1983).

6. See Steve Biko's testimony at the SASO/BPC trials during May 1976 (Arnold 1978).

REFERENCES

Adam, Heribert, and Kogila Moodley. 1986. *South Africa Without Apartheid*. Berkeley: University of California Press.

Alexander, Neville. 1985. "The National Situation." In *Sow the Wind: Contemporary Speeches*, ed. N. Alexander, 23–40. Johannesburg: Skotaville Publishers.

———. 1986. "Aspects of Non-Collaboration in the Western Cape, 1943–1963." *Social Dynamics* 12(1):1–14.

Arnold, Millard, ed. 1978. *Steve Biko: Black Consciousness in South Africa*. New York: Random House.

Brewer, John D. 1986. "Black Protest in South Africa's Crisis: A Comment on Legassick." *African Affairs* 85, no. 339 (April):283–94.

Brooks, Alan, and Jeremy Brickhill. 1980. *Whirlwind before the Storm*. London: International Defense and Aid Fund for Southern Africa.

Charney, Craig. 1986. "Thinking of Revolution: The New South African Intelligentsia." *Monthly Review* 38 (December):10–19.

Crapranzano, Vincent. 1985. *Waiting: The Whites of South Africa*. New York: Random House.

———. 1987. "Ending Apartheid: The Whites of South Africa." Lecture sponsored by the African Studies Program, Indiana University, Bloomington, March.

CUSA/AZACTU. 1987. "Remarks to the Special Committee Against Apartheid of the United Nations, 26–27 February." Photocopy.

Davis, Dennis, and Robert Fine. 1985. "Political Strategies and the State: Some Historical Observations." *Journal of Southern African Studies* 12(1):25–48.

Fatton, Robert, Jr. 1984. "The African National Congress of South Africa: The Limitations of a Revolutionary Strategy." *Canadian Journal of African Studies* 18(3):593–608.

Fisher, Fozia. 1977. "Class Consciousness among Colonized Workers in South Africa." In *Perspectives on South Africa,* ed. T. Adler. Johannesburg: University of the Witwatersrand.

Friedman, Steve. 1986. "Black Politics at the Crossroads." South African Institute of Race Relations Topical Briefing.

Gastrow, Shelagh, ed. 1985. *Who's Who in South African Politics*. Johannesburg: Raven Press.

Gerhart, Gail M. 1978. *Black Power in South Africa: The Evolution of an Ideology*. Berkeley: University of California Press.

Gorz, Andre. 1973. *Socialism and Revolution*. Trans. Norman Denny. Garden City, NY: Anchor Books.

Gouldner, Alvin W. 1979. *The Future of Intellectuals and the Rise of the New Class*. New York: Seabury Press.

Hirsh, Arthur. 1981. *The French New Left: An Intellectual History from Sartre to Gorz*. Boston: South End Press.

Hirson, Baruch. 1979. *Year of Fire, Year of Ash*. London: Zed Press.

Howard, Dick. 1984. "A Political Theory for Marxism: Restoring Politics to Political Economy." *New Political Science* 13 (Winter):5–26.

Innes, Duncan, and Stephen Gelb. 1987. "Towards a Democratic Economy in South Africa." *Third World Quarterly* 19(2):545–82.

James, Wilmot G. 1984. "Class, Race and Democracy: Nolutshungu's South Africa." In *On the Political Economy of Race: Proceedings of the Conference on Economic Development and Racial Domination*. Paper no. 18. Bellville, South Africa.

———. 1986. "Nolutshungu's South Africa." *Social Dynamics* 12(1):43–48.

Jordaan, K. A. 1968. "The Communist Party in South Africa: Its Counter-Revolutionary Role." *World Revolution* 1(2):12–20.

Kotane, Moses. 1981. "Letter Calling for Africanisation of the Party from Moses Kotane in Cradock to Johannesburg District Party Committee Dated February 23, 1934." In *South African Communists Speak: Documents from the History of the South African Communist Party, 1915–1980*. London: Inkululeko Publications.

Laclau, Ernesto. 1979. *Politics and Ideology in Marxist Theory*. London: Verso Editions.

Lekota, "Terror" Mosiuoa Patrick. 1986. "A Personal Account." In *30 Years of the Freedom Charter*, comps. Raymond Suttner and Jeremy Cronin. Johannesburg: Raven Press.

Lijphart, Arend. 1987. "The Ethnic Factor and Democratic Constitution-Making in South Africa." Paper presented at the Forty-first Annual Meeting of the Western Political Science Association, Anaheim, California, 26–28 March.

Lodge, Tom. 1983. *Black Politics in South Africa since 1945*. London: Longman.

———. 1985. Introduction to *Who's Who in South African Politics*, ed. Shelagh Gastrow. Johannesburg: Raven Press.

Mafeje, Archie. 1978. "Soweto and Its Aftermath." *Review of African Political Economy* 11 (January–April).

Marcum, John A. 1972. "The Exile Condition and Revolutionary Effectiveness: Southern African Liberation Movements." In *Southern Africa in Perspective: Essays in Regional Politics*, eds. Christian P. Potholm and Richard Dale, 262–75. New York: Free Press.

Maree, Johann. 1986. "A Democratic Economy with Independent Trade Unions." *South African International* 17, no. 2 (October).

Marks, Shula. 1986. *The Ambiguities of Dependence in South Africa: Class, Nationalism, and the State in Twentieth-Century Natal*. Baltimore and London: Johns Hopkins University Press.

Mbeki, Thabo. 1984. "The Fatton Thesis: A Rejoinder." *Canadian Journal of African Studies* 18(3):609–12.

New York Times. 1989. 16 October.

Nolutshungu, Sam. 1982. *Changing South Africa*. Manchester: Manchester University Press.

O'Meara, Patrick, and Brian Winchester. 1987. "South Africa." In *Encyclopedia Americana Annual*, 462–65. New York and Chicago: Americana Corporation.

Padmore, George. 1972. *Pan-Africanism or Communism*. Garden City, NY: Anchor Books.

Saul, John. 1986. "South Africa: The Question of Unity in the Struggle." *South African Labour Bulletin* 11, no. 1 (September):5–13.

Sitas, Ari. 1985. "From Grassroots Control to Democracy: A Case Study of the Impact of Trade Unionism on Migrant Workers' Cultural Formations on the East Rand." *Social Dynamics* 11, no. 1 (October):32–43.

Toussaint. 1979. "'Fallen Among Liberals': An Ideology of Black Consciousness." *African Communist* 78:18–30.

Walshe, Peter. 1971. *The Rise of Nationalism in South Africa: The African National Congress, 1912–1952*. Berkeley: University of California Press.

Webster, Eddie. 1985. "Competing Paradigms: Towards a Critical Sociology in Southern Africa." *Social Dynamics* 11(1):44–48.

5

Democratizing the United Democratic Front: The Muddy Slope

KARL S. BECK

The history of resistance to white domination in South Africa will note 29 March 1986 for an important event in the struggle against apartheid. On that day in Durban, *New Nation* editor Zwelakhe Sisulu faced a thousand young revolutionaries in an incendiary atmosphere. Sisulu urged the youth to eschew violence and school boycotts and to join with adult opponents of apartheid in strengthening grass-roots organizations to oppose the political program of the National party government.

At the time, 1.7 million black youths were boycotting schools in the false hope that liberation was just around the corner. The brutalizing effects of thirty-five years of apartheid rule and its devastation of educational, social, and economic conditions affecting black South Africans had caused deep resentment among blacks throughout the country. Young blacks were particularly angry because they saw themselves being trained for inferior roles in a failing economy that offered few prospects for a secure future. Yet if the youths had continued the boycott, black South Africa would have faced the prospects of a generation of illiterates and a significant setback in the struggle for black political empowerment.

In 1985–86 many of the young *comrades*, the term used generally for youth supporters of the antiapartheid United Democratic Front (UDF), believed incorrectly that more riots and chaos in black neighborhoods were all that was needed to bring down the South African government. But in the eyes of large numbers of their fellow blacks, the comrades posed a more immediate danger than the government they opposed.

The same youths were the core of the UDF, the internal political association that shared the aspirations of the then banned African National Congress (ANC). The UDF, a federation of more than 600 organizations, was formed in 1983 to protest the South African government's attempts to reconfigure apartheid and make it more acceptable to black South Africans and the international community. Given the numbers and energies of the youth, the UDF needed to hold on to their support as much as it needed to stop the chaos that they were causing. At issue were the survival of the internal movement and the future of South Africa's black youth.

The 1986 Durban Conference

The occasion of Zwelakhe Sisulu's bold speech was a conference of the National Education Crisis Committee (NECC), an organization formed in late 1985 by a group of mostly adult UDF supporters to try to resolve the education crisis. Following an initial meeting in Johannesburg in December 1985 under the auspices of the Soweto Parents Crisis Committee, the NECC undertook an intense schedule of consultations with local and external groups, including the ANC, aimed at developing a national consensus on the need for black youths to go back to school.

The Durban conference began in danger and excited expectation. The conference site was changed three times following bombings and threats of more violence. Finally the identity of the hall where the meeting actually occurred was kept secret even from those who were on their way there. One thousand people were led to the unknown destination in convoys after dark. The conference proceedings did not begin until after ten o'clock and continued through the night. The boisterous singing and frantic stomping of the *toi toi* dance of the revolution could hardly have been more antithetical to the dry logic of Sisulu's speech.

The thirty-five-year-old Sisulu, heir to a great South African political legacy, argued that the comrades' zeal threatened to create obstacles to achieving the freedom they sought. Opposing a continuation of school boycotts and seeking an opening for expansion of the forces of the revolt, Sisulu said: "We will not defeat apartheid while the youth alone carry on the struggle against Bantu education or other aspects of racist rule" (National Education Crisis Committee 1986b:33).

Sisulu faced young political activists who had been in the front lines of resistance politics since the Soweto uprising ten years earlier. Some had burned schools, government buildings, and government collaborators' properties. They had experienced violent confrontation, and they had boycotted South Africa's "Bantu education" schools for all or part of several previous years. Many also had directed or perpetrated threats and acts of violence against other blacks in order to promote consumer, school and election boycotts in communities where individual levels of black political awareness varied widely.

In attendance at the Durban conference was the upper echelon of the young activists who since 1983 had also blocked acceptance by blacks of the cornerstones of the South African government's reform program, the tricameral parliament, which introduced separate houses for whites, "coloreds" (mixed race), and Indians, and locally elected administration of black urban areas. Their success had reawakened in the minds of South Africans and international decision makers the possibility that South Africa would one day have a majority government. But despite their successes, Sisulu's listeners included elements of the UDF that were a radical force, out of control and in danger of self-destruction.

Most of the comrades had believed in 1985 that 1986 would be the year of liberation. They were committed to sowing "ungovernability" in black areas as the means of achieving freedom. In the parlance of the black townships, they were the *siyayinyova*, ("we are causing chaos"). In urging them to alter their strategy, Sisulu argued for a return to the ANC tradition of *umzabalazo*, a disciplined approach which since 1961 has included targeted violence as one of numerous tactics but which recognizes the need for a long-term strategy of multifaceted struggle against the system of white domination.

In the Nguni languages, the different meanings of the infinitive verb roots of the two expressions offer a colorful contrast. *Ukuyinyova* is to resort to uncontrollable violence in the way a disinherited wife might break up the funeral feast for her dead husband who has left his property to another woman. Shouting insults, kicking over pots of food, and assaulting the heiress, the aggrieved widow makes everyone aware of her anger, but she gains nothing of lasting value for herself. *Ukuzabalaza*, on the other hand, describes the exercise of strength and cunning such as that which is needed to climb up the slippery slope of a muddy riverbank. In the latter situation, lashing out in anger carries the risk of tumbling back into the water below.

Sisulu spoke bluntly to the young radicals: "We are not poised for the immediate transfer of power to the people. The belief that this is so could lead to serious errors and defeats. We are however poised to enter a phase which can lead to transfer of power. What we are seeking to do is to decisively shift the balance of forces in our favor. To do this we have to adopt the appropriate strategies and tactics, we have to understand our strengths and weaknesses, as well as that of the enemy, that is, the forces of apartheid reaction" (National Education Crisis Committee, 1986a:5). *Weekly Mail* reporter Patrick Laurence described Sisulu's address as "not the product of a temperate moderate so much as a disciplined radical" (Laurence 1986).

The speech Zwelakhe Sisulu read was the product of a drafting committee, but the choice of Sisulu as keynote speaker was rich in symbolism. Son of giants of the "struggle," Walter and Albertina Sisulu, Zwelakhe carried onto the stage of the Rajput Center hall the mantle of a family whose leading participation in the resistance encompasses several significant tendencies of post–World War II black politics.

Walter Sisulu was a founder of the African National Congress Youth League, which critically altered the direction of the elitist-led congress in the 1940s and helped turn it into a mass organization. From 1949 to 1954, Walter Sisulu was ANC national secretary-general and one of the organization's principal strategists. Although banned in 1954, he continued to influence ANC operations from behind the scenes until he was arrested in 1963 at the Rivonia headquarters of the ANC's military wing, *Umkhonto we Sizwe* (Spear of the Nation) (Karis and Carter 1977:143–45). Walter Sisulu was sentenced to life imprisonment with Nelson Mandela in 1964 and spent the next 25 years in prison until his release on 15 October 1990. He is second only to Mandela on the roster of revolutionary heroes. Black South Africans sometimes remark that in Zwelakhe's face they see the gaze of the "people's secretary."

Zwelakhe's mother, Albertina, is the most powerful woman in South African politics. For two decades, and despite ten years of house arrest and prison terms, including long periods of solitary confinement, the indomitable Albertina Sisulu was one of a handful of internal activists who kept the ANC alive in the black South African psyche. Nothing the government did could diminish either her opposition to apartheid or her ability to analyze coolly where she and the movement were and what they should do next. A master political organizer, Albertina Sisulu is Transvaal president and national copresident of the UDF. Four months before the Durban meeting, she and eleven other UDF leaders were acquitted of charges of high treason in a much publicized supreme court trial that was the South African government's first major judicial assault on the UDF (Gastrow 1987:281–83).

The story of Albertina Sisulu's life of sacrifice, steadfast defiance of National party rule, and unemotional organizational development of the Charterist movement—named for its allegiance to the ANC's Freedom Charter of 1955, which defined demands for nonracial government—is known to millions of young blacks. The youth whom Zwelakhe Sisulu hoped to influence could be counted on to know that the ideas he presented were those of the highest political authority of the resistance.

Zwelakhe Sisulu himself entered the NECC conference with a personal history of political involvement that linked him to the major currents of contemporary black politics and to those whom he hoped to persuade. During the 1970s when the ground was being prepared for the advances and crises that occasioned the Durban meeting,

Zwelakhe was influenced by Black Consciousness, which opposed the psychological colonization of blacks and revitalized the internal resistance. At the time, some Charterists were cool to Black Consciousness and viewed it as a rival ideology.

A Harvard-trained journalist, the younger Sisulu was from 1980 president of the Black Consciousness Media Workers Association of South Africa, a position that placed him in the vanguard of efforts to achieve advances for blacks through the newly legal black trade unions. In 1985, Sisulu launched the *New Nation*, a Catholic-funded newspaper that is the unofficial voice of the UDF. By the mid 1980s, the younger Sisulu, like many UDF activists at the conference, had confirmed his political loyalties to Charterism. Like them also, Sisulu brought with him into the Charterist camp attitudes of pride in black culture and concern for black self-development, which were hallmarks of Black Consciousness.

If the choice of Sisulu as keynote speaker was a brilliant coup, the decision to hold the conference in Durban, the principal town of Natal, was a provocation seemingly calculated to sustain the UDF's reputation for militancy even as it sought to brake the violence of its most militant supporters. Natal is the home turf of Mangosuthu Buthelezi, KwaZulu's chief minister and president of Inkatha, the Zulu-based political organization. The UDF's program of defiance and Buthelezi's policy of selective collaboration are antipodes of modern black politics. In the UDF's and Buthelezi's respective demonologies, each is the other's principal devil. The organizers of the conference must have known that both their comrades and Buthelezi would view the choice of Natal as an affront to the thin-skinned Inkatha leader. Given the history of bloody confrontation between the UDF and Inkatha in Natal, the UDF also should have known that Inkatha would not resist the temptation to attack the conference. Yet in the minds of the UDF comrades, an assault on the proceedings would be a powerful benediction on the conference results.

Buthelezi's forces wasted little time in attacking the delegates, who apparently were armed and ready. On the first night of the assembly, two Inkatha militants lay dead outside the meeting hall. Buthelezi assailed the conference as a bid by its organizers to demonstrate that he could be affronted in his home base. Commenting on the four separate attacks on conference delegates by Inkatha loyalists, Buthelezi said: "If there were Inkatha youths with Inkatha uniforms involved in the eruption of anger, why must I be blamed for their behavior? The National Education Crisis Committee itself came here to court anger" (Laurence 1986).

Despite Sisulu's propitious background and Buthelezi's backhanded blessing, Sisulu faced a daunting task. His audience had sparked and sustained the longest and most widespread revolt against white South African rule in this century. They were intensely proud that they had shaken the South African government, and they were intoxicated by international media attention to their clashes with both the security forces and their black opponents. Some were not strangers to political murder of those whom they viewed as "sellouts." Anyone who opposed them—even Zwelakhe Sisulu—could not be entirely immune from such an allegation. Among those in the hall also were certainly police informers, although the police did not need to be present to learn what Sisulu said. All South Africa would know that Sisulu had instructed black youth in how to undertake a successful revolution. The boldness of the endeavor is staggering.

Sisulu's prescriptions for success were discipline, grass-roots organization, solidarity, and time. Calling the occasion "a crossroads of the struggle," Sisulu said: "We hold the future in our hands. The decisions we take at this conference will be truly historic, in the sense that they will help determine whether we go forward to progress and peace, or whether the racists push us backwards and reverse some of the gains that we have made, towards barbarism and chaos" (National Education Crisis Committee 1986b:4).

Two factors impelled the changes that Sisulu proposed. Despite virtually universal agreement among blacks that Bantu education is bad, adult blacks wanted their children back in classrooms. The specter of masses of youth with no skills haunted black South Africa. In addition adult blacks, especially those with jobs, were tired of the confusion and insecurity in their daily lives caused by boycotts, demonstrations, and political warfare in black neighborhoods. Such feelings were reinforced by a culture that assigns to adults, not to youths, decision-making authority.

Acknowledging his listeners' successes, Sisulu attributed to their activism the phenomenon whereby "the initiative passed into the hands of the people" and out of the hands of the government (National Education Crisis Committee 1986b:7). Sisulu noted that blacks had challenged the legitimacy of the National party regime and that South Africa faced its worst economic crisis ever.

Sisulu's speech analyzed two results of the 1983–86 youth rebellion. In two areas, the Eastern Cape and the East Rand region, which adjoins Johannesburg and Pretoria, ungovernability and the consequent absence of functioning local governments had produced situations in which black people in some townships seized opportunities to assume for themselves some functions of government through a system of representative structures called street committees. Sisulu probably had in mind places like Port Alfred, Alexandra, and Duduza, from which government authorities temporarily withdrew out of fear for their lives and property. It is interesting to note that during this period of "alternative government" the street committees managed to lower local crime rates, particularly in Alexandra. Many blacks felt that under the established order prior to alternative government the attitude of the police seemed to encourage blacks to attack and kill each other as long as they were not targeting government supporters. The second outcome of the youth rebellion was a tendency for various local challenges to state authority to converge into campaigns with nationwide implications. Sisulu argued that the UDF should strengthen and accelerate both processes.

Sisulu told the comrades that the developments that had resulted from their actions were "positive tendencies," but he warned of "counter tendencies which threaten to reverse our struggle" in the absence of efforts to deepen breakthroughs and assure that temporary gains were transformed into fundamental and long-lasting features of the struggle. He also warned of the state's "new methods," such as reliance on vigilantes and death squads (National Education Crisis Committee 1986b:12–13).

As the means of sustaining the positive tendencies and of countering the government's new methods of repression, Sisulu proposed "people's power" by which blacks would begin to govern themselves even while the National party government was still in office. He emphasized that such developments "were only possible because of the development of democratic organs, or committees, of people's power" such as neighborhood-based formations that incorporated all segments of black society, youth and adults, and were accountable to the people living in each area (National Education Crisis Committee 1986b:14–19). Sisulu termed such power of the people as both "defensive and offensive," and he concluded that the extension and consolidation of people's power would enable the movement to withstand what he foresaw as a massive onslaught from the state. He later was proved prescient in both these predictions.

The delegates approved thirteen resolutions ranging from a condemnation of U.S. involvement in Angola on the side of Jonas Savimbi to a call to all students to return to school. Sisulu's calls for discipline and wider involvement of people of all ages were not addressed directly, but they are implicit in several resolutions (National Education Crisis Committee 1986a:13–21). Perhaps most significant was Resolution 11, which urged community action on education struggles and noted that the source of problems in the black community—"gutter" education and high rents, taxes, and living costs—is the same. The delegates resolved to "urge all communities and democratic organizations to launch appropriate regional and/or national mass action campaigns, by considering all forms of rent, consumer and other boycotts" (National Education Crisis Committee 1986a:19).

Prior to the Durban NECC conference, large numbers of adult blacks, including many leading activists, had come to fear the young comrades. Sisulu's position was risky. If he had failed to persuade the youth, the UDF would have fallen apart. The young would have been alienated from the older UDF leadership, and the UDF's adult sympathizers would have seen no future for themselves in an organization dominated by extremists. As it was, not all adult Charterists favored a reduction in violence. While planning the NECC initiative, those who wanted to redirect the youth faced no less a counterinfluence than Winnie Mandela, whose public statements in support of necklacing and bombing differed from her husband's views.

The importance of Sisulu's speech and of the audience to which it was addressed cannot be overemphasized. Youth groups made up more than half of the UDF's 600 affiliated organizations, and individual youths formed the majority of the UDF's active supporters. It is likely that the UDF lost some support at Durban. Sisulu was hissed at by youths who rejected his analysis. The hissers probably formed part of the 300,000 black students—out of 1,700,000—who did not return to school the following July.

Building Community Structures

The ideas that Sisulu espoused at the NECC conference gained rapid acceptance among Charterists. Indeed, the ground for such acceptance had already been prepared by some of the UDF's most respected leaders. In the months after the conference, youths and adults sought to implement Sisulu's proposals in what would be one of the most eventful periods of modern South African history. In the process the struggle moved indoors, and the township streets that had seen so much violence and bloodshed in the two previous years were left to the police, the army, the vigilantes, and gangs of "out-of-discipline comrades," the phrase used by UDF leaders to describe the youths who continued to seek violent confrontation with the authorities and other blacks.

Operating in the NECC's and Sisulu's favor was the realization that had already dawned on some youths, that schools in session are valuable assembly points for politicization and mass organization. Eventually the South African government also seemed to reach the same conclusion, with the consequence that in some places in July and August 1986 comrades who were former school boycotters were working feverishly to block the government from closing schools as a means of barring their attendance.

The Charterists turned to practical politics in an attempt to show black South Africans how democracy works and to demonstrate to the widest possible group of black adults that the UDF could achieve positive things for them. As part of that process, in early 1986 the UDF set out to duplicate nationwide the community structures that Port Elizabeth UDF regional vice president Henry Fazzie had started building in the Eastern Cape in November 1985 and which copied the ANC's local networks of the 1950s.

Typically such structures consisted of street or block committees grouped under area committees and reporting to township civic associations. These usually were made up of elected representatives, but in some places police interference prevented elections. Elsewhere, fear of police infiltration served either as a pretext or a valid reason for committees to be self-appointed. Lots of familiar UDF/ANC faces appeared in the new community leadership. Significantly, they were joined by sizable numbers of people who had previously not participated in elected organizations with civic responsibilities.

According to a veteran Cape Town activist who favored the UDF's new direction, at the bottom of the UDF's desire to replace ungovernability with alternative structures was the UDF's analysis that 70 to 80 percent of blacks were sympathetic to the Charterists, but only a much smaller percentage were willing to suffer the risks of overt political involvement under the pre-1986 conditions. A further element was the UDF's recognition that large numbers of blacks, especially in the over-forty age group, had doubts about how they would fare under a majority government. This group also hated apartheid and white domination, but they were confused about the present and afraid of the future.

Although Sisulu did not mention the Congress of South African Trade Unions (COSATU) in his address, it is likely that the UDF was particularly concerned to get the comrades under control as a prerequisite for cooperation with this new superunion federation. The formation of COSATU on 30 November 1985, four months before the NECC's Durban conference, offered an opportunity to thrust the liberation struggle into the South African economy with considerably more potential for effective results than fighting among blacks in their segregated neighborhoods could ever produce. COSATU's membership, however, was made up of many adult workers who shared the generalized fear and anger toward the violence of the comrades. The Charterists could not afford to alienate COSATU workers by permitting young hotheads to direct the UDF.

The three dozen unions that joined COSATU at its launch constituted a combined membership of half a million black workers. Never before had any South African union federation, black or white, brought together so many members (Lewis and Randall 1985). COSATU, however, was not united on issues of politics and ideology. The federation represented a convergence of two South African trade union traditions, the South African Congress of Trade Unions, a pre-1960 ANC ally, and the Federation of South African Trade Unions, whose formation in 1979 coincided with the Black Consciousness activism of the 1970s. The latter had a history of wariness about alliances with political movements (Laurence 1986). In addition to containing both Charterist and Black Consciousness tendencies, in Natal there were many Zulu COSATU members who also supported Inkatha. The leaders of COSATU must have found it necessary to proceed carefully.

COSATU's five founding principles—nonracialism, one union/one industry, worker control, representation on the basis of paid-up membership, and cooperation between affiliates at the national level—manifested a preponderance of labor direction but betrayed, in the first principle of nonracialism, a definite inclination toward the Charterists. An important issue between the UDF and COSATU would be the extent of workers' tolerance for the loss of workdays for political rather than labor reasons.

Despite the need of COSATU leaders to steer a delicate course, the new COSATU president, Elijah Barayi, a former ANC Youth League member from Cradock in the Eastern Cape wellspring of black political activism, viewed COSATU as an essential part of the liberation struggle (Gastrow 1987:14–16.). A day after his election, Barayi linked COSATU's agenda to one of blacks' most fervent demands. At a mass rally in King's Park, Durban, Barayi declared: "COSATU gives Botha six months to get rid of passes. If that does not take place within six months, we will burn the passes of the black man" (Laurence 1986). Barayi's challenge to South African President P.W. Botha held open the possibility that COSATU could quickly join the forefront of black resistance.

Similarities in structures and methods between the COSATU unions and the UDF local community organizations, which were called civic associations, or civics, and which coordinated the street and area committees, provided an important intersection between the two groups despite their not entirely similar agendas. Workers who had experienced COSATU organizational techniques could feel at home in the UDF's grass-roots entities. Moreover, the street committees and civic associations, like the mine shaft and factory floor committees, had dual purposes of getting the leaders' messages to the people and the people's views to the leadership. In the case of the civics, this was accomplished at incessant meetings, typically in church halls, where blacks were encouraged to consider themselves part of a national campaign. The sessions usually included a news report that linked local issues to those of other regions. Guest speakers from distant places reported on the struggle in their areas and urged people to bear sacrifices in support of political action. Concurrently the UDF launched a "Call to Whites" in an attempt to use the same techniques in the white neighborhoods of Johannesburg and Cape Town, which had the largest numbers of whites who inclined toward nonracial government.

Leadership of the civics varied from place to place. Youths, priests, members of the black upper and middle classes, and, significantly, trade unionists were heavily involved, as were the revered former political prisoners and other old-time ANC operatives who were still around. Civic activists also included teachers and nurses who were South African government employees. Numerous—maybe several hundred—leaders of civics saw their houses bombed and were the targets of early-hours raids by the security forces. A few were kidnapped and tortured or killed. In Port Elizabeth, UDF regional vice president Henry Fazzie, a sixty-two-year-old veteran of the period before 1961 when the ANC was still legal, and youth leader Mkhuseli Jack were banned due to their involvement with street committees.

The South African government lifted the partial state of emergency on 4 March 1986. For a while in some areas the authorities seemed surprisingly tolerant. The appearance of tolerance was probably due in part to the frequent presence in South Africa during the same period of the Eminent Persons Group (EPG), a committee of prominent figures from several British Commonwealth countries who were seeking to promote negotiations between the South African government and opponents of apartheid, principally the ANC and the UDF. Some in the South African government saw the EPG as a shield against further sanctions. The tolerance also might have been due to the government's inability at first to cope with the unprecedented volume of black political activity.

Many civic associations succeeded in taking over some functions that previously had been the responsibilities of government. Youths collected trash and created "people's parks." Neighborhood and family conflict-resolution processes and crime prevention squads were organized, and "people's courts," some working under the supervision of Charterist attorneys, responded to deeply felt grievances about racial bias in the official legal system. Kindergartens and community advice offices sprang up, and in a few places the civics took over schools. In Port Alfred, the civic association began to collect taxes. In the Transvaal, one of the chief functions of the civics was to extend and sustain rent boycotts, which continued in four dozen towns for several years and affected millions of urban blacks.

During the heyday of the civics in 1986, Charterist activists learned that the exercise of self-rule was not easy. Educated, modern-sector civic leaders often found themselves dealing with the superstitions and problems of the uneducated oppressed. Allegations of witchcraft became the topic of some civic meetings at which the UDF had hoped to sensitize the rank and file about the benefits of rent or consumer boycotts. Often the people were more interested in discussing their grueling poverty or local disputes, and the Charterist leaders were confronted directly by the horrific problems of blacks caused by ignorance, destitution, and four decades of apartheid misgovernment.

All the while there was a constant tugging at the limits of discipline by youths who were impatient with revolution building. Suspicion of police infiltration at times incited the comrades to violence. One such occasion was a Western Cape UDF meeting where adult leaders watched helplessly while youths killed a suspected informer. Some youths favored coercion to alter the behavior of adults. A UDF lawyer in Mamelodi recalled an all-night session in which he opposed youths' plans to prohibit men's beer parties. The youths saw the drunken parties as causes of crime and tensions. The lawyer realistically foresaw the potential for alienation of adult men and consequent possible collaboration between them and the police. Indeed, in some places, most notably in the Cape Town squatter camp of Crossroads, the police manipulated tensions between conservative black men and the comrades to produce open conflict. Crossroads was the best-known example during early 1986 of the government's determination to exploit "black-on-black" violence to defuse political activism. Crossroads, however, was only the most publicized incident of a fairly widespread phenomenon.

The civic associations intended both to defy and supersede the government's black township councils. As the means of accomplishing this, some civics, like the Duncan Village Residents Association in East London, entered into negotiations with the white city council about eventual amalgamation under nonracial local government. Meanwhile the NECC met several times with the Department of Education and Training (DET) with the objectives of gaining community control of black schools and getting authorization for the implementation of people's education in government-funded schools. The joint city council/civic meetings and the negotiations between the NECC and the DET were probably the only functioning direct communications between the internal Charterists outside prisons and the South African government at that time. Those lines were exceedingly fragile, but they constituted some chance for peaceful reconciliation. Eventually that chance was lost due to the government's refusal to recognize the Charterist leaders.

Of greater and more enduring significance was the effect on millions of South African blacks of participating for the first time ever in representative organizations that gave them some say over their own lives. The memory of the exercise would remain even after its functioning was repressed.

A Turbulent Stalemate

For several months, the South African government hesitated while hitting out sporadically at the Charterist challenge. In April 1986, the government announced that it would no longer enforce the pass system. The preceding February it had published full-page newspaper ads signed by State President P. W. Botha that proclaimed: "Revolutionaries may stamp their feet. The communists may scream their lies. Our enemies may try to undermine us."[1] The ads went on to state that the pass laws would be scrapped by July 1 and that the government was committed to power sharing and a single education policy for all. They concluded: "South Africa will never hand this country over to those who would see it destroyed, to those under the misapprehension that solutions lie in anarchy." Botha asked blacks, "from my heart, to share in the future, to share in the new South Africa." Barayi and others could be forgiven if they felt for a moment that the Charterists had the government on the run.

Then on 19 May 1986, the South African Defence Force raided Botswana, Zambia, and Zimbabwe, all three Commonwealth countries, thus effectively ending the mediation work of the EPG and foreshadowing a government repositioning that became clear three weeks later with the declaration of the first nationwide state of emergency since 1960. Under the terms of the June 1986 state of emergency declaration, the South African government assumed more drastic powers to eliminate political opposition than had ever been exercised since the country's independence from Great Britain in 1910. Conciliatory measures and limited tolerance were finished. Almost immediately 30,000 activists, most of them Charterists and including Zwelakhe Sisulu, were jailed. Incrementally stiffer prohibitions on political activity over the next thirty months made overt opposition even more dangerous and difficult. Eventually Sisulu would spend two years in jail because of his work with the NECC and his activism as an antiapartheid newspaper editor. He was never charged or brought before a court.

Although the government described the purpose of the emergency as the reduction of violence, it seemed clear that the real purpose was to crush the UDF. What followed was a turbulent stalemate until the dramatic developments of 1989–90 that led to the government's de facto acknowledgment of the Charterists as its principal interlocutor on South Africa's future. For the three years following the state of emergency declaration the government could not get black support for its program of limited reforms based on an unexplained concept of power sharing among groups separated by race. Meanwhile the Charterist opposition could not move beyond the point reached in 1986 when it demonstrated that it commanded the support of the majority of black South Africans. It is significant, however, that the 1986 emergency and its successors in 1987, 1988, and 1989 did not eliminate resistance. Indeed, after an initial pause for several months following the June 1986 declaration and a subsequent pause after the February 1988 restrictions on the UDF, COSATU, and sixteen other organizations, the opposition regrouped each time and went on with its political work.

By mid-1987, resistance political organizing had resumed throughout the country. For the first time, the Charterists managed in 1986–87 to organize modern-day Soweto, South Africa's largest black city, into street, area, and zone committees. In several areas the UDF elected regional officers to replace those in detention. They also concluded a year-long drive to organize youth into the South African Youth Congress (SAYCO), which was launched in February 1987 and claimed 2 million members. The durable effect of Zwelakhe Sisulu's ideas was demonstrated in a statement published at the launch of SAYCO. It declared that adult workers should lead the struggle.

During the same period, the UDF kept students in schools despite the provocative presence of soldiers on many schoolgrounds. It also sustained massive boycotts in Soweto and more than fifty other townships of rent payments to government councils, which own most black housing. Perhaps most important was the propulsion of COSATU into a leadership role in black opposition politics. In August 1987, the National Union of Mineworkers (NUM), a COSATU affiliate, called the largest and longest-lasting mine strike in South African history. Although the costs in lost jobs and profits were painful to both the unions and the mining companies, the point was made to government and business that blacks' political demands cannot be kept separate from business and the economy.

Without the mass politicization that Zwelakhe Sisulu proposed at Durban, it is unlikely the UDF would have survived the successive states of emergency. The fact that the Charterists withstood the assault by the state was demonstrated in October 1988 when only 3 percent of black South African adults voted in township council elections, which both the government and the Charterists saw as a crucial test of their relative strengths. The government also failed to win support for its black collaborators like Isaac Mokoena and Thamsanqa Linda who it hoped would replace the Charterist leadership in the townships while the government kept the Charterists in jails. Meanwhile no black of any stature, including homelands leaders, agreed to join the National Council that the government proposed as a way to include blacks in national government while still denying them representation in Parliament. Even Chief Gatsha Buthelezi repeatedly declared that he would not participate in the council as long as Nelson Mandela was held in prison and denied a right to take part.

The Tragic Story of Raymond Mavuso

All the while, acts of brutality committed by the police, army, and vigilantes probably enhanced support for the Charterists. The tragic story of one Eastern Transvaal comrade who attended the Durban conference is a case in point. UDF youth leader Raymond Mavuso[2] was buried 17 May 1987, on a hillside near the remote KwaZulu village of Ntumbane. Mavuso could have been an "Everyman" of black youth during the 1980s. His history exemplifies both the inequities within South Africa and the spiraling nature of blacks' reactions to apartheid rule. The Mavuso family and their neighbors are only a few of many traditional, rural people who were profoundly touched by South African politics in the 1980s. Many were politicized to a degree that would have been unthinkable at the outset of the decade.

In 1983 Raymond Mavuso, age twenty-three and employed as a "Bantu operator assistant" at the ESCOM power plant near the small Transvaal town of Bethal, was elected president of the Bethal branch of the South African government–sponsored Zwelitsha ("New World") Youth Organization. At the time Raymond felt it was right to channel his community spirit through a government program. The reasons for Raymond's popularity were evident in his ever-smiling manner and easy assumption of responsibility.

In 1984 Raymond became disillusioned with the government authorities' unwillingness to respond to his pleas to negotiate with youths about problems that had led to boycotts of Bethal's black schools. Raymond shifted his allegiance to the new UDF, but his passage to antigovernment politics was a difficult one because his eldest brother, George, was a South African police sergeant. Eventually there were strains between Raymond and George. In 1985 Raymond participated in the burning of the shop of a township councillor who later also joined the UDF and eventually attended Raymond's funeral.

In June 1986, at the time of the nationwide state of emergency declaration, Raymond was on leave from his job while attending a Black Sash course in Johannesburg in preparation for setting up a community advice office in Bethal. Raymond, like many of his UDF comrades, had heeded Sisulu's call to positive activism. After the declaration of the state of emergency, Raymond and thousands of other comrades went into hiding. He lost his job at the power plant. When he was arrested he was held in solitary confinement for eight months. In a letter smuggled out of jail, Raymond wrote that he was suffering from severe depression. During Raymond's imprisonment, his brother George influenced the family, most of whom live at Ntumbane, 300 kilometers from Bethal, not to visit him.

On his release in March 1987, the police told Raymond to stay in Bethal. They also told him they would not protect him from the vigilantes. Two weeks later, on a warm evening, Raymond was led into an ambush by someone he trusted. The murderers, ironically, were UDF supporters from a distant town who had been hired by agents of the Bethal township council and told they would be used to kill vigilante supporters of the government. There was strong suspicion that George Mavuso helped recruit the youths who shot Raymond. No one was arrested for Raymond's killing.

Police found Raymond minutes after the shooting. But he was left unattended for several hours before they took him to the black section of the Bethal hospital, five minutes by car from the street corner where he was shot. The Bethal hospital is not well equipped, but Raymond was kept there in critical condition for a week before he was transferred to the hospital for blacks at Tembisa, near Johannesburg, where better medical facilities are available.

Raymond's visitors at the Tembisa hospital were summoned by the white hospital superintendent to be questioned why they had come to see "that sort of person." Policemen harassed Raymond while he appeared to be getting well. Then suddenly, a month after the shooting he died. Only two nights before, he had been sitting up and talking in his usual rapid way. The nurse who was taking care of him said he was on his way to recovery.

Raymond Mavuso's funeral was a delicate balance of Zulu ritual, fundamentalist Christian rites, and revolutionary politics, forces usually ill at ease with one another. Raymond's family and other barefoot Nazarene Zionists shared the ceremonies with a contingent of township comrades. Zionists and activists took turns carrying the body from the family compound through the high grass of late summer to the village graveyard while singing shifted between hymns and political chants in praise of the ANC. A police vehicle drove back and forth along a ridge across a valley from the cemetery, but the police did not attend the funeral or attempt to disrupt it.

In accord with traditional rites, Raymond's family and his childhood neighbors buried all his clothing with the body and laid stones on the fresh grave. Nazarene men smashed the casket and inserted the pieces next to the corpse, which was wrapped in a shroud and laid in a shelf to the side of the grave shaft. The comrades danced the *toi toi*, filling the afternoon air with billows of dust. A dozen adult women joined them, taking the place of their children who were in jail.

The eulogizers were villagers, youth activists, the former Bethal township councillor who converted to the UDF, and another Mavuso brother, Samson, who described the shooting of Raymond by vigilantes and his subsequent treatment by police and hospital personnel. The largely rural Zulu congregation responded audibly to Samson Mavuso's remarks. Sergeant George Mavuso, as the eldest man of the family, had the lead role at the funeral. Standing on the mound of earth next to Raymond's grave, George appeared uncomfortable as the comrades sang about government collaborators as the "dogs of Botha" and as the villagers murmured their angry reactions to Samson's account of how Raymond died.

Following the graveside ceremonies, the mourners returned to the family kraal to wash their hands and share a meal. Raymond's mother and Samson sat in the hut that is the family's parlor and planned their journey to Johannesburg to ask a lawyer to open an inquest into Raymond's death.

The Impasse in South African Politics

Like the Mavusos and their fellow villagers at Ntumbane, millions of black South Africans were affected in the mid-1980s either by direct experiences of the state of emergency oppression or by the suffering of family members and friends who were jailed, tortured, or killed. Added to those experiences, of course, were the mundane conditions of deprivation, alienation, and denial of dignity and justice that are the lot of nearly all black South Africans. In the context of the heightened political awareness that the UDF and the trade unions had achieved, the oppressive tactics of the South African government had the effect of consolidating and extending blacks' opposition to apartheid and its enforcers. Those tactics thus became a formula for the impasse that still characterizes South African politics.

The violence of the rebellion of the mid-1980s ceased, but the potential for widespread violence like that of the mid-1980s is palpable both to the government and to its opponents. Meanwhile continued repression, rapid population growth, escalating unemployment, and a declining economy are exacerbating the unfavorable social conditions that help inspire antigovernment sentiments. Many blacks now consider South Africa and its economy to be badly misadministered and view themselves as the chief victims of the government's follies. Meanwhile the whites who cling to power claim they must do so to prevent misadministration under black rule.

Faced with massive and growing opposition, the failures of official efforts to coopt blacks, the stalemate caused by state of emergency repression, and the debilitating effects of international economic sanctions, the South African government has recognized that talking to leaders like Nelson Mandela, Walter Sisulu, and hundreds of others who are in prison or under restriction orders offers the only possible alternative to insecurity, international isolation, and economic depression. By releasing the Charterists' leaders the government has taken a crucial step away from its obsession with white domination and toward acceptance of the need to negotiate with black leaders about how to build a society in which all South Africans would have equal rights. The future course will not be easy, but for now, the prospects for lasting peace in South Africa are higher than before.

NOTES

The judgments and most of the descriptions related in this chapter result from personal observations.

1. See, for instance, the *Sowetan*, 7 February 1986.

2. Raymond Mavuso and I were friends. We often talked about politics and South African society. After Raymond was shot, his other friends and I visited him in the hospital regularly until the authorities forbade our visits. This account relates parts of our conversations and my observations at his funeral.

REFERENCES

Doke, C. M., and B. W. Vilakazi. 1972. *Zulu-English Dictionary*. Johannesburg: Witwatersrand Press.

Dreyer, Peter. 1980. *Martyrs and Fanatics*. New York: Simon and Schuster.

Fischer, Arnold. 1985. *English-Xhosa Dictionary*. Cape Town: Oxford University Press.

Gastrow, Shelagh, ed. 1987. *Who's Who in South African Politics*. Number 2. Johannesburg: Raven Press.

Karis, Thomas, and Gwendolen M. Carter. 1977. *From Protest to Challenge*, Volume 4. Stanford, CA: Hoover Institution Press.

Laurence, Patrick. 1986. "Back to School for Spirit of Defiance." *Weekly Mail* 2, no. 13 (4–10 April).

Lewis, Jon, and Estell Randall. 1985. "Superunion Finds Its Wings." *Weekly Mail* 1, no. 24 (29 November–5 December).

National Education Crisis Committee. 1986a. *Report on the Second National Consultative Conference on the Crisis in Education*. Johannesburg: National Education Crisis Committee.

―――. 1986b. *Second National Consultative Congress. Keynote Address*. 29 March. Johannesburg: National Education Crisis Committee.

Weekly Mail (Johannesburg). 1986, 1987, and 1988.

Wilson, Monica, and Leonard Thompson. 1971. *The Oxford History of South Africa*. Volume 2. Oxford: Clarendon Press.

6

Worker Solidarity, Differentiation, and the Manipulation of Ethnicity: Conflict at Vaal Reefs, 1984–1986

ROBERT SHANAFELT

If we go back and we count up all the number of clashes that we have records for from 1973 up until last year the most common form of clash is in fact between Sotho and Xhosa, I think we know this.

—Kent McNamara, anthropologist and labor consultant, testifying before an Anglo American Corporation inquiry into unrest at Vaal Reefs mine, 7 August 1987 (Bregman 1987: Pt134/5035)

It is necessary to raise the consciousness of people so that they realize the people of Lesotho, Botswana, and South Africa are one; it is the whites who have deceived us by dividing us into different tribes.

—Letter to the editor of *Leselinyana la Lesotho* ("Lipolitiki ke eng?" (What is politics?) 21 March 1986) written by mineworker from Lesotho[1]

Management wishes to reassure its workers that they care a great deal for them and do not want any violence or lawlessness whatsoever which will interfere in their well-being...Remember management is here to look after you and not abuse you and hurt you...Without happy workers on a mine the mine becomes an unpleasant place to be. All people work on a mine to earn money for their families. Mining underground is a tough and dangerous job—management want their workers to be as comfortable as possible when on surface.

—Brief to workers from mine manager of Vaal Reefs east division following violent clashes at compound 1, 6 December 1986 (Bregman 1987: Memorandum following Exhibit J)

Migrant workers in South Africa's mines, a work force characterized as politically quiescent in the 1970s, were unionized in the 1980s at one of the fastest rates in the world (Crush 1989:6). The National Union of Mineworkers (NUM) grew from just a few thousand members in 1982 to about 250,000 registered members in 1986 (*Africa Report*, March–April 1986:10). Yet it would be an oversimplification to suggest that the growth of the union has come about merely because workers are conscious of a set of common material interests. Indeed, even if all individuals in collective groups can be shown to have the same material interests, unity in action still remains problematic. Economist and theorist of group action Mancur Olson (1965), for example, points out that it is not economically rational for individuals to participate in endeavors in which there are collective interests—in such cases individuals can simply "free ride" on the efforts of others. In Olson's view the problem of free riders in collective action generally has to be overcome either by the offering of selective incentives to attract support or by the use of coercive force against those who refuse to cooperate.[2]

Among workers in industrial firms the problem of the free rider is exacerbated by the varying interests of a differentiated labor force. In South Africa white policymakers have taken advantage of such differentiation by attempting to co-opt black workers occupying relatively elite positions (Pycroft and Munslow 1988). Through the introduction of a job-grading system, the so-called Patterson Plan, the mining establishment has attempted to stabilize the work force and reinforce status distinctions among workers. More contentiously, the Patterson system has provided proportionally higher pay increases and selective incentives to blacks working in positions of authority (Pycroft and Munslow 1988:166). This differential pay has led to protest and conflict within the work force. As we shall see, union members and supporters have resorted to coercive force against clerks and team leaders to counter management's incentives.

Union solidarity is most evident when the struggle with management is over questions of pay and working conditions. The massive support given by the rank and file to the 1987 mineworkers' strike over wages is evidence of the kind of solidarity that can be achieved. However, beginning in 1985, union leadership began to formally address larger political issues and to see itself playing a vanguard role in the political education of workers. As NUM Secretary-General Cyril Ramaphosa said during the formation of the Congress of South African Trade Unions (COSATU) in December 1985: "When workers are paid their wages, it is not only an economic issue, it is a political issue...As unions we have a solemn duty to develop consciousness among workers of their exploitation as workers" (*Africa Report*, March–April 1986:10). As the struggle moved out of the realm of the direct material concerns of all workers and into the realm of the struggle for national liberation, solidarity became more problematic.

For the NUM leadership workers are workers and their distinct national or ethnic backgrounds are viewed largely as irrelevant. Ethnic or linguistic differences among workers are seen primarily as factors manipulated by management to hamper worker solidarity. Yet it was perhaps a miscalculation on the part of NUM not to realize that the newly proclaimed national political agenda of the union made migrants from foreign countries particularly vulnerable to threats of repatriation and endangered the solidarity achieved in struggles for improvements in wages and working conditions. The fragility of this solidarity became evident in the outbreak of violence that occurred between mineworkers as the union became more overtly political.

In 1985 and 1986 many of the South African gold mines were hit with what are variously referred to as "faction fights" or "riots" on the one hand and "intergroup" or "class" conflicts on the other. According to Kent McNamara, anthropologist and former employee of the Chamber of Mines, "Of the 330 mineworkers who lost their lives in inter-group clashes since 1974, fully one-third (118) died during 1986 alone" (1988: 33). In the South African media and in government reports such violence is often associated with ethnic antagonism. Xhosa and Sotho speakers, who make up the majority of mineworkers, have frequently been on opposite sides of mineworker clashes. Between 1974 (when workers from Lesotho began protesting the mandatory deferred payment system) and 1977 conflict was particularly widespread. A South African government inquiry into mine "riots" leaked to the press in 1978 blamed the situation both on the migrant labor system itself and on primordial ethnic attachments (Pallister et al. 1988:140–42). In an effort to forestall such conflict (and make riot control less problematic) the Anglo American Corporation implemented a new housing system in which blocks of rooms were no longer assigned to single "tribes." Instead, the blocks were "integrated," although individual rooms remained linguistically homogeneous (McNamara 1980:397). For its part, NUM had been campaigning against tribalism since 1982 and urging workers to see one another in terms of their common interests. Prior to 1986, interethnic conflict was indeed on the wane. Many workers gave NUM credit for promoting a new sense of solidarity.

The class background to so-called tribal violence is frequently noted by workers and academic observers. Close examination of contemporary cases generally shows that such conflict at the mines correlates with disputes over pay, racial discrimination, working conditions, and competition for scarce jobs allocated on an ethnic basis (McNamara 1988). Historian Terence Ranger has pointed out that similar economic factors can be causally linked to ethnic conflict that took place at a mine in 1914 (Ranger 1978). Nowadays, workers often say management deliberately provokes fights among them in order to ensure management's continued control. In the recent incidences of violence, one miner from Lesotho stated bluntly, "The cause of these fights which are famed for being 'tribal' are not 'tribal' at all; the fighting is about the union, period" (*Litsoakotleng* 1987).[3] This control is facilitated by the *induna* (unit supervisor) system, which automatically allocates authority and privilege on an ethnic basis. From this perspective so-called ethnic conflict at the mines is simply another example of the old story of divide and rule. As one labor leader remarked in 1975, "If labour forces on individual mines were homogeneous, mines would run the risk of strikes being total instead of partial" (South African Labour and Development Research Unit 1976:24).

Yet even if the ethnic differences of workers are manipulated by management, the question that remains to be addressed is in what way workers respond to it. It may be that many workers do not see themselves only as workers; places of origin and the shared life impressions generated from them—what Bentley (1987), after Bordieau, calls shared "habitus"—may also be important. Still, Sotho and Xhosa differences in this regard should be quite minor. How, then, are Sotho- and Xhosa-speaking miners possibly subject to manipulation and division?

To answer this question, unrest at the Anglo American Corporation's Vaal Reefs mines will be examined. At Vaal Reefs in 1986 dispute over a variety of issues including pay, racial discrimination, the Transkei elections, and the privileges of team leaders, indunas, and clerks led to periodic incidents of violence, including a number of clashes between club- and sword-wielding "Sotho" and "Xhosa" that left some thirty-five workers dead.[4] Testimony before the Bregman (1987) commission of inquiry into the unrest conducted under the auspices of the Anglo American Corporation reveals a picture of considerable complexity.[5] Nonetheless, it is clear that ethnic-related violence that the Bregman commission investigated, if such it is, emerged only after a whole series of other conflicts. These other conflicts are the fuel that fired a process of schismogenesis that only later took on an ethnic form.

Background

Vaal Reefs is an extremely large mining complex, perhaps the largest gold mine in the world (Pycroft and Munslow 1988:167). It is situated on the West Rand, near the "white towns" of Klerksdorp and Orkney and the African townships of Kanana and Joubertina. Managed by the Anglo American Corporation, the complex consists of nine separate, deep-level shafts. (A tenth shaft, Afrikaner Leases, is treated as part of Vaal Reefs for management purposes, although it is actually on the other side of Klerksdorp.) Each of these shafts has its own compound where several thousand workers are housed and fed. These compounds are quite distinct and located some distance apart. Workers from one compound often use taxis or buses to visit another. The entire Vaal Reefs complex covers some eighty square kilometers (Bregman 1987: PT1/26). For management purposes, it is divided into an east, a west, and a south division, with two to four shafts per division. According to a report published in the *South African Labour Bulletin* (Golding 1985:100), in 1985 these divisions were organized as follows: the west division controlled shafts no. 6 with 2,900 miners, no. 7 with 2,500 miners, no. 3 with 4,000 miners, no. 4 with 4,100 miners; the east division controlled shafts no. 2 with 4,000 miners, no. 1 with 4,500 miners, no. 5 with 3,000 miners, no. 10 with 1,500 miners; and the south division controlled shafts no. 8 with 12,000 miners, no. 9 with 6,000 miners.

Not all workers live in the compounds. White miners may live at the mines in segregated housing, while many senior-level African personnel and their families live at a major complex referred to as the Black Married Quarters (BMQ) or Umuzimuhle Village. The BMQ contains approximately 1,010 houses with 5,370 official residents. Unofficially, probably twice that number stay at the BMQ at any one time (Bregman 1987:PT8/449). In addition, about sixty black employees and their families live in the married quarters near no. 4 shaft and no. 7 shaft (Golding 1985:100). Much of the mineworkers' informal economy, like the African beer trade, is centered at Umuzimuhle Village. Mine security identifies this area with vice and crime. For example, one senior Vaal Reefs security officer described the BMQ as a "Sodom and Gomorrah" (Bregman 1987:PT9/451).

Private security at the mines is organized to protect mine property, guard the extracted gold and uranium, and maintain order among the work force and their visitors. At each of the shafts a white security officer oversees day-to-day affairs. In 1987 all but one of these men were former members of the South African police force, the lone exception being a former South African Railways policeman (Bregman 1987:PT7/363). At east division, where most of the conflict took place, there were 162 men on the security force. Most of the senior officers were white, but the junior ranks were largely black (Bregman 1987: Transkei Memorandum, 3). The South African police and defense forces, which are easily and rapidly mobilized from the nearby towns, and an Emergency Protection Unit composed of 100 white company employees augmented the mines' private security. The security police had at their disposal an array of weapons including attack dogs, handguns, shotguns, semiautomatic rifles, tear gas, and hand grenades. They were mobilized for mass action in riot vans and a variety of armored personnel carriers. During recent years they have generally shot tear gas and rubber bullets when firing; no one was reported to have been shot by live ammunition in the 1986 disturbances. Security monitors the compound gates twenty-four hours a day, but workers on their own time are generally allowed to come and go as they please. According to an agreement reached with NUM, union representatives are supposed to be given access to the mine compounds and allowed office space there.

Events

Union Organization at Vaal Reefs

NUM began organizing at Vaal Reefs in 1982. One regional organizer reported that when he first began working at Vaal Reefs no. 6 shaft in October of that year, he had only seven active supporters. Workers often insulted him and chased him away, believing that he was actually promoting some sort of insurance fraud (Golding 1985:100–101). Union organizers maintain that management used indunas and team leaders to spread disinformation about the union and discourage others from joining.

Despite the initially slow start, union membership soon mushroomed. An issue to which many workers responded readily was that of alleged abuses of power by management, especially with respect to what were perceived as unfair dismissals (Golding 1985:100–101). By February 1983 thousands of miners had joined the union. At the west and east divisions management conceded that membership exceeded 50 percent of the workers. Therefore, according to the recently enacted labor legislation, Vaal Reefs was forced to recognize NUM as a legitimate representative of the workers at these divisions. By September 1984 NUM was confident enough at the industrywide level to launch its first legal strike.

Workers' Allegations Regarding 1984 Disturbances

A management spokesperson at the Bregman inquiry argued that, aside from the September strike, 1984 was a relatively quiet year at Vaal Reefs (Bregman 1987: Memoranda/Dicks Affidavit, 2). Some miners told a different story, however. An unnamed NUM source told the Lesotho magazine *Litsoakotleng* (1988:14) that before the strike shaft stewards at no. 4 shaft foiled a management-instigated plan to cause ethnic clashes among them. They claimed to have intercepted four men—two workers and two other men thought to be associated with the criminal gang commonly known as the Russians—who confessed to receiving 500 rands each from mine security as payment for starting interethnic fighting. The same NUM source also implied that fights which broke out at shafts no. 1 and no. 3 at about that time, leaving more than eight men dead, were a consequence of similar tactics.[6]

Political Protest, Dissent, and Conflict in Early 1985

During 1985 protests and strikes at the mines were frequent and widespread. In early March Vaal Reef workers rallied against management's decision to give pay increases to a select few employees by working short shifts. This coincided with a campaign by militants at the mines to attack the entrenched hierarchy of the workplace. To this end protestors disrupted dining halls segregated according to occupational status and boycotted liquor outlets on the mine complex. They also boycotted taxi and concession stores in protest against poor food quality, poor service, and high prices.

Some of the mineworkers, including shaft stewards, were allegedly associated with the militant youth known as the comrades. Comrades who were not mineworkers probably were involved in a number of the mine protests of 1984 to 1986. During the inquiry there were allegations that they were involved in such incidents as spilling the groceries of miners who broke a shop boycott, disrupting the balloting for Transkei elections held at the mines, and assaulting black office workers. Management claimed that the national political agenda of some activists was clouding work-related affairs. They also argued that the short shifts were illegal and that many workers were the targets of threats and intimidation.

In April 1985 a series of work stoppages occurred. At no. 6 shaft ordinary workers protested against the special privileges offered to an induna and a group of team leaders; at no. 1 shaft, workers protested against the "piccanin" system;[7] at no. 7 shaft workers were objecting to working hours and overtime without pay (Golding 1985:107). The protests at shafts no. 8 and no. 9 (south division) had the most serious consequences as they led to the dismissal of 14,000 to 17,000 workers—at the time the largest dismissal of workers in South African history. Union sympathizers say black workers were protesting the job-reservation system by refusing to set dynamite charges (Golding 1985). Blasting has long been done by blacks but the job category has until recently been officially reserved for whites. This protest at south division resulted in dramatic losses in production. Management, however, did not acknowledge this as the central issue leading to the massive dismissals. They claimed instead that miners were dismissed for illegal short shifts, sabotage, boycotts, intimidation, and holding unauthorized meetings (Bregman 1987: Memoranda/Dicks Affidavit, 3).[8]

Another dramatic event occurred at no. 5 shaft in July after a period of protest against the quality of food served at the compound dining halls. This protest, coupled with the general NUM campaign of "equality for all," resulted in a serious rift and fight between team leaders and other workers. The mine manager claims that team leaders at no. 5 came to him with complaints of intimidation. He stated in an affidavit that "during July 1985, No. 5 Shaft team leaders and unit supervisors alleged intimidation by gangs of NUM members and office bearers singing songs outside their rooms containing such statements as: 'Vaal-Maseru buses will be filled with (your) dead bodies'" (Bregman 1987: Memoranda/Dicks Affidavit, 4). For its part NUM alleges that mine management regularly used team leaders and others recruited from outside the mines to attack the union and its representatives.[9] According to one report sympathetic to the union, tension was exacerbated by a search conducted by security police of all rooms except those belonging to team leaders (*Work for Justice,* June 1988:8). Shaft stewards say they feared an attack was being planned against them. To forestall this, they maintain, a group of miners attacked the team leaders first. A mob descended upon rooms shared by team leaders, attacking them with clubs and handmade swords. Four team leaders were hacked to death and their bodies set alight.

Violent Confrontations in 1986

Much of the conflict that occurred at east division in 1986 can be traced to these murders. In February 1986 nine men were arrested in connection with the killings. Shaft stewards and their supporters in the east division organized a sympathy strike (illegal in South Africa), saying that shaft stewards who took no part in the killings were selected for arrest simply because of their position in the union. On 26 February a Sotho-speaking mineworker known as Seven broke the strike at no. 1 shaft by leading a group of twenty-three new recruits down to work. Strike sympathizers complained that Seven and his group were armed and, although this violated company regulations, their weapons were not confiscated. They suggested that if the mine authorities wished to ensure the safety of those who wanted to work an escort should have been provided for them by mine security.

Because Seven was staying at the quarters of the Sotho induna, many felt the Sotho induna—and perhaps other indunas—were associated with his actions. On the night of 4 March the automobiles of the three indunas for the Sotho, Swazi, and Shangaan units were bombed (Bregman 1987: PT40/1724–25).[10] Undoubtedly in the minds of many workers this was connected with the breaking of the strike, but the perpetrators were not found.

The following day action in sympathy with the defendants from no. 5 shaft was continued in the form of short shifts. Management obtained an injunction from the South African Supreme Court declaring this action illegal and ordering the miners back to work. About this time a rumor circulated among the miners that the hostel would be attacked by thugs hired to break the union. Workers were reportedly walking about armed (Bregman 1987: PT75/2729).

On the morning of 7 March miners were lined up in the presence of security and asked to sign a form reaffirming the conditions of their employment. Due to the vast number of workers the oath signing continued throughout the day and on into the next morning. The following night a bomb exploded near the Sotho induna's house. The Sotho induna, known as Mpalinyana, claimed he heard someone who was outside say "Let it burn" in Xhosa. This is the first hint of a meaningful ethnic dimension to the conflict.

Mining operations returned to normal on 9 March, but this semblance of normality was not to last. Two days later clashes occurred of an apparently interethnic sort. These were the first such conflicts to be investigated by Bregman's commission. Mine manager K.V. Dicks summed up one perspective on the origins of these clashes: "A pervasive fear grew amongst the employees caught between the threat of possible bodily harm or even death for non-cooperation with the NUM and the threat of dismissal for participating in illegal activities. In my view, this fear and tension caused polarisation along tribal lines and the first faction fights between Xhosa/Sotho occurred on 11 March 1986 leaving 3 dead at No. 1 Shaft. This faction fighting spread to No. 3 Shaft where 9 people lost their lives on 16 March 1986" (Bregman 1987: Memoranda/Dicks Affidavit, 5–6). Dicks supports his position by citing statements allegedly made at the time to security by mineworkers in fear for their lives.[11] One such statement, purportedly made by a miner housed at room 404 in no. 1 hostel, relates an account of some of the fighting along with the alleged eyewitness's explanation:

> We went outside and saw that Basutho [sic], in blankets, were running in the direction of the shaft. They were chased by Xhosas, dressed in white sheets, they had in their hands spears in [sic] steel. We all ran away towards the hostel gate. The Sotho were over [a] hundred[;] the Xhosas were far in the majority. The Xhosas kept beating the Basuthos [sic] chasing them. At the gate we were met by security. They

told us to wait. We then went back, behind the security
vehicle. We met with the Xhosas who ran way. As we proceeded we found two bodies, of Sothos. The security tried to
bring us together to discuss the problem. At that time the
Basotho were [on] one side [and] the Xhosa were on the
other side. Security urged the Xhosas to return to their
rooms. The Xhosas refused. The security asked the Basotho.
We Basotho told them that we could not go to our rooms
because the risk to be killed. We advised security to go with
us and to stay with us until morning. Security remained and
protected us. The whole situation developed since the previous week when the shaft stewards supported by the Xhosas
urged and forced us to refuse to work. A few days later the
shaft stewards blamed the Basotho to be the pimpi [collabo-
rators] of the Whites...The Xhosas said that if the Basotho
do no [sic] cooperate they will be killed. This was said by all
Xhosas who stated it is better to kill the Basotho as they
were the collaborators of the Whites. (Bregman 1987:
Memoranda/KVD40)

In the inquiry itself more details emerged indicating that this fight was
not simply a fight between a unified block of Sotho sympathy-strike
opponents against a unified block of Xhosa sympathy-strike advocates. A miner alleged that one of the Xhosa men killed was pointed
out by security police before being attacked. Mine and hostel management itself emphasized that the dispute had much to do with a power
struggle between the Sotho induna and the Xhosa induna and their
supporters.[12] Sotho speakers also suspected that their induna's house
had been singled out because of his association with Seven. The Xhosa
induna, nicknamed Machain, allegedly was threatened and chased
around the compound the night before the killings by a group of
Sotho speakers (Bregman 1987: PT36/1578; PT40/1701–02). Xhosa
and Sotho factions spent the following day buying or handcrafting
weapons.

The incident in which Machain was chased and that in which the
first three miners were killed were both preceded by the blowing of a
whistle. This is a rallying signal generally associated at the mines with
the Sotho (Bregman 1987: PT40/1711).[13] One miner, who identified
himself both as a shaft steward and as an Mpondo, told the inquiry of
his participation in the fight and described the scene immediately preceding it (Bregman 1987: PT40/1714–15):

> *Mr. Chairman:* So when the whistle blew did the Xhosa
>   advance to the Sotho or the Sotho advance
>   to the Xhosa?

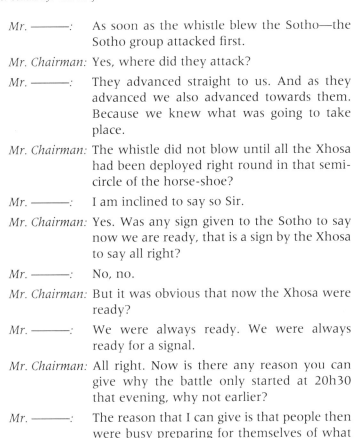

Mr. ———: As soon as the whistle blew the Sotho—the Sotho group attacked first.

Mr. *Chairman:* Yes, where did they attack?

Mr. ———: They advanced straight to us. And as they advanced we also advanced towards them. Because we knew what was going to take place.

Mr. *Chairman:* The whistle did not blow until all the Xhosa had been deployed right round in that semi-circle of the horse-shoe?

Mr. ———: I am inclined to say so Sir.

Mr. *Chairman:* Yes. Was any sign given to the Sotho to say now we are ready, that is a sign by the Xhosa to say all right?

Mr. ———: No, no.

Mr. *Chairman:* But it was obvious that now the Xhosa were ready?

Mr. ———: We were always ready. We were always ready for a signal.

Mr. *Chairman:* All right. Now is there any reason you can give why the battle only started at 20h30 that evening, why not earlier?

Mr. ———: The reason that I can give is that people then were busy preparing for themselves of what would take place later on.

Mr. *Chairman:* So they needed time to prepare.

Mr. ———: Yes, it is true that they need time to prepare for themselves because all the faction fights on the mines start at night.[14]

Miners working underground were informed by white workers that a fight had broken out at no. 1 hostel. Some prepared weapons while still beneath the surface, but all refrained from fighting there.[15] Workers returning to the compound after finishing the second shift were stopped by security at the gates. Although many Sotho had been pushed out of the compound during the initial fighting, only Sotho were allowed to enter. In fact, the Lesotho delegation to the inquiry found that the Sotho were actively encouraged to join the fighting by two senior white officials (Bregman 1987: Memoranda/Lesotho Delegation, 2). However, about half of all workers chose to remain outside.

The workers who chose to go into the compound were told by

security to go to the mess hall, where allegedly they were fed an unusually nice meal and told not to allow the Xhosa in to eat. One miner testified that he heard the hostel manager, a white man nicknamed *Tsotsi* (gangster), encourage the new group to join in the fight. Tsotsi is said to have promised to take the side of the Sotho because he blamed the Xhosa for instigating the recent short shifts (Bregman 1987: PT76/2758, 2761). As the fighting proceeded the Sotho combatants, now with the support of security, were able to reverse their earlier loss and drive the Xhosa faction out of the mine compound. They then set about looting rooms known to belong to Xhosa speakers.

A group of shaft stewards who testified at a special session of the inquiry on 31 July 1987 gave a different perspective on these events. They said the March confrontation was not merely between Sotho and Xhosa and their indunas but between indunas and shaft stewards as well. Stewards admitted that indunas often hate them because of the union's campaign to take away the indunas' special privileges (Bregman 1987: PT122/4529). For this reason, on 11 March the Sotho induna's followers, allegedly with security's collusion, came after a Sotho-speaking steward named Thabang because he was seen as siding with Xhosa militants against the Sotho induna. A steward said the March fight was "a fight between the Basuto [sic] who supported the Union and the Basuto who supported the Induna" (Bregman 1987: PT123/4572). Another steward admitted that the majority of Sotho workers supported the induna in this particular case (Bregman 1987: PT123/4573). He went on to add, in a revealing statement that in general men from Lesotho "do not believe that we are one thing as workers. They still want to continue to isolate themselves as a Basuto ethnic group" (Bregman 1987: PT123/4580).

Despite these admissions, the shaft stewards maintained that the whole Xhosa/Sotho fight was created by management. They argued that security actually came into the compound on the night of 11 March *before* fighting broke out (Bregman 1987: PT122/4556). Security provoked a fight along ethnic lines by arbitrarily dividing the workers into Sotho- and Xhosa-speaking groups before firing rubber bullets at the Xhosas. "Even those Basothos who were mixing up with Xhosas were also shot by the rubber bullets," a witness stated (Bregman 1987: PT115/4344).

State of Emergency, Protest, and the Slaying of Shaft Stewards

South Africa declared a state of emergency on 12 June 1986 to combat the wave of protest sweeping over the country. In the first week of July, two shaft stewards from Vaal Reefs were detained in terms of the emergency regulations. Many miners felt that the arrest of one of

these stewards was connected with an earlier incident in which black
and white workers had clashed underground.[16] In August NUM and
other activists renewed their political campaign by staging marches
that involved singing, dancing, and waving union banners as they trot-
ted through the hostels. It is alleged that some of the participants wore
tires around their necks—an ominous sign of the notorious "neck-
lace"-style killings employed against supposed collaborators with the
white regime (Bregman 1987: Memoranda/Dicks Affidavit, 7).

The next incident to receive extensive treatment by the Bregman
inquiry occurred at no. 1 shaft in late September during the balloting
for Transkei elections being held in the compounds. A group of
singing mineworkers marched upon the hall at no. 1 shaft where balloting was scheduled. They overturned tables and scattered ballots
before making off with one of the black mining clerks officiating the
election. He was then paraded through the compound, and possibly
assaulted. Tension reportedly rose sharply at no. 1 hostel after three
men, including a shaft steward, were dismissed from their jobs and
subsequently arrested in connection with this incident (Bregman
1987: Memoranda/Dicks Affidavit, 7).

On 8 October security forces were sent down no. 1 shaft on information that a sit-down strike was about to begin. The mine manager
maintains that such a strike was attempted at level 65. It was for this
reason that twenty-seven workers were arrested and five subsequently dismissed from their jobs (Bregman 1987: Memoranda/Dicks
Affidavit, 7). For their part, union representatives deny that any such
strike took place. They say all that happened is that some men working underground received unprovoked beatings from security men
(Bregman 1987: PT20/1047–48; PT58/2205).

Many workers were angry about this incident. The situation again
grew tense in no. 1 hostel. Some six to eight days after the below-
ground arrests were made, rumors spread that an attack by vigilantes
supposedly associated with the Russian gang on no. 1 hostel was
imminent. A provoked "tribal" clash was feared.[17] In order to prevent
this, shaft stewards and others spent the night of the 16th and 17th
patrolling the compound. On the night of the 17th two white men in
a Mitsubishi sedan and a van full of black men were allegedly seen
entering the compound. Further, "people were seen climbing over
into the bar, they were climbing the fence into the bar" (Bregman
1987: PT50/2041). There were no attacks, however, and in the next
few days tension subsided somewhat.

In early November some 700 miners crowded into the compound
meeting hall and voted to boycott the mines' liquor outlets. For many
the boycott was seen as the only forceful way left to protest the dismissals and arrests connected with the October conflicts (Bregman

1987: PT21/1070). All previous appeals made by NUM through official channels had been rejected (Bregman 1987: PT48/1978–79, 1990). Critics among the workers, however, charged that the boycott lacked a clear mandate and was being foisted upon them by shaft stewards (Bregman 1987: PT52/2044–47). The boycott was to lead to complex political maneuvering and, eventually, to more violence and bloodshed.

The day after it was called the boycott was broken by half a dozen men identified by other miners as Mpondo (Bregman 1987: PT21/1072). They were recognized also as members of the hostel's *umtshongolo* dancing group (PT21/1078). They entered the bar attired in white sheets, which identified them as Xhosa speakers and, possibly, as belonging to the *ndlavini* Xhosa subculture.[18] One of the shaft stewards, himself an Mpondo, went to the liquor outlet to talk with them. They told him they were not respecting the boycott because they had received no recompense from the looting that took place during the March fighting (Bregman, 1987: PT21/1080; PT58/2229). After the boycott was broken by the Mpondo group, it was agreed to call it off temporarily. Supporters of the boycott said they wanted to avoid a confrontation; less-enthusiastic boycotters simply may have welcomed a return to routine drinking.

The boycott was resumed on Wednesday, 19 November. It was respected on the 20th but violated the following day by a group of other miners identified as Mpondo. This time there were between thirty-five and forty-five men involved (Bregman 1987: PT59/2242–43). They were armed with staves, clubs, *panga* knives, and swords. Security was called but did not disarm them. The reaction of the security police indicated to many miners that the boycott-breakers had the approval of management (Bregman 1987: PT 77/2814; Transkei Memorandum, 17–18).

As the Mpondo dance group and a few others continued to drink that Friday afternoon, someone thought by the drinkers to be a shaft steward threw a firebomb into the bar. This act so angered the drinkers that they set off en masse on a hunt for the alleged culprit as well as the other nine shaft stewards. Some of these armed men ran immediately into the hall next door where a movie was being shown and threatened those inside. Frightened moviegoers "crashed through closed windows in a stampede as they desperately looked for escape routes" (Bregman, 1987: Transkei Memorandum, 13).

The group of Mpondo drinkers chased most of the shaft stewards out of the compound, but they succeeded in capturing one. Perhaps because he was also a team leader, he was not killed, but he was beaten and sustained serious injuries. The battered corpse of another man, a suspected comrade, was found in room 386 that evening (Bregman 1987: Transkei Memorandum, 14). White security officials and the hostel manager Tsotsi were reportedly seen in the liquor outlet praising and shaking the hands of men in the Mpondo group after these attacks occurred (Bregman 1987: Lesotho Delegation Memorandum, 3).

The hunt for shaft stewards continued the following afternoon, after the first shift. A group of about 400 men, Mpondo prominent among them, were reported to have converged on the BMQ sometime between 2:00 and 5:00 P.M. in search of stewards hiding there. Allegations were made that the Mpondo leaders increased their numbers by threatening other workers and forcing them to join in the hunt (Bregman 1987: Transkei Memorandum, 14). Workers from other hostels were probably also recruited (Bregman 1987: Lesotho Delegation Memorandum, 5). On Saturday and Sunday gang members are said to have shouted that they had been given six days to finish their job; common wisdom in the hostel was that they had been instructed by management to eliminate shaft stewards (Bregman 1987: PT28/1296–97). Indeed, it is difficult to imagine how a group of 400 armed men marching on the BMQ in the middle of the day could go undetected. Once at the BMQ the armed men conducted a house-to-house search. Apparently they succeeded in finding at least one steward. The body of shaft steward Mhlamvu Alton was found at the BMQ on the following morning.

While the armed men were rampaging through the BMQ the men remaining in the hostel prepared to defend themselves. Xhosa and Sotho speakers initially joined in a common defense. When the marauders returned from the BMQ this Xhosa/Sotho alliance fought them and succeeded in driving them out of the compound. About an hour later, however, an apparently unprovoked murder broke the unity of the Xhosa/Sotho group. A Sotho-speaking man allegedly killed a Xhosa in cold blood, saying he was tired of his victim speaking Xhosa and not Sotho (Bregman 1987: PT27/1275). After this the Xhosa men abandoned the Sotho and joined the Mpondo group that had been driven out of the hostel in the fighting. This is reportedly how the ethnic fighting began (Bregman 1987: PT27/1276).

With its renewed support the so-called Mpondo faction had the upper hand. They were aided further by a man (probably from the group of defectors) who opened the back gate leading to the liquor outlet. The combatants from outside were able to enter the compound secretly and attack the main body of Sotho from behind. They forced the Sotho fighters out of the hostel, then turned to looting rooms known to belong to Sotho speakers. Some of these rooms were occupied by men who had chosen not to fight or who were unsure about what side to take. A number of these relatively defenseless men were found and killed. While this was happening, security prevented the

Sotho combatants from reentering the compound, threatening to shoot anyone who tried to do so (Bregman 1987: Lesotho Delegation Memorandum, 5). In total thirteen people were killed on the 22nd and 23rd.

On Friday, 5 December, a further round of fighting was sparked off when a Sotho man spotted a Xhosa man wearing clothing that he claimed was his own (Bregman 1987: Memoranda/Minutes of December 7 Meeting Between Management and NUM Representatives). While the specifics of that fight are unclear, on the following evening, according to the Sotho, a horn sounded and, "all of a sudden, they found that the Xhosas were heavily armed with lethal weapons" (Bregman 1987: Lesotho Delegation Memorandum, 6). This fight had been preceded by another buildup of tensions. A Sotho spokesperson claimed later that "from Wednesday [Mpondos] started moving into the hostel with dangerous weapons and security did nothing. Two days ago [the day before the fighting], security were in the hostel and they saw Xhosa with dangerous weapons but did nothing" (Bregman 1987: Memoranda/Minutes of December 7 Meeting Between Production Manager, Sotho, and Xhosa Delegation). Most of the Sotho men fled through the main gate, but a few were trapped inside. These men were systematically hunted down and murdered, allegedly in sight of mine security (Bregman 1987: Lesotho Delegation Memorandum, 6).

The next day 587 miners, mostly Sotho speakers, decided to return to their homes (Bregman 1987: Dicks Affidavit, 9). The Lesotho miners' understanding of the situation at that time was summarized as follows: management had wanted to use them against Xhosas in March and they refused; management had now found a willing group to be used, i.e., Mpondos, and this group was being used against them (Basotho); there could not therefore be any protection that could be expected from management in the circumstances (Bregman 1987: Lesotho Delegation Memorandum, 8). After a few weeks many of these miners returned to the mines, but they were reinstated at low-level positions, regardless of their previous status. At the time of the inquiry, shaft stewards still feared for their lives. Apparently one person was charged with threatening a shaft steward in November, but at the time of the inquiry he was free on bail and back working and living in the same hostel. Nonetheless, as evidenced by the ability to mobilize workers for the September strike of 1987, the power and influence of NUM was not broken by these incidents.

Interpretation

This short discussion obviously cannot do complete justice to the complex series of events that took place at Vaal Reef in 1984, 1985, and

1986. There is evidence in the transcripts from the Bregman inquiry to support a number of different interpretations. Some of the evidence is contradictory and there is a great deal of self-interested evasion. Yet apart from problems of truthfulness and evasion, it is clear that much of the evidence is colored by the differing ideological perspectives of the participants. There is a "Rashoman" effect at work here. For example, one could take a hard-line antiwhite/antimanagement view and argue that all the so-called tribal fighting was created by white management's machinations. There is little doubt that management encouraged, tolerated, and promoted much of the violence. It was in management's interest to promote ethnic hostility in order to weaken the union and the more revolutionary groups associated with it. Such hostility took the form of Sotho/Xhosa fighting because these are the dominant groups represented at the mines. They are consequently the people usually involved in the struggles for power and authority in the induna system of compound management.

Some shaft stewards themselves admitted that worker unity was an ideal rather than a reality at no. 1 hostel. Workers from Lesotho were mentioned particularly as clinging to ethnic consciousness; Mpondo workers are another group at the mines with whom a well-defined set of ethnic characteristics is associated. Part of the reason for the conflict between shaft stewards and other workers is that political identities are changing. There is generational conflict at work here too. Many militant young Sotho and Xhosa speakers do see themselves primarily as workers. But this puts them in conflict with those older men who have become established at the mines and who have used their wages to build up the rural resources to which they have access. When it comes to issues of wages and working conditions, there is no conflict between the two groups and worker unity is great. But many workers are less willing to support radical "comrade-style" tactics. Team leaders and office personnel at no. 1 shaft, for example, could hardly be expected to endorse vigorously a sympathy strike for people suspected of harassing and killing others in their position at no. 5 shaft.[19]

Worker unity may or may not be growing in the wake of the 1987 strike. Incidents of ethnic and racial tension continue to be reported from the mines. For example, a miner from Lesotho recently wrote to the newspaper *Moeletsi oa Basotho* (18 July 1989, 6) describing conflict between Xhosa and Shangaan workers at Western Deep Levels in the Transvaal. According to his report, this fight began in early May after the headless body of a young Xhosa-speaking worker was found underground. The young man had been missing for several days. His team leader, identified as a Shangaan, admitted killing the youth at the instigation of his white boss. For unknown reasons, the white miner reportedly was seeking the *head* of a black man. What is significant here is that Xhosa-speakers retaliated against other workers whom they identified as "Shangaan" and six of them were killed.

APPENDIX

Chronology of Events at Vaal Reefs in 1984–1986

September 1984	Legal strike launched by NUM. Miners allege "Russian" gang members were hired to provoke ethnic conflict.
November 1984	Local shops are boycotted.
11–14 March 1985	Miners work short shifts in protest of pay hikes for select employees.
21–22 April 1985	Workers at south division protest working conditions and refuse to do blasting "reserved" for whites—14,000 to 17,000 miners are dismissed.
July 1985	NUM "equality-for-all" campaign begins, including protests at senior dining halls. Serious rift develops between team leaders and NUM militants at no. 5 shaft. Four team leaders are murdered.
December 1985	Black administrator's car is bombed.
18 February 1986	Nine workers are arrested in connection with July killings.
25 February 1986	East division (shaft nos. 1, 2, 5) goes out on strike in sympathy with those arrested.
26 February 1986	A mineworker named Seven and twenty-three other workers break strike. Seven associated with Sotho induna.
4 March 1986	Automobiles of three indunas are bombed.
5 March 1986	Miners work short shifts in sympathy with those arrested. Some workers allege union or comrade intimidation.
7 March 1986	Three black administrators are allegedly assaulted and forced to run through compound with NUM banner for not respecting short shift.
8 March 1986	Sotho induna's house is bombed.
9 March 1986	Normal production resumes.
11 March 1986	First "faction fights" take place. Three workers are killed at no. 1 shaft. Sotho men loot Xhosa workers' rooms.

16 March 1986	Fighting breaks out at no. 3 shaft; nine more men are killed.
7 July 1986	Confrontation erupts between black and white workers underground. Protest of state of emergency and arrest of shaft stewards take place.
August 1986	NUM/COSATU militants and comrades campaign in hostels.
September 1986	Transkei elections are disrupted.
8 October 1986	Alleged sit-down strike takes place. Workers claim they were beaten for nothing.
6–7 November 1986	Liquor outlets first boycotted at no. 1 hostel. Boycott is broken by Mpondo dance group.
19–20 November 1986	Liquor boycott is renewed and broken again by Mpondo faction.
21–22 November 1986	Fire bomb is thrown into liquor outlet; shaft stewards are suspected. Hunt for shaft stewards begins. Two men are killed.
23 November 1986	Shaft stewards are hunted down at BMQ. Battle is fought at compound. Security allegedly takes little action; twenty men are killed.
5–6 December 1986	Fight over possessions leads to renewed fighting at no. 1 hostel. Sotho workers claim compatriots were brutally murdered while security looked on; thirteen men are killed.

NOTES

1. "Ho lokela ho hlaka likelellong tsa batho hore batho ba Lesotho, Botswana, le Africa Boroa ke sechaba se le seng se mpang se arotsoe ke batho ba Juropa ho re thetsa hore re lichaba tse fapaneng."

2. Of course other, less self-interested factors, like group symbols and norms, also need to be considered in analyses of social solidarity. For an elaboration of Olson's perspective see, for example, Hardin (1982) and Hechter (1987). For the author's perspective on the theoretical issues raised by this paper see Shanafelt (1989).

3. "Sesosa sa lintoa tsena ho tummeng hore ke tsa merabe: ha ho merabe ea letho. Ho itoants'etsoa union feela qha."

4. In mining accounts of the incidents Tswana and Sotho speakers are often lumped together, as are various subdivisions of Xhosa-speaking peoples (listed below as Mpondo, Pondomise, Xhosa, Baca, and Hlubi). For management, tribal categorization is often a function of numbers. For

example, nationality gets precedence over ethnic background for the relatively few Malawians; therefore, all Malawians are referred to as members of a single "tribe." On the other hand, various subdivisions of Xhosa speakers are considered salient apparently because there are many Xhosa speakers to contend with. As defined by management, the ethnic composition of the residents at Vaal Reefs no. 1 hostel was as follows:

TRIBE	31 JAN. 1985	31 JAN. 1986	23 NOV. 1986
Lesotho	1,749	1,660	1,192
Mpondo	145	138	135
Pondomise	114	137	106
Xhosa	637	574	700
Baca	196	123	125
Hlubi	117	135	114
Tswana	1,027	1,049	1,034
Zulu	185	192	185
Swazi	246	297	349
Shangaans	242	423	451
Malawi	40	53	60
Pedi	110	115	106
Venda	49	55	54
Ndebele	76	81	51
Totals	4,933	5,032	4,662

Source: Bregman 1987: Memoranda/Exhibit L

5. Some 8,000 pages of testimony were taken during an investigation of the disturbances conducted under the authority of advocate D. A. Bregman and the auspices of the Anglo American Corporation. The investigation was established as a private fact-finding commission rather than a state-sanctioned criminal inquiry. While Bregman was engaged to conduct a "one-man commission" of inquiry into the disturbances, the actual proceedings involved a number of other professionals. Lesotho and Transkei sent official delegations as did NUM and the management of Vaal Reefs. Witnesses who testified included various levels of mine security and management, and numerous workers, shaft stewards, and other union representatives. All of the testimony from miners was taken on the grounds at Vaal Reefs. The author wishes to thank Dunbar Moodie for bringing these documents to the attention of other scholars.

6. A story told to the author by a veteran miner indicates that some ethnic clashes can be provoked by seemingly minor incidents. The miner recalled that a fight once broke out between Shangaan and other miners during the showing of a movie. A scene was shown of a black man acting exceedingly meek to a white man. Someone shouted out in Fanakalo that this must be a Shangaan worker because only Shangaans are so meek. Shangaan viewers became upset and an argument and fistfight ensued. Workers do have ethnic stereotypes of each other, but these stereotypes cannot be adequately understood unless the nature of interaction at the workplace is considered.

7. *Piccanin* is the name used in Fanakalo to refer to a black miner who acts as a white miner's servant. These black miners, in practice if not in law, set most of the dynamite charges.

8. Mine officials often fail to acknowledge the issues that motivate mass worker action. This is not necessarily cynical manipulation on their part; it may be a manifestation of an ideological system that defines miners as illiterate and primitive. For a good example of this type of management ideology in operation see Prior (1977).

9. For examples see *Work for Justice* (June 1988:7–8).

10. A senior black administrative official also had his car bombed in December of 1985. This occurred after he intervened in an incident in which miners reportedly disrupted a senior staff dining hall (Bregman 1987: PT32/1426).

11. One miner wrote to the Lesotho paper *Leselinyana* (21 March 1986:2) at about this time, alleging that NUM had lost its focus on issues of the workplace and was now merely a front for the African National Congress.

12. They may have been competing for the position of chief induna for the hostel. The Sotho induna's position was vulnerable because of the declining number of Sotho men hired. See note 4.

13. In contrast, a horn (*isibaba*) is often used to rally Xhosa speakers.

14. The name of the witness has been deleted here. His testimony was taken in Xhosa, but the original Xhosa was not transcribed in the Anglo American documents.

15. The decision not to fight underground is probably related to the expectation that security reaction is swifter and more ruthless when the means of production is threatened (see Bregman 1987: PT75/2751). In this case, a miner testified that Sotho and Xhosa workers actually helped each other make weapons while they were still underground, although they expected a fight along ethnic lines (Bregman 1987: PT75/2749–50).

16. Black workers reportedly retaliated after a white shift boss assaulted a coworker. The next day the white mine captain threatened black workers with a loaded revolver. At the end of the shift, he refused to let—in his words—"Kaffirs" surface until all whites had done so. When the elevator eventually returned for them, the black workers refused to board. They only agreed to surface after a shaft steward went down and convinced them to do so. This shaft steward was one of the two detained under the state of emergency (Bregman 1987: Lesotho Delegation Memorandum, 3).

17. A worker explained it this way: "When the Russians get into the hostels they attack Xhosas and Xhosas would presume that they are being attacked by Basothos and then a faction fight would erupt" (Bregman 1987: PT50/2046).

18. The Mpondo (*amaMpondo*) are a Xhosa-speaking people traditionally associated with the Mpondo chieftaincy. The *umtshongolo* is a type of dance done by some Mpondo men at the mines. *Ndlavini* are Xhosa-speaking men, frequently brought up in rural areas, who embrace

modern South African popular culture without completely rejecting Mpondo customs. For an insightful discussion see Beinart (1987).

19. A team leader testified that team leaders were sympathetic to those killed at no. 5 shaft and were against the actions of shaft stewards in this regard. They participated in the March short shifts because they were afraid for their safety (Bregman 1987: PT73/2678–81). This is not easily dismissed as testimony of a man telling the commission what he thought they wanted to hear. For example, he also argued that he was in favor of the union and that all the "tribal" fighting had been created by management's clever use of Russian vigilantes (PT107/4000).

REFERENCES

Africa Report. 1986. "Organizing the Struggle: Cyril Ramaphosa, General Secretary, National Union of Mineworkers." (March–April):10.

Beinart, William. 1987. "Worker Consciousness, Ethnic Particularism and Nationalism: The Experiences of a South African Migrant, 1930–1960." In *The Politics of Race, Class and Nationalism in Twentieth-Century South Africa,* eds. Shula Marks and Stanley Trapido, 286–309. New York: Longman.

Bentley, G. Carter. 1987. "Ethnicity and Practice." *Comparative Studies in Society and History* 29: 24–55.

Bregman, D. A. (commissioner). 1987. "Anglo American Corporation Commission of Enquiry, Vaal Reefs Exploration and Mining Co." Unpublished proceedings of commission of inquiry on unrest at Vaal Reefs. Held January–October in Vaal Reefs and Johannesburg.

Crush, Jonathan. 1989. "Migrancy and Militance: The Case of the National Union of Mineworkers of South Africa." *African Affairs* 88(1): 5–23.

Golding, Marcel. 1985. "Mass Dismissals on the Mines: The Workers' Story." *South African Labour Bulletin* 10(7) 97–117.

Hardin, Russell. 1982. *Collective Action.* Baltimore: Johns Hopkins University Press.

Hechter, Michael. 1987. *Principles of Group Solidarity.* Berkeley: University of California.

Leselinyana la Lesotho. 1986a. "E Bona Mahe ha e Bone Leraba" (It Sees the Eggs Without Noticing the Trap). 21 March, 2.

———. 1986. "Lipolitiki ke eng?" (What is politics?) 21 March, 2, 4.

Litsoakotleng (Lesotho). 1987. "Lintoa tsa Merabe" (Inter-Group Fighting). 2: 23–24.

———. 1988. "Ho estsahala'ng Merafong" (What's Happening in the Mines?). 2:14.

McNamara, J. K. 1980. "Brothers and Work Mates: Home Friend Networks in the Social Life of Black Migrant Workers in a Gold Mine Hostel." In *Black Villagers in an Industrial Society,* ed. P. Mayer, 305–40. Cape Town: Oxford University Press.

———. 1988. "Inter-Group Violence among Black Employees on South African Gold Mines: 1976–1986." *South African Sociological Review* 1(1): 23–38.

Moeletsi oa Basotho (Lesotho). 1989. "Litaba tsa Mona le Mane—Africa Boroa" (News from Here and There—South Africa). 16 July, 6.

Olson, Mancur. 1965. *The Logic of Collective Action: Public Goods and the Theory of Groups*. Cambridge: Harvard University Press.

Pallister, D., S. Stewart, and I. Lepper. 1988. *South Africa Inc.: The Oppenheimer Empire*. London: Simon and Schuster.

Prior, Andrew. 1977. "Managerial Ideology: A Case Study of an Incident in a South African Gold Mine: 13th August, 1975." *South African Labour Bulletin* 3(8): 67–71.

Pycroft, Christopher, and Barry Munslow. 1988. "Black Mine Workers in South Africa: Strategies of Co-optation and Resistance." *Journal of Asian and African Studies* 23(1–2): 156–179.

Ranger, Terence. 1978. "Faction Fighting, Race Consciousness and Worker Consciousness: A Note on the Jagersfontein Riots of 1914." *South African Labour Bulletin*. 4(5): 66–74.

Shanafelt, Robert. 1989. "Talking Peace, Living Conflict: The Mental and the Material on the Borders of Apartheid." Ph.D. Diss. University of Florida.

South African Labour and Development Research Unit. 1976. *Conflict on South African Gold Mines, 1972–1976*. Cape Town: University of Cape Town.

Work for Justice (Lesotho). 1988. "Basotho Mineworkers Sentenced for 'Faction Fighting.'" (June): 7–8.

7

Decolonization in Southern Africa and the Labor Crisis in South Africa: Modernizing Migrant Labor Policies

PEARL-ALICE MARSH

The decline of migrant labor as a significant portion of the South African labor force over the past decade can be associated directly with a major political phenomenon in Southern Africa, that being the decolonization of Mozambique and Angola and the ending of white rule in Rhodesia. The fact that the migrant labor system has been restructured in *direct response* to a reordering of interstate relations in the region is evidence of the original social and political foundation of the regional system based principally on race.[1] In the colonial "fraternal economy" of Southern Africa, white supremacy served as the social imperative for regional economic integration. Relations among states were relations among white settler authorities, leaving blacks out of the configuration of political and economic power.

This reliance on race as a dominant criterion for economic and industrial organization in the region paralleled the reliance on the same factor in South Africa's domestic economy. Further, South Africa's internal stability was perceived as dependent upon the regional racial order. The rise of black nationalism throughout Africa and the demise of colonial rule in Southern Africa generated a growing hostility toward white-ruled South Africa. The response of the South African government in both the regional and domestic situation was to develop a "total national strategy" of white survival. South Africa attempted to supplant previous colonial authorities in bordering states with new interstate structures that strengthened regional dependence on South Africa.[2] The subsequent regional strategy relied heavily on economic coercion.[3] Equally important, however, was South Africa's desire to respond to the growing black unemployment within its borders. The exact number of unemployed in South Africa at any given time is difficult to assess given the government's pattern of statistical data gathering (e.g., homelands statistics are not included in the data, and statistics from other rural areas are extremely unreliable). However, estimates in the early 1970s put the figure at 750,000 and rising at the rate of 100,000 per year.

The existence of a dominant economic power in a region is not in and of itself totally undesirable. In fact, a powerful economic presence in a cooperative environment can be a magnet attracting foreign investments, tourism, and trade into a region. Where hostilities do not exist between the dominant power and neighboring states, the stronger state can, in fact, see its own self-interest in strengthening the entire regional economy, thereby enhancing its own position vis-à-vis the world economy. But Southern Africa is different. South Africa's racially structured social order and the hostilities of bordering countries to the apartheid system precluded such regional organization. Normalizing relations with an apartheid-ruled South Africa—that is, forming common regional economic, military, and security structures that foster expansion of the status quo—is anathema to the majority-ruled states. Thus, Southern Africa has been caught up in the grip of South Africa's power as the latter seeks to maintain dominance of the region's economic structure under emerging state relations. At the same time, the majority-ruled states through the Lusaka Declaration have committed themselves "to pursue policies aimed at economic liberation, primarily from South Africa, and integrated development of our national economies."

The American sociologist W.E.B. Du Bois argued that "the problem of the twentieth century is the problem of the color line—the relations of the darker to the lighter races of men" (Du Bois 1970:10). The end of colonialism and settler domination of states in Southern Africa reflects major movement toward overcoming this "problem" on the continent of Africa. While empirically the conjunction between race and economic power is still evident throughout the region,[4] the absence of formal structures governing race relations in all states except South Africa makes the future of *racial power* more ambiguous —indeed, possible to overcome. Changes in the migrant labor system reflect this phenomenon.

The remainder of this chapter will discuss (1) how the interstate system developed in Southern Africa, (2) how the interstate system was reflected in the regional labor system, (3) how the transformation of the region from a race-based regional economy to a national-based one occurred, (4) how this change impacted migrant labor relations in the region, and (5) how the organization of black labor in South Africa will affect the future of race and state. While the organization of regional labor *reflected* interstate racial policies in the past, black labor power now will help determine "race relations" in the present and future.[5]

Race, State, and Migrant Labor

During the period 1882–1898, over 5 million Southern Africans and over 1 million square miles of Southern African soil came under European rule as Britain, Portugal, and Germany gained control over the territory, resources, and labor (Schreuder 1980:2). The successful expansion of settler communities and the presence of powerful European companies created "subimperial forces" which, while engaged in conflict with the metropolitan centers over their own political autonomy, were quite essential to the disruption of the economies and societies of the indigenous people. In particular, the aggressive Boer frontiersmen of South Africa posed serious problems for British policymakers wishing to minimize disorder and competition among whites in the region in order to settle the "native question."[6]

The immediate "native problem" was to transform the indigenous peoples into a work force while suppressing their workplace, social, and political demands. As a contemporary source noted: "The [native problem] seems to refer to the Kaffirs becoming aware that their labour is really worth a good deal more than the two shillings a day they have been accustomed to get for it at the mines. The white man gets from five to ten times as much—ten to twenty shillings—and the newspapers, in commenting on the matter, frequently assert that in point of physique and efficiency for hard manual labour, the Kaffirs are as good as the whites" ("Indicus" 1969:49). The translation of this potentially troublesome labor force into a docile one would require concerted efforts on the part of both British and Boers and between mining concerns and settler governments. The unifying economic interests were "rationalized" through the unity of race—the white race against the Africans.

The European concept of race (later translated into racial administration) carried enormous force during the forging of new group relations in Southern Africa in the nineteenth century. Not only were the physical attributes of peoples sufficient to form prejudices on which to base discrimination, but the powerful racist perceptions of Africans as noninhabitants and African land as supposedly vacant denied the region capabilities of social and political organization equal to those of Europe. During the heady period of settler expansion, the practical problem the presence of Africans posed was not "how to live with them" but, more instrumentally, "how to use them." This attitude toward the African reflected two phenomena: (1) the industrial-capitalist mode of production that defined labor in stark commodity terms and (2) the centrality of race as a legitimating basis for conquest, domination, and political order.

Comparison of these social and economic relations during the period of colonial conquest and subsequent domination in Southern Africa with social and economic relations in Europe during the eighteenth and nineteenth centuries illustrates how the race variable qualitatively altered the outcome of the political and economic development processes. In Europe, as new technologies revolutionized the economies relations among social groups were also transformed. Emerging agricultural capitalism and industrialization ruthlessly disrupted European societies, altering social relations and creating a new class structure. In England, as in Southern Africa, how to "use" rather than "live with" labor became the question. William Cobbett, responding to the growing power of commercial interests in England, described the changing scene in a rural farmhouse: "Everything about this farm-house was formerly the scene of *plain manners* and *plentiful living*" (quoted in Horn 1987:20–21; italics in original). He goes on to describe the "plentiful living" as peasants and owners interacting within the main household. But on this particular visit, finding the house nearly bare of people and of social interaction among workers and owners, he describes the latter as having been "transmuted into a species of mock gentlefolk" and the laborers as having been "ground down into real slaves":

> Why do not farmers now feed and lodge their work-people, as they did formerly? Because they cannot keep them upon so little as they give them in wages. This is the real cause of the change. There needs no more to prove that the lot of the working classes has become worse than it formerly was. All the world knows that a number of people, boarded in the same house, and at the same table, can, with as good food, be boarded much cheaper than those persons divided into twos, threes, or fours can be boarded. Therefore, if the farmer now shuts his pantry against his labourers and pays them wholly in money, is it not clear that he does it because he thereby gives them a living *cheaper* to him, that is to say, a *worse* living than formerly?

Such living together, characteristic of European preindustrial relations, was no longer possible in industrial England. New systems of political order accompanied these new modes of production. Bureaucratic administration became the foundation of the modern state. Strong central governments emerged in Europe that broke down divisions among the multiple political authorities and created new political systems, transforming the environment of the individual. While the countryside was being ravaged by agricultural capitalism, individuals—particularly the youth—could urbanize and assimilate in the new industrial centers. This process of assimilation occurred rather completely in Europe.

The utility of the concepts of wage labor so central to the advance of industrial capitalism in the metropole was equally important in the settler colonies. However, the prospect of assimilation when taking over people so different in terms of appearance, culture, and society was out of the question. While industrial and agricultural capitalism transformed the indigenous peoples of Southern Africa into wage-laboring groups, they were not assimilated into new national societies. Settler communities became enclaves of European cultures, norms, and customs, impermeable to the surrounding African cultures, norms, and customs while thoroughly exploiting African labor in the local and regional economies. Through religious proselytism and missionary education, African traditions were attacked and many individuals drawn to Christianity, furthering the breakdown of indigenous culture that brutal conquest had begun.

As a matter of colonial practice, urbanization of Africans and assimilation among Africans and Europeans were not socially or politically desirable outcomes. Africans were not racial kin nor were they neighbors. Africa was "discovered" as virgin soil and the African "discovered" as an unharnessed labor source. Throughout Southern Africa in particular, governments established elaborate "native location areas" in urban areas and rural trust territories to segregate Africans from Europeans. As industrial capitalism expanded and went abroad, Southern Africa lent itself well to settler control. The question that emerged was, how could the settlers use the "natives"? It is relevant at this point to examine the ways in which the wage-labor and social interaction models from Europe were reflected and transformed in colonial/settler Southern Africa within the context of race ideology.

The Development of Settler States

The European political rhetoric concerning Southern Africa deemed the region "white man's country" from the outset. There was no question about that. The only problem was how to resolve the competing European interests in order to exploit the region's resources, including its labor.

Rapid expansion into the interior of Africa required administrative mechanisms to fulfill the goal of economic expansion. The British government initially created a charter system that sponsored the activities of commercial trading companies as part of the extension of the British empire. The charters granted wide-ranging administrative authority to private companies (often headed by a single individual) over land confiscated from indigenous inhabitants. Companies thus became vehicles for promoting emigration and colonization, generating trade and commerce, developing the mining industry, and directing the construction of railway and communication lines. Although the charters included lists of minimal rights for the "natives" that were to be preserved when disputes arose, the metropolitan authorities virtually always took the side of the companies and settlers over that of the indigenous population.

The British South Africa (BSA) Company's conquest and subsequent administration of Southern Rhodesia illustrates the relationships among the companies, the metropoles, and the settlers.[7] In 1890 the company moved north with a column of 200 settlers accompanied by the company's own police force. Upon reaching what became Fort Salisbury (present-day Harare), each member of the so-called Pioneer Column received a claim for fifteen mining sites and a farm—all of which was seized from the local African population. Company administration was characterized by enormous hostility and aggression toward Africans that provoked a war in 1893 and a major rebellion in 1896.

While the BSA Company served British imperial interests by establishing control over south-central Africa, its roughshod methods proved embarrassing to the British government. As one British official lamented: "I am dead against any attempt to rip up the past, but, between ourselves, it is a bad story. On the one hand, land was alienated in the most reckless manner to companies and individuals, on the other hand, a lot of unfit people were allowed to exercise power . . . with regard to the natives, in a manner which cannot be defended" (quoted in Schreuder 1980:263).

The aggressiveness and crudeness of the company men made the concept of settler governance increasingly attractive to the British government, for it hoped that a settler government would follow the Cape Colony policy of guaranteeing equal rights for all "civilized men." The solution became a partial devolution of administrative authority to settlers. Lord Ripon, the colonial secretary arguing for this policy, stated: "In the self-governing colonies the more fully we can accept their self-government in the fullest sense, and leave them to deal with the natives in their own way, on their own responsibility, the better for our relations with them and for the maintenance of their loyalty" (quoted in Schreuder 1980:256).

Within South Africa, Britain found hostile and formidable opposition among the Boers. Not only did they oppose British domination, whether from the metropole directly or via a British settler group, but they were also extremely aggressive in pursuit of new lands further into the interior. Ultimately, the conflict between British and Boer interests led to the Anglo-Boer War (1899–1902). Britain's military victory left the British in control of all of South Africa. Britain's subsequent overall strategy was to flood the region with British settlers sufficient to establish a majority of the voting population and to grant government to a people loyal to the imperial government. But while Britain was encouraging white settlement, it also feared the independence of these same local settler groups. It used a professed concern for the treatment of Africans as a means to stay in the region as an imperial power, particularly as white settlers became increasingly aggressive in proposing local white political control.

By 1923, the "scramble" for Southern Africa had generated the present geographic entities recognized today as the sovereign states of the region. South Africa had effectively won its independence with the formation of the Union of South Africa in 1910. After World War I, German Southwest Africa (now Namibia) became a League of Nations–mandated territory of South Africa. Nyasaland (Malawi), Bechuanaland (Botswana), Basutoland (Lesotho), and Swaziland remained under British administrative authority as "protectorates," while Northern and Southern Rhodesia (Zambia and Zimbabwe) were self-governing territories under settler-dominated legislative bodies. Mozambique and Angola remained under the colonial rule of Portugal.

Fraternity and Economy

Rhodesian, Portuguese, and South African settlers saw their collective interests as whites superseding any they might have shared with members of the indigenous black populations within their respective national geographic domains. What resulted was an interstate "fraternal economy," one which delineated major regional economic, social, and political interests along racial rather than national lines.

The late nineteenth-century South African mining boom spawned a land grab by whites throughout the region. Blacks were alienated from their land while whites developed large-scale agricultural enterprises and the mining industry. The mining-based economy generated enormous wealth for those who controlled the technologies and the means of production and who had the power to control the African majority. The infrastructure developed rapidly to extract the wealth, and settlers throughout the region prospered, establishing contractual and treaty agreements for distributing the profits among themselves. The port of Lourenço Marques (now Maputo), for instance, became a thriving city as port terminus of the Transvaal rail line, its position bolstered by a treaty guaranteeing the Portuguese a share of profits from rail traffic. The BSA Company and other private concerns reserved authority to occupy and take even more land from indigenous inhabitants and to use their position to develop further the infrastructure and the political economy of the region to serve European interests.

Individual colonial governments organized displaced blacks into labor pools for South African mines and to serve the region's agricultural needs. In fact, the large demand for African workers in the South African mines set up competition over labor between mining companies and local farmers. At times, white farmers throughout the region experienced labor shortages and attempted to block the labor drain from their areas of Southern Africa. There were, however, two factors working against restraining this flow of labor. First, the wages paid by farmers could not compete with those paid by the mining companies. There was thus a natural market flow of labor away from agriculture. Second, in order to gain the support of the governments of the region, mining companies developed lucrative payment-repatriation schemes to benefit those governments. Thus, South Africa's prosperity generated economic growth in neighboring countries. Profits from the mining enterprises in South Africa, for instance, helped develop mining and agriculture in both Southern and Northern Rhodesia. South Africa, the most developed of the states, also became the source of imported goods for the region.

The Migrant Labor System

The extensive use of organized migrant labor in South African mines formed the economic foundation of the interstate system. The rapid development of diamond and gold mining required a massive infusion of labor over a short period of time. Blacks who were displaced from land did not automatically translate into a wage-labor force. In fact, during the first decade of the mining boom the industry experienced a labor shortage. In order to meet the demand, migrant workers were pooled from the region, forming the massive labor-supply system necessary for generating South Africa's extraction-based economy.

The migrant labor system evolved over several important phases of South African industrial development. During the initial period, migrant workers entered South African mines as free labor, recruited by individual mining companies. During this stage, workers were able to exercise a choice among their peasant-based economic activities, jobs on white commercial farms, and working in the mines. Africans moved from one type of work to another as personal need demanded. The availability of labor depended upon the desire and need of Africans to engage in wage-earning activities. Production, however, was being driven by the demand for minerals. Labor availability was sporadic and not responsive to market forces. Thus, those individuals willing to work in the mines were able to drive up the wages of workers. To suppress wages and guarantee a labor force, the mining industry developed recruitment practices that virtually forced blacks from throughout the region into mine labor. By the turn of the century, formal private recruitment agencies had been established and conferred with legal powers by the South African government. These agencies were empowered to establish formal agreements between the Chamber of Mines and neighboring colonial governments. Formal recruitment through these recruitment organizations began in Mozambique in 1897, in Zimbabwe in 1911, in Angola in 1928, and in Malawi and Zambia in 1938.[8]

As mining consolidated into large individual conglomerates and demands for a more coherent and efficient system grew, recruitment for mining labor was "rationalized" and negotiated through formal interstate agreements between South Africa and supplier states. The first such agreement was between South Africa and Mozambique in 1928. These government-to-government arrangements included minimum service periods, minimum recruitment quotas, compulsory deferred-payment schemes, health and identification requirements, transportation liabilities, conditions for repatriation, restrictions on occupational and area mobility while in South Africa, and termination of contract conditions. The deferred-payment schemes were very important to the economies of neighboring states. Under agreed-upon terms, half of the miners' wages were received by the settler governments; on returning home, miners received these remittances in local currency. This became a major source of foreign exchange for countries sending labor to South Africa.

The South African government viewed control of the foreign African labor supply as essential to the overall control of the African population in South Africa. Foreign Africans were more attractive as a labor force because they could not establish permanent residence or political status in South Africa. They were not allowed to bring their families to South Africa because this would exacerbate the already existing "native problem." As a further "safeguard," urban tenancy other than in hostels was prohibited. As early as 1911, the Native Labour Regulations Act No. 15 defined black foreign workers as *prohibited immigrants* who did not meet the standards of life suitable to white South Africans. This act was followed by the Admission of Persons to the Union Regulation Act No. 22 in 1913 (revised in 1972) and the Aliens Act No. 1 of 1937. These regulations and their subsequent revisions established conditions that would allow foreign white workers entry into South Africa on a permanent basis but made it virtually impossible for Africans to enter other than as migrant workers. The terms of their employment were (1) a service contract with an employer, (2) continued maintenance of employment, (3) departure upon expiration of the contract, and (4) limited costs to the South African state.

Migrant laborers were housed primarily in compounds hardly fit for habitation. Pre–World War II dormitories did not have beds but only concrete slabs to sleep on. No dining facilities were provided; men had to eat outside or in the dormitories. On each compound were cells in which men who broke laws, rules, and regulations could be locked up. Severe discipline was an essential part of daily life in the mines: "The use of the *chikote* or *sjambok* to force production and minimize 'loafing' was the central feature of compound discipline. Occasionally these whippings were undertaken by the compound 'police'—on the explicit instruction of the compound manager—but usually the compound manager chose to administer the lashes himself. Many of these whippings were so brutal that they required more than one man to administer them: the worker was held down at wrists and ankles by the compound 'police' while the lashes were administered by the compound manager" (van Onselen 1976:144).

The primary purpose of these regulations was to maintain the foreign African workers as the main supplement to a local labor market. Foreign African workers were restricted or prohibited from certain areas of employment and from designated geographic regions. Foreign workers have never been eligible for unemployment compensation. All social costs of migrant labor were the responsibility of supplier countries.

Much of what concerned the local settlers, then, was the division of regional labor and laws regulating the exploitation and habitation of blacks as workers. The extensive demand for workers in mining, particularly gold mining in South Africa, fundamentally shaped the interstate labor system.

Migrant Labor: 1911–1975

Competition over labor between the northern territories and South Africa was a serious factor in the development of the migrant labor system, even though there was a general consensus regarding the question of race and labor in the regional economic system. During the 1930s, South Africa experienced a boom in gold mining that drove up the demand for labor. Again, while the northern governments did not necessarily support lifting an earlier ban, it was clear that if they opposed it South Africa could accomplish its recruitment goals simply through raises in the wage structure. Britain supported South Africa in establishing a "regulated flow of labor" into the mines. The concessions to Northern Rhodesia and Nyasaland were that they would have first access to their own labor, that "tribal life" would not be interrupted, and that transport and remittance would be the responsibility of South Africa. By 1939, South Africa had established its unilateral domination over migrant labor in the region. The Witwatersrand Native Labour Association sought raises of 100 percent or more in its labor quotas from Nyasaland and Northern Rhodesia, from 8,500 to 15,000 and 1,500 to 5,000, respectively (Chanock 1977:220–22). Labor recruitment took place throughout the Southern African region, as shown in Table 7.1.

Between 1896 and 1972, mining labor increased sevenfold from 54,000 to 381,000 workers. The largest increase in labor came from outside South Africa—Lesotho and north of latitude 22° south. If 1896 percentages had held constant, the 1972 labor population from these two sources would have been less than 50,000 workers. However, of the 381,000 workers employed in mining in 1972, these two sources accounted for some 193,000 laborers. When combined with other non–South African labor, the total foreign migrant labor was nearly 300,000 workers, representing almost 78 percent of the mining labor force (see Table 7.2).

This was the highest percentage reached since 1905, when 85 percent of the laborers were foreign (Hanlon 1986:76). The largest single-country source was Mozambique, from which the number of miners often exceeded those from within South Africa itself.

Mining quotas for each country within the region were to remain steady until well into the 1970s. However, major political changes in South Africa—the African labor unrest beginning in 1973 and the unrest in the townships—and changes in the political reality of the region—the independence of Mozambique, Angola, and Zimbabwe—created conditions for altering the country's migrant labor policies.

Table 7.1.   Distribution of Recruitment Station by Country and Agency, 1946

COUNTRY	WNLA STATIONS[a]	NRC STATIONS[b]
Angola	–	–
Botswana	5	9
Lesotho	–	9
Malawi	11	–
Mozambique	20	–
Rhodesia	1	–
South Africa	6	83
Southwest Africa	2	–
Swaziland	–	7
Zambia	4	–

Source: From map in Wilson (1972:x).
[a]Witwatersrand Native Labor Association.
[b]Native Recruiting Corporation.

Table 7.2.   Geographical Source of Black Labor
Employed by Chamber of Mines

COUNTRY/AREA	1896–98 (%)	1936 (%)	1972 (%)
South Africa			
Transvaal	23.4	7.0	1.8
Natal and Zululand	1.0	4.9	1.2
Orange Free State	–	1.1	1.6
Cape Province	11.1	39.2	17.7
Subtotal	35.5	52.2	22.3
Swaziland	–	2.2	1.4
Lesotho	–	14.5	18.5
Botswana	3.9	2.3	5.2
Mozambique	60.2	27.8	21.4
N. of latitude 22°S	0.5	1.1	32.2
Total (%)	100.1	100.1	101.0
Total (000s)	54.0	318.0	381.0

Source: Wilson (1972:70–71)
Note: For the years 1896–98, the figures for the Cape Privince, the Orange
Free State, and Lesotho are combined (11.1 percent), as are those for Natal,
Zululand, and Swaziland (1.0 percent).

Independence of Mozambique, Angola, and Zimbabwe

The early and mid-1960s saw the emergence of "independent Africa."
One by one, countries formerly under colonial rule—British, French,
and Belgian—established their own governments. The change, however, seemed to stop at the Belgian Congo, sitting in the heart of
Africa. Though Lesotho, Botswana, and Swaziland were granted their
independence in the 1960s, this did little to change the political land-
scape of the Southern African region, which remained solidly under
the control of the Portuguese government, the Rhodesian settlers, and
the apartheid regime. South Africa maintained strong economic control over the region because of the economic dependence established
during the colonizing days, the infrastructural arrangements that
accompanied the dependency system, and its overwhelming security
domination through its military, secret service, and death squads. The
independence of Malawi (Nyasaland) and Zambia (Northern
Rhodesia) also failed to alter the economic and political balance in the
region. Below the Ruvuma and Zambezi rivers, Portuguese and settler
colonies continued to thrive, maintaining the *cordon sanitaire*, and so
did apartheid, migrant labor patterns, and the fraternal economy.

The collapse of Portugal's dictatorship in 1974 began to change the
face of Southern Africa overnight. The following year both Angola and

Mozambique became independent. After a bloody revolution, Zimbabwe gained its independence in 1980. Suddenly South Africa was faced with a ring of black states that would provide sanctuary to its primary foe, the African National Congress (ANC), and would establish a means of politically influencing labor in South Africa through politicized migrant laborers. South Africa's sole remaining ally was Rhodesia, sitting in the center of the region and providing vital control against any insurgency. With the end of white rule in Rhodesia, the apartheid regime launched its destabilization campaign to make the region even weaker and more dependent on South Africa. In 1980, South Africa established the Lesotho Liberation Army with the express aim of overthrowing the prime minister. The South African Defense Force (SADF) repeatedly attacked Mozambique, armed the insurgent RENAMO movement, and was implicated in several assassinations and assassination attempts. The SADF launched major attacks into Angola and attempted to establish a rebel force in Zimbabwe; Botswana was the target of repeated attacks from South Africa. This military aggression in the region was the backdrop against which the changes in the migrant labor system were unfolding. Concern over the internal instability in industrial relations was compounded, in the government's view, by this external political environment in the region. The national liberation movements that were leading neighboring countries to independence were seen as potential threats to the stability of South Africa. And indeed, South Africa's political agenda of white supremacy had created enormous antagonisms between that country and its neighbors. South Africa's response was to reduce its dependence on foreign labor and to concentrate the majority of that labor which was left in the traditional migrant sector, mining.

Restructuring Migrant Labor in South Africa: From External to Internal Migration

Migrant labor became vulnerable to South Africa's aggression after the national independence period. In order to buffer its labor force from the influences of workers from newly independent black states and to stave off the alarming unemployment in the country, South Africa began a policy of repatriation in the late 1970s. When Lesotho refused to sign a nonaggression pact with South Africa, the latter threatened to reduce the quota of workers allowed to cross its borders. After Mozambican independence in 1975, South Africa's Chamber of Mines cut recruitment to 45,000 Mozambican workers per year—far below the minimum of 60,000 set in the interstate agreement and the average of well over 100,000 per year. In 1981 South Africa discontinued recruit-

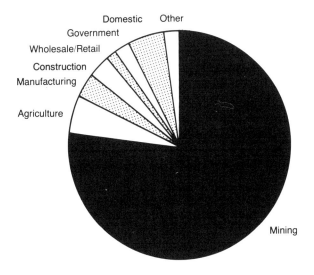

Figure 7.1. Distribution of Migrant Labor by Economic Sectors, 1983

ing mineworkers from Zimbabwe. The South African Institute of Race Relations (1984:260) reported that a decline in the foreign work force had reduced the overall numbers from 501,000 migrant laborers in 1974 to 282,000 in 1982. In agriculture alone, there was a decline from 144,000 foreign workers in 1964 to 15,000 in 1982. During 1983, South Africa repatriated 23,450 migrant workers to five neighboring states (the distribution of migrant labor by sector for 1983 is shown in Figure 7.1).

To compensate for the loss of foreign nationals and to respond to the demands of the growing unemployment problem in South Africa, South Africa shifted to "commuter workers" and migrants from the South African national states (bantustans). Between 1970 and 1982, the number of commuter workers increased from 290,800 to 773,000. Of these, 662,400 were employed in urban areas and 110,600 were employed in rural areas (Republic of South Africa 1986:239). Table 7.3 lists official figures for migrant laborers, South African workers, and "independent" homeland workers by economic sector for 1983.

By 1985, there were 584,700 migrant workers[9] employed from the six national states,[10] and 1.8 million workers from the TBVC[11] countries, approximately 371,000 legal workers from neighboring states, and 1,129,000 illegal workers. Most of the legal contract workers were in the mines. The illegal workers crossed the border and were absorbed in agriculture, casual urban labor, service jobs, and so forth, thus making it more difficult to account for their presence. The South African Police control forty-four border posts along the borders of Botswana, Lesotho, Swaziland, Angola, and Mozambique, while pass-

Table 7.3.   Sources of Labor by Economic Sector, 1983

SECTOR	SOUTH AFRICA	TBVC	FOREIGN NATIONALS	TOTAL
Mining	170,067	252,525	217,856	640,448
Agriculture	419,018	154,761	15,435	589,214
Manufacturing	613,888	165,172	9,017	788,077
Construction	314,152	117,483	9,157	440,792
Wholesale/retail	309,519	99,634	4,106	413,259
Government	385,014	131,776	6,632	523,422
Domestic	428,029	176,003	13,432	617,464
Other	198,172	86,317	6,635	291,124

Source: Summarized from tables in South African Institute of Race Relations (1983:136).

port-control services are provided by the South African Police at four-teen designated smaller aerodromes. This leaves extraordinarily long border areas over which illegal migrants can cross undetected.

While South Africa's threat had an impact on all countries in the region who had workers inside South Africa, the distribution by country demonstrates where the most extreme vulnerabilities lay. Lesotho accounted for 50 percent of all migrant workers in South Africa. These workers, in turn, accounted for 50 percent of Lesotho's active work force. The second most vulnerable country was Mozambique, accounting for 22 percent of South Africa's migrant labor force. These workers, however, represented only 5 percent of Mozambique's active work force. The third most vulnerable country was Botswana, accounting for 9 percent of South Africa's migrant labor force. These workers represented 30 percent of Botswana's active labor force. Fourth was Swaziland, accounting for 6 percent of South Africa's migrant labor force; these workers represented 15 percent of Swaziland's active work force. Lesotho, Botswana, and Swaziland together accounted for 65 percent of the migrant work force in South Africa. When combined with foreign labor from Mozambique, work-ers from these four countries accounted for 87 percent of South Africa's migrant labor force. Lesotho, Swaziland, and Mozambique were and continue to be the weakest economies in the region.

After 1985 migrant labor figures stabilized and have remained con-stant through the present.

Internal Factors: South African Labor Unrest

At the beginning of the 1970s, the South African government faced a series of internal crises that affected the organization of migrant labor. First, the government needed to support major industrial expansion and maintain a dynamic economy in order to complete its "separate development" (homelands) policy. The industrial decentralization policies, begun in 1968 and designed to alleviate problems of internal

African migration to the cities, sought to create "black jobs" in border industries located near homeland territories. It was projected that South Africa would have to produce a minimum of 14,000 new jobs each year to make the decentralization policy work. However, after an initial 10,000 new jobs in 1971, only around 6,500 new jobs were created per year during subsequent years (*Financial Mail* 1974:1132). Second, it became clearer that the South African economy—minus the fictitious homeland economies—was permanently dependent on indigenous African labor. The labor force that had been evenly divided between Africans and whites in 1934 was dominated by African labor three to one by World War II. By the mid-1950s, African labor represented 75 percent of the labor force (Greenberg 1980:177). Third, the type of labor needed changed in relation to the changes in the sectorial composition of the economy. While the composition of the labor force was changing, the relative size of the manufacturing sector was increasing as well. Manufacturing doubled by World War II and doubled again by the mid-1950s, thus superseding the combined strength of the mining and agricultural sectors. Manufacturing's labor needs were different from those of mining, demanding workers with mobility, education, and skills. Fourth, the industrial relations system—the relations among state, labor, and capital—were sorely strained by the rigidity of the "Industrial Conciliation" laws that restricted the capacity of the system to adjust to the new demands. In the 1960s, while industrialists and economists described South Africa's economy as ready to "take off" as the manufacturing sector achieved dominance, the government was attempting to implement its radical industrial decentralization program that was suited for the purpose of "separate development" but not for economic growth (Grenville-Grey 1975:188).

The nexus of these crises became the industrial relations system. By 1980, the most acute factor destabilizing the government's industrial scheme was the renewed activism of African industrial labor begun in the 1970s. The labor tranquillity of the 1960s, brought on through the repressive policies of the government, was brought to an end by a decade of worker unrest. A wave of strikes swept through South Africa beginning in Natal in 1973. Between 1970 and 1980, South Africa recorded 1,993 strikes and work stoppages involving a total of 397,578 African workers, or 93 percent of all striking workers (South African Institute of Race Relations 1982:183). Strikes were first centered in manufacturing, transport, and service industries. Workers in food, automobile, transportation, shipping, textiles, steel, metals, transport, retail, clothing, and other industries downed tools and formed unions. Mining companies also began to experience serious conflict with African workers, and by that time, due to internal labor-force restructuring, the majority of migrant laborers were in mining, thus raising the same challenges that faced other sectors. Predictions were, however, that because of the rigid controls built into the mining industry reinforced by the ethnic- and nationality-based organization of the mining compound system, it would not be possible to achieve the same kind of labor organization in the mines that had been realized in other sectors of the economy. These predictions proved to be wrong, and by 1985 the National Union of Mineworkers (NUM) was born. However, in 1982, the Chamber of Mines had already granted permission for union organizing of black mineworkers. In 1985, the government recognized the Federated Mining Explosives and Chemical Workers Union (for African and colored workers) and the broadly supported NUM.

Throughout Southern Africa, national labor bodies responded to the labor crisis in South Africa. In February 1986 the Southern African Trade Union Coordination Council was formed to "pursue socio-economic and political actions to liberate South Africa and Namibia." Its members include the Angolan Organization of Workers; Botswana Federation of Trade Unions; Swaziland Federation of Trade Unions; Lesotho Congress of Free Trade Unions; Congress of Malawi Trade Unions; Organization of Mozambique Workers; Zambian Congress of Trade Unions; Zimbabwe Congress of Trade Unions; National Union of Tanzanian Workers; Azania Trade Union Coordination Center (a Pan-Africanist Congress affiliate); South African Congress of Trade Unions (an African National Congress affiliate); and the National Union of Namibian Workers.

While employing repressive tactics to suppress African labor's dissent, the South African government was cognizant of the need for structural changes in industrial relations. The incompatibility of the existing system of industrial management, dominated by industrial laws initiated in the 1920s, strained relations between labor and capital to a crisis point. Both African labor and management demanded changes. The government established the Wiehahn and Riekert commissions to study the labor situation and to make recommendations for future policy. Both commissions took up the question of migrant labor[12] as a part of their general inquiry (Wiehahn 1979; Riekert 1979).

The Wiehahn Commission found that the fundamental issues involved (1) maintaining the state-to-state agreements in order to regulate the flow of migrant workers between countries, (2) structuring African trade unions, and (3) including (or excluding) migrant labor in the collective bargaining process. Included in the discussion of state-to-state agreements were three categories of countries: the "national states"—homelands that had not achieved "independence," independent states—homelands that had been granted independence, and historical states in the region. It was recommended by the commission that these agreements remain intact in order to maintain recruitment, travel documents, tax collection, service contracts, terms for repatriation, and terms of deferred payments. However, it was also recommended that the local industrial management system be over-hauled with two specific major changes suggested: (1) that the gov-ernment eliminate "race" as a defining characteristic of the labor force, since it had declared itself moving away from discrimination based on race, opting instead for definition by sector, skill level, and nationality,[13] and (2) that migrant workers be allowed freedom of association, thereby eliminating distinctions between migrant and South African workers in terms of collective bargaining. Responding to the criticism that migrant workers represented a political threat to South Africa and should be excluded from unions, the Wiehahn Commission argued the opposite: excluding migrant workers from unions would mean these workers would pose a greater threat to domestic peace. They could become a point of clandestine organizing, thus transforming an industrial problem into a security concern. To the argument that foreign workers would overwhelm the trade unions and thus their inclusion should be regulated, the commission argued that the trade unions themselves, out of their own self-inter-est, would control the degree of influence the migrant workers would have. Permanent South African workers would be much more attrac-tive to unions than transient migrant workers.

The Wiehahn Commission took up the issue of mine workers specifically and concluded that the mining industry did not warrant special or different treatment from that of any other sectors. In effect, the recommendations the commission made regarding manufactur-ing, service, transport, sales, and so forth should be applied to mining. Further, the commission anticipated that the development of African trade unions in mining would soon follow the pattern established in the rest of the trade union movement, regardless of laws disallowing such organization. In the meantime, the commission proposed an industrial council system for the mines (conciliation boards, wage boards, local industrial councils, etc.) until black worker organizations formed in the future. It went on to recommend that given the short-age of skilled labor in the mines, Africans should be trained for skilled jobs—irrespective of their national origins. In 1985, the government agreed in principle to the Wiehahn recommendations and set up negotiations with government, the Chamber of Mines, and white unions to work out a plan.

The Riekert Commission was appointed to deal with the nuts and bolts of labor regulation and to make recommendations regarding labor legislation and particular regulations and administrative prac-tices. Findings of the Riekert Commission paralleled the findings of Wiehahn. First, there was emphasis on deracializing the industrial relations system. Concerning migrant labor, the Riekert Commission concluded that provisions governing endorsements in the travel documents of black workers from independent African states should be removed from the Natives Abolition of Passes and Coordination of Documents Act of 1952 because the provisions were "tantamount to statutory discrimination on the grounds of colour between citizens of the same independent African state" and that such endorsements should be of a "non-discriminatory nature." In other words, there should be no racial distinction made between black and white workers from the same country. The commission further recommended that a new employment and training act be provided that would extend to all workers whether from "independent states or from black states [bantu-stans] in the Republic of South Africa and workers of all population groups resident in the Republic of South Africa outside the Black States" (Riekert 1979:234). The flow of workers entering from "independent states" and leaving South Africa was to continue to be regulated under interstate agreements; in fact, the regulation of these agreements was to be decentralized to include bantustan governments. Third, the commission recognized the detrimental effects of section 3 of the Environment Planning Act (1967), which established a 2.5:1 white to black worker ratio in the (white) metropolitan areas. This section of the act was intended to squeeze industry to expand to border areas where such ratios were not in effect. The Riekert Commission found that "since the coming into operation of Section 3, unemployment particularly among Blacks and especially Black juveniles has increased considerably in the controlled areas owing to the general economic position" (Riekert 1979:233). The commission recommended that section 3 be repealed and replaced by a provision for industrial zones.

The findings and recommendations of these two commissions constituted a major conceptual shift in formal industrial and interstate labor relations from a race-based system to a class-based one for the indigenous population and a national/class-based one for migrant workers, though in reality African workers continued to be the major work force affected by and affecting industrial relations. And the inclusion of migrant workers in the conceptual shift signaled the formal redefining of the regional labor force on a national rather than racial basis, in response to independence in neighboring states.

Conclusion

Until the 1970s, the era of independence for Southern African countries and of the labor crisis inside South Africa, Southern Africa's migrant labor was manipulated through a fraternal economy. Today, the regional migrant labor system has been transformed to reflect the shift in the regional economic system from a colonial "fraternity" to a deracialized interstate system (with the anachronism of apartheid still dominating in military power). From a global perspective, independent Southern African states have been recognized as equal members in the international system. Likewise, the regional labor system has been transformed into a new de jure deracialized system attempting to accommodate the political and industrial demands surrounding South Africa while allowing the apartheid government to maintain a high degree of control. While the interstate agreements continue to provide a basis for the importation of labor from supplying countries, the South African trade union movement has provided a basis for workers' rights for migrant laborers.

NOTES

1. I want to draw comparisons between the ideology of race, which describes the political delineation of people with different skin color, hair texture, facial features, etc., and race as an analytical category, that attempts to use "race" as a social science construct. I contend that race, in both instances, has little value except to reify negative political and social behavior and to promote "race" policies. This idea is echoed in Miles (1982) and is further elaborated in his discussion of "the racialization of the Irish."

2. South Africa, Lesotho, Botswana, and Swaziland form the Southern African Customs Union (SACU), which allows the free flow of goods throughout the four states. SACU's provisions were originally intended for the entire region, but the decolonization process and the introduction of the Southern African Development Coordination Conference (SADCC) cut off the union's potential for reaching outside the four countries. In 1977, South Africa proposed in a defense white paper a "Constellation of Southern African States" (CONSAS) as part of a comprehensive regional strategy. The purpose of the proposal was "to maintain a solid military balance [sic] relative to neighboring states and other states in southern Africa" and called for "economic action in relation to transport services, distribution and telecommunications to promote political and economic collaboration among the states of southern Africa" (Hanlon 1986:14).

3. See Johnson and Martin (1986) for an extensive discussion of this tactic.

4. Note, for instance, Anglo American Corporation's ownership of the mining industry; indeed, white ownership of industry throughout the region is still in evidence.

5. As evidenced by the formation of the Southern African Trade Union Coordinating Conference (SATUCC) in February 1986, a group of regional trade unions whose express purpose is "to pursue socio-economic and political actions to liberate South Africa and Namibia."

6. Resolution of metropole-settler conflict in South Africa emerged after the Boer War, when the "settlers" were given full dominion over South

Africa. While independence did not come to the white settlers in Southern Rhodesia until the mid-1960s under the Unilateral Declaration of Independence (UDI), they received the status of responsible government in 1923.

7. See Gann (1965) for full details on the BSA Company era in Southern Rhodesia.

8. As British protectorates, Lesotho, Botswana, and Swaziland had less formally regulated migration of labor.

9. Though there were a total of 1.5–2.0 million migrant workers a year in South Africa, there were only 500,000+ at any one time based on the continued state-to-state system and the six-month to one-year contract (Republic of South Africa 1986).

10. KwaZulu, Qwaqwa, Lebowa, Gazankulu, KwaNgwane, and KwaNdebele.

11. Transkei, Bophuthatswana, Venda, and Ciskei.

12. South Africa has three categories of "migrant/commuter workers." Frontier commuters are those workers who reside in a national state and who cross the "frontier" (border) between South Africa and the bantustan at regular or frequent intervals; migrant workers are from independent or self-governing states (i.e., the bantustans) and are temporary residents whose presence has been authorized under one of several acts, (e.g., Aliens Act of 1937) and who have been authorized to enter into a labor contract for a specified period of time (usually six months to a year) that may be renewed; and those workers who are citizens of another country and enter South Africa on a labor contract.

13. This, of course, was still problematic since South Africa defined workers from the bantustans as nationalities.

REFERENCES

Benson, John, ed. 1985. *The Working Class in England, 1875–1914.* London: Croom Helm.

Berger, Elene L. 1974. *Labour, Race and Colonial Rule: The Copperbelt from 1924 to Independence.* Oxford: Clarendon Press.

Blatchford, Robert. 1984. *Dismal England.* New York: Garland Publishing.

Butler, Jeffrey, Robert I. Rotbert, and Johns Adams. 1977. *The Black Homelands of South Africa: The Political and Economic Development of Bophuthatswana and Kwazulu.* Berkeley and Los Angeles: University of California Press.

Chanock, Martin. 1977. *Unconsummated Union: Britain, Rhodesia, and South Africa, 1900–45.* Manchester, U.K.: Manchester University Press.

Denoon, Donald. 1983. *Settler Capitalism: The Dynamics of Dependent Development in the Southern Hemisphere.* Oxford: Clarendon Press.

Du Bois, W. E. B. 1970. *The Soul of Black Folks.* New York: Washington Square Press.

Financial Mail (Johannesburg). 1974.

Gann, L. H. 1965. *A History of Southern Rhodesia: Early Days to 1934*. London: Chatto and Windus.

Ginswick, J., ed. 1983. *Labour and the Poor in England and Wales, 1849–1851*, Volume 3. London: Frank Oass Publishers.

Greenberg, Stanley. 1980. *Race and State in Capitalist Development: Comparative Perspectives*. New Haven: Yale University Press.

Grenville-Grey, W. 1975. "The Argument that Economic Growth Will Produce Fundamental Change—The Oppenheimer Thesis," and Leo Katzen, "The Debate about Growth." *The Policy Debate*. Uppsala: Study Project on External Investment in South Africa and Namibia.

Hanlon, Joseph. 1986. *Beggar Your Neighbors: Apartheid Power in Southern Africa*. Bloomington: James Currey/Indiana University Press.

Horn, Pamela. 1987. *Life and Labor in Rural England, 1760–1850*. London: Macmillan Education.

"Indicus." 1969. *Labour and other Questions in South Africa: Being Mainly Considerations on the Rational and Profitable Treatment of the Coloured Races Living There*. New York: Negro University Press.

Jabbour, George. 1970. *Settler Colonialism in Southern Africa and the Middle East*. Palestine Books no. 30. Beirut: University of Khartoum and Palestine Liberation Organization.

Jeeves, Alan H. 1985. *Migrant Labour in South Africa's Mining Economy: The Struggle for the Gold Mines' Labour Supply 1890–1920*. Kingston and Montreal: McGill Queen's University Press.

Johnson, Phyllis, and David Martin, eds. 1986. *Destructive Engagement: Southern Africa at War*. Harare: Zimbabwe Publishing House.

Katzen, Leo. 1964. *Gold and the South African Economy: The Influence of the Goldmining Industry on Business Cycles and Economic Growth in South Africa, 1886–1961*. Cape Town: A. A. Balkema.

Kowett, Donald Kalinde. 1978. *Land, Labour Migration, and Politics in Southern Africa: Botswana, Lesotho, and Swaziland*. Uppsala: Scandinavian Institute of African Studies.

Lewis, Stephen R., Jr. 1990. *The Economics of Apartheid*. New York: Council on Foreign Relations Press.

Libby, Ronald T. 1987. *The Politics of Economic Power in Southern Africa*. Princeton, NJ: Princeton University Press.

Miles, Robert. 1982. *Racism and Migrant Labour*. Boston: Routledge and Kegan Paul.

Miller, Shirley. 1982. *Trade Unions in South Africa, 1970–1980*. Saldru Working Paper no. 45. Cape Town: South African Labour and Development Research Unit.

Phimister, I. R., and Charles van Onselen. 1978. *Studies in the History of African Mine Labour in Colonial Zimbabwe*. Volume 6. Salisbury: Mambo Press.

Republic of South Africa. 1986. *South Africa 1986: Official Yearbook of the Republic of South Africa*. Pretoria: Government Printers.

Richardson, Peter. 1982. *Chinese Mine Labour in the Transvaal*. London: Macmillan Press.

Riekert, P. J. 1979. *Report of the Commission of Inquiry into Legislation Affecting the Utilisation of Manpower (Excluding the Legislation Administered by the Departments of Labour and Mines)*. Pretoria: Government Printers.

Rule, John. 1981. *The Experience of Labour in Eighteenth-Century Industry.*
London: Croom Helm.

Schreuder, D. M. 1980. *The Scramble for Southern Africa: 1877–1895.*
Cambridge: Cambridge University Press.

South African Institute of Race Relations. 1982, 1983, 1984. *Survey of Race
Relations.* Johannesburg: South African Institute of Race Relations.

van Onselen, Charles. 1976. *Chibaro: African Mine Labour in Southern Rhodesia,
1900–1933.* London: Pluto Press.

Wiehahn, Nicholas. 1979. *The Complete Wiehahn Report: Parts 1–6 and the White
Papers on Each Part with Notes by Professor N. E. Wiehahn.* Pretoria: Lex Patria
Publishers.

Wilson, Francis. 1972. *Migrant Labour in South Africa.* Johannesburg: South
African Council of Churches and SPRO-CAS.

8

South Africa and SADCC: Economics of the Southern African Region

JAMES COBBE

The main features of the Republic of South Africa's domination of the economy of Southern Africa are well known. It is worth summarizing, however, a few of the salient features and their proximate historical causes in terms of the contrasts between South Africa and the member states of the Southern African Development Coordination Conference (SADCC), namely Angola, Botswana, Lesotho, Malawi, Mozambique, Swaziland, Tanzania, Zambia, and Zimbabwe.

SADCC's member nations comprise about four times the land area of South Africa and are home to a little more than twice the republic's total population. In conventional economic terms, however, South Africa has about two and a half times SADCC's total economic output (GDP), so South Africa has an average national per capita income of between five and six times SADCC's (according to World Bank data, about $2,340 versus $375 in 1984 GNP per capita). Structurally, there are also substantial differences between South Africa and SADCC nations in the sectors of the economy that produce output. South Africa resembles a high-income economy with respect to agriculture, which in 1986 produced only 6 percent of GDP; but a very large proportion of South Africa's GDP comes from mining. In total, 46 percent of South Africa's GDP originated in "industry" (including mining) in 1986; less than half (22 percent) of that 46 percent was from manufacturing (International Bank for Reconstruction and Development, 1988). Contrary to popular belief, manufacturing in South Africa produces a lower proportion of GDP than in the average "upper-middle income" country with which the World Bank classifies South Africa, and thus lower than in many individual countries South Africans often think they are ahead of (e.g., Brazil, South Korea, Mexico, Argentina, Singapore). The depth of the recession in South Africa in the 1980s has also made industrial production in January 1990 still only 2.5 percent above the average level of 1980 (Standard Bank Investment Corporation Limited 1990:4).

There is great variety in structure in SADCC nations with respect to sectorial origin of GDP, with the proportion originating in agriculture ranging from over half (in Tanzania) to only 4 percent (in Botswana) in 1986. Generally, however, agriculture is more important and both industry and manufacturing less important than in South Africa, although mining in Botswana and manufacturing in Zimbabwe in proportional terms are comparable in importance to the corresponding sectors in South Africa (International Bank for Reconstruction and Development 1984, 1987, 1988).

In terms of macro statistical data, the contrasts are, as one would expect, starker if we look at labor force and population data. Data for 1980 from the World Bank indicate that 17 percent of South Africa's labor force was in agriculture, 35 percent was in industry (including mining), and 49 percent was in services (International Bank for Reconstruction and Development 1988:283). These figures reflect the normal differentials in productivity among these sectors (output per worker is usually lower in agriculture than in the rest of the economy, and especially industry), exacerbated in South Africa's case by the extraordinarily low levels of productivity in bantustan agriculture. The bantustans in 1980 contained 37.6 percent of South Africa's population but in 1978 produced a mere 4.3 percent of the country's output (Van der Berg 1989:201). The corresponding percentages for the combined labor force of SADCC nations were, for the region as a whole, 72 percent in agriculture, 11 percent in industry, and 17 percent in services. The ranges were 59 percent (Angola) to 86 percent (Malawi) in agriculture, 5 percent (Malawi) to 18 percent (Mozambique) in industry, and 9 percent (Malawi) to 25 percent (Angola, Lesotho, and Zimbabwe) in services. Similarly, in 1985, 56 percent of South Africa's population was reported as urban, compared to only 20 percent of SADCC nations' combined population, with a range from 11 percent in Malawi to 48 percent in Zambia. Furthermore, the official statistics on urbanization in South Africa understate the actual extent of black urbanization when one takes into account "the phenomenon of 'displaced urbanization'. . . [a] term [which] describes the concentration of black South Africans, over the last ten to fifteen years in particular, in huge rural slums which are politically in the Bantustans and economically on the peripheries of the established metropolitan labour markets" (Murray 1988:111).

Foreign trade is quantitatively important throughout the region. Measuring its importance by the ratio of exports plus imports to GNP, it has been somewhat more important in SADCC nations at 50 percent versus the 42 percent for South Africa (1983 data in both cases; in 1986 the ratio was over 50 percent for South Africa). However, this is somewhat misleading because the SADCC countries differ very markedly in their size and structure, resulting in a very wide range for this ratio across countries, from only 17 percent in Mozambique to 167 percent in tiny Swaziland. In total, South Africa's exports are about three times the value of exports for all SADCC nations, and its imports are well over twice the value of imports for all SADCC countries. South Africa also benefits in particular from its trade relations with its immediate neighbors, particularly its partners in the Southern African Customs Union (SACU)—Botswana, Lesotho, and Swaziland. Direction-of-trade data published by those three countries indicate that because most of Botswana's and Swaziland's exports go outside the union while most of all three countries' imports come from South Africa, South Africa earns about $1.5 billion a year in hard currency from SACU. (Lesotho produces negligible commodity exports, relying on migrant labor for the bulk of its foreign earnings). It is much more difficult to get precise data on trade between other African countries and South Africa, but it is known that South Africa is an important trade partner for Zimbabwe, Zambia, Malawi, Mozambique, and Zaire. In 1986, over 21 percent of Zimbabwe's imports came from South Africa, and in 1985 over 38 percent of Malawi's imports had the same origin (Economist Intelligence Unit 1987). It has been suggested that in 1984 South Africa's trade surplus with these countries was worth an additional $238 million in foreign exchange to South Africa (Lewis 1987:56); official South African data report trade surpluses with "Africa" (excluding SACU and Namibia) of $252 million in 1984 and $512 million in 1985 (Economist Intelligence Unit 1987). Moreover, the region's limited transport routes and South African–assisted sabotage of the Benguela Railway and the various rail routes through Mozambique force the inland SADCC states and Zaire to ship a high proportion of their overseas trade over South African Railways and through South African ports. Lewis (1987:17) estimates South Africa's surplus on transport and other nonfactor services with the SADCC states in the mid 1980s at $300 to $500 million a year.

Migrant labor links also remain important in Southern Africa. Botswana, Lesotho, and Mozambique are the three countries most significantly affected, although Malawi, Swaziland, and Zimbabwe still have considerable numbers of workers in South Africa. For Lesotho, access to South African labor markets is absolutely vital; in the cases of Botswana and Mozambique, the problem is far less important from a macroeconomic point of view but is nevertheless significant. Botswana would face substantial problems with respect to labor markets if its workers did not have access to South Africa, and Mozambique sorely needs the foreign exchange generated by its workers in South Africa, whose numbers are declining. Illegal migrants from these countries also work in South Africa, with Mozambique the source of by far the largest numbers recently apprehended and repatriated by the authorities. In 1987, 26,870 workers were repatriated to Mozambique, representing over 71 percent of all foreign African workers repatriated from South Africa (South African Institute of Race Relations 1988:315).

The causes of this situation are well known and firmly rooted in the process by which capitalism, colonialism, and Afrikaner nationalism have transformed the subcontinent over the last 150 years. More immediately, the current situation results from the dynamics of capitalist development in Southern Africa and the deliberate policies of the South African government in response to the withdrawal of British and Portuguese control of what are now the SADCC states. South African attitudes toward those states are somewhat schizoid. They are seen simultaneously as the natural extended economic hinterland for the more advanced and dynamic South African economy and as a threat to political stability within South Africa. The implications of these two views are sometimes reinforcing, sometimes contradictory.

Consider the implications of SADCC countries as economic hinterland: SADCC member states can provide markets for South Africa's manufactures, services, and commercial agriculture, permitting greater economies of scale in South Africa with proximity substituting for low-cost production, thereby giving South Africa comparative advantage relative to overseas suppliers; SADCC countries provide additional demand for South Africa's railways, ports, and financial and commercial services; SADCC nations can supply additional sources of migrant labor that is potentially, at least, more docile and flexible than domestic labor, thereby strengthening employers vis-à-vis labor within the South African economy; and SADCC states can provide opportunities for South African businesses to expand and invest abroad in areas where they can at least expect to have advantages of local knowledge and expertise over overseas alternatives.

To the extent that South Africa actually succeeds in drawing SADCC states into these roles vis-à-vis its economy, it also makes these states even more dependent on it economically and therefore vulnerable to economic pressure in pursuit of South Africa's political aims. The obvious extreme example is Lesotho, a small state completely enclosed within the Republic of South Africa, but there are an ample number of other instances that can be cited. South Africa, and more particularly its private and parastatal sectors, however, have not in the vast majority of cases built up these economic links to increase Pretoria's political leverage; Pretoria may have encouraged the links for that purpose, but the links were forged because they were of commercial advantage to the South African participants as well as the SADCC ones. Economic dependence is never one-way when based on exchange, not gifts; thus, actually using the leverage threatens costs not only to the threatened SADCC state but also to the South African economy and the particular actors within that economy who are the South African end of the link that may be broken or curtailed. When the links are broken, costs are imposed at both ends; if the common beliefs about the nature of such dependent links between unequals are true, the absolute costs may be greater at the South African end than at the SADCC end. Relatively, of course, the costs will be much lower to the South African economy as a whole because of its greater size. From a policy point of view, however, this is almost irrelevant, because in particular cases the costs may well be heavily concentrated on particular actors or groups of actors, and they may not be willing to bear those costs without compensation or extreme pressure.

The migrant labor situation provides a clear example. It is obvious from the extent of black unemployment within South Africa and from the statements of The Employment Bureau of Africa (TEBA), the Chamber of Mines' recruiting organization, about its ability to supply recruits from the bantustans that in the long run the South African economy as a whole does not need foreign migrant workers. However, the existing corps of migrants, now mostly long service, experienced, and often skilled, cannot be disposed of without very heavy costs to the mining industry. Thus, when the South African government, through the State Security Council, threatened in November 1985 to repatriate migrants if sanctions were imposed against it by the West, the Chamber of Mines howled in protest and the government backed away from an immediate decision, although it opened consultations with major employers of foreign workers on contingency plans should repatriation become "necessary." Similarly, after the South African government supposedly imposed a ban on all Mozambican labor in October 1986, the Chamber of Mines was reportedly able to negotiate a temporary deal to save the jobs of half the Mozambican miners in South Africa—namely, those in skilled and semiskilled jobs—and give mines with heavy reliance on unskilled Mozambicans three years over which to phase them out (South African Institute of Race Relations 1988:314).

In this case as in others, it is also important to distinguish carefully between long-run implications of a change for an extended period and the short-run costs of a temporary change. It is here that the far greater overall strength and wealth of the South African economy gives Pretoria substantial leverage over the SADCC states as a result of their economic interdependence. South Africa's economy is strong enough to withstand the costs of temporary (weeks to months) inter-ruptions of many of these links without difficulty, whereas in many cases the economies—and polities—of the SADCC states involved are sufficiently weak that interruptions of indefinite duration (that may turn out to be only temporary) cannot be withstood for more than very short periods. Considering again the extreme case of Lesotho, the permanent loss of exports to that country would be costly to South Africa, although bearable; an interruption for a few days or weeks has almost negligible costs because the sales involved are merely postponed, not lost. But as the events of January 1986 demonstrated, Lesotho was unable to withstand an interruption of supplies of key imports that lasted for only a few weeks (Cobbe 1988).

South Africa is thus in a position to exploit its economic advantage for political gains because in the medium term it does not anticipate having to bear costs from interruptions of economic intercourse for more than a fairly short period. In contrast, the SADCC state at the other end will likely have capitulated politically. Of course, the exercise of such power will have costs in the long run: it will make the SADCC states more determined to delink from South Africa in order to reduce such vulnerability to economic pressure. In the short to medium term, however, the implication is that although South Africa is unlikely to sever its economic links with SADCC nations on a permanent basis (e.g., why would South Africa refuse permanently to supply SADCC states with goods as a result of sanctions, thereby reducing its own exports?), it can be expected to interrupt such links on a short-term basis in order to pressure the SADCC states to comply with its wishes, or to influence the actions of other states. Thus, as Richard Weisfelder (private communication, November 1985) has pointed out, Botswana, Lesotho, and Swaziland in particular may now be more literally "South Africa's hostages"—because South Africa could do them severe damage by cutting off supplies and repatriating migrants in retaliation for sanctions—than they were when the phrase was first applied to them in the 1960s.

With this background in mind, it is now appropriate to move to an examination of the effects on the region in economic terms of recent events within South Africa. The key relevant aspects are the following:

1. the slowdown in economic growth within South Africa, exacerbated by limited sanctions and disinvestment by the West and the loss of confidence in the South African economy on the part of foreign investors, foreign banks, and portions of the white population itself;

2. the stance that the South African government has adopted toward its neighbors of being willing to use not only crude economic pressures in order to achieve compliance with its wishes with respect to policy in those countries toward the ANC and itself, but also to use support of rebel movements

such as UNITA in Angola and RENAMO in Mozambique and outright military attacks to keep neighboring countries economically and militarily weak; and

3. the potential spillover effects on SADCC states of moves by outside parties to influence what happens in South Africa, as in the case of sanctions.

The South African Economy

South Africa has an overall population growth rate of about 3 percent per annum. Its economy therefore needs to grow at at least that rate in order to prevent average per capita income from falling. Structurally, the South African economy remains heavily dependent on foreign capital and technology to support growth. Gavin Relly, chairman of Anglo American Corporation, summarized the conventional wisdom on the country's macroeconomy: "Without foreign capital inflows, the South African economy can grow at little more than 3.5 percent per annum. In fact, recent growth has been even lower, averaging only 2.5 percent during the last decade and a shocking 1.1 percent during the last five years. Contributing to these dismal statistics have been the cessation of capital inflows over the last decade and the increase of capital outflows recently" (Relly 1986).

Relly's numbers represent estimates of long-term trends and may even be overestimates—in June 1987 Standard Bank estimated growth of real GDP in South Africa since 1975 at only just over 2 percent per annum and argued that 2 percent might well represent the underlying long-term growth rate with South Africa's current structure, particularly its high propensity to import capital goods and intermediates and the consequent balance-of-payments constraint on growth. In the short run, growth depends on some factors Relly does not mention, most notably the gold price (which heavily influences export earnings), diamond and other mineral prices, and government fiscal, monetary, and exchange rate policy. For example, real GDP fell 1.5 percent in 1985 and rose only 0.7 percent in 1986. In 1987, the short-term performance of the South African macroeconomy was better than it had been for some time, largely as a result of the gold price being around $450 per ounce and the boost to export earnings finally coming through from the prolonged depreciation of the rand. In terms of the U.S. dollar, the external value of the rand fell from $1.29 in 1980 to a low of $0.35 during 1985; it then recovered somewhat and fluctuated between about $0.45 and $0.49 until late 1988, without appreciating against the yen or major European currencies, before falling again in 1989, dropping to about $0.36 by the end of May; by June 1990 it had recovered a little to about $0.375. Real growth continued at about a 3 percent rate in 1988, but by May 1989 forecasts again suggest a slowing in 1989 (to under 2.5 percent) and 1990 (to less than 1 percent) (Volkskas Bank 1989:3). The major underlying problems continue to be the balance-of-payments constraint and the large government budget deficit, together with shortages of skilled labor. Inflation continues to grow at a rate of 12 to 15 percent a year, the gold price has declined again to the $360 to $380 region, and some sources suggest that real disposable incomes have been falling since 1980—and economic concerns, particularly those of pensioners, farmers, and wage earners, were an important factor in white politics in the run up to the 1989 election (*New York Times*, 4 June 1989, sec. 1, p. 10).

The effects of these macroeconomic developments on real income per person, particularly when broken down by racial group, were becoming quite marked by as early as 1986. From 1980 to 1984, real personal disposable income per capita fell 10 percent for whites, but it rose by more than 12 percent for Coloreds and Africans and by more than 15 percent for Asians; between 1984 and 1986, it fell a further 6 percent for whites but fell by more than 10 per cent for the other groups, leaving them much where they were in 1980 (Volkskas Bank 1987:4). Although one should not read too much into such necessarily rough estimates or put too much reliance on crude economic determinism, a substantial increase in real incomes over four years followed by a return to previous levels in just two years, apparently experienced by Africans, Asians, and Coloreds alike, is surely a recipe for considerable discontent. Furthermore, the continuing fall in real per capita disposable incomes for whites is perhaps not unconnected with changing political attitudes among them, as exemplified by the electoral gains of the extreme right-wing Conservative party in the May 1987 parliamentary elections and the October 1988 local elections.

South Africa's macroeconomic difficulties can be said to have three major causes:

1. Structural: South Africa has developed an economy heavily dependent on gold, diamond, and other mineral exports but with a large manufacturing sector that is highly intensive in its use of both imported capital goods and imported intermediate goods. This situation is due at least in part to government policy and black labor unrest that have produced effective costs to the private sector that are artificially high for labor and low for capital. Relative skill scarcities that have reinforced the unequal racial income distribution also contribute to this situation and have their origins in

race-biased education and training provisions. The extreme disparities in income and wealth are also connected with consumption patterns on the part of the high-income groups, largely white, that imply a high propensity to import, further exacerbating the economy's foreign exchange difficulties.

2. The strong inflationary pressures in the economy, due in part to the large security expenditures of the government, the large bureaucracy required to enforce government policy, the large state-owned sector, and the inefficiencies induced by race- and security-based restrictions on freedom of movement, occupation, employment, residence, and establishment of economic activities.

3. To some extent, the imposition of sanctions on trade with and investment in South Africa by other countries, the movement by some foreign investors to divest, the loss of production caused by strikes, labor unrest, and "stayaways" that are connected to the political situation, and losses of skills and capital resulting from loss of confidence and the emigration of skilled workers.

A major irony of the current and prospective economic situation is the probable racial incidence of the costs of these difficulties. There has to be considerable uncertainty about this, as it is difficult to be certain of the appropriate hypothetical alternative with which to make comparisons. It seems at least plausible, however, that contrary to the arguments of many opponents of actions against South Africa, much of the cost is likely to be borne by whites rather than blacks (and this is consistent with the data on real personal disposable income per capita by race cited above). Some of the reasoning behind this assertion is simple, other of it more subtle. At a simple level, it is clear that in the medium term if the South African government is to maintain its policies and its intransigence, it will have to extract more real resources from the economy by either taxation or inflation. But the ability of government to extract additional resources from blacks is limited, given the small cushion above subsistence at which most of them already live, the evident militancy of wage employees in recent years, and the stated objectives of the government's limited "reform" policies to reduce race-based inequities. Further, as van der Berg (1989:198–200) persuasively argues, the sheer arithmetic of the current inequalities of provision imply that if government is to move toward parity in social expenditures for the different racial groups, not only are rapid increases in spending on blacks required, but also dramatic decreases in spending on whites—which politically may be extraordinarily difficult, if feasible at all.

More subtly, if the government is to avoid stagnation, it will need to shift the structure of the economy so that it is less capital-intensive and less import-intensive. Currently, the white labor force is effectively fully employed, and it is whites who have the more import-intensive consumption patterns. The implication is that a shift in the direction required to permit faster growth would, relatively speaking, bring benefits to blacks, not whites, except with respect to capital income. The net effect is uncertain, but it is at least plausible that the overall effect of the current macroeconomic difficulties in South Africa may be, in relative terms, to shift the distribution of income in favor of blacks.

Interactions with SADCC

There are three components of South Africa's interactions with SADCC. The first pertains to the negative effects on SADCC states of South African destabilization policies. The second has to do with the effects on SADCC states of economic developments within South Africa. Finally there is the question of prospects for the future.

Destabilization

One of the greatest negative effects of South African destabilization policies is their impact in the area of transport and trade. South African support of UNITA and RENAMO has had the effect of forcing the great bulk of the overseas trade of the inland SADCC states over South African rail routes and through South African ports. This raises transport costs for the states concerned, while increasing their dependency on South Africa. It has also indirectly almost certainly increased the volume of direct trade between South Africa and the inland SADCC states, other than the members of SACU, by increasing the comparative advantage of South African suppliers relative to overseas sources. It also has had the incidental effect of increasing service imports by SADCC states from South Africa. It is difficult to estimate accurately the economic cost of these transport diversions, but it is almost certainly in the hundreds of millions of dollars per year. Involved are direct increases in transport costs, higher interest charges on larger volumes of goods in the longer transit pipeline, and insurance, clearing, and forwarding charges. The gains to South Africa are less than the costs to SADCC states, and the diversions cause the region a net loss. Restoring the transport routes that are independent of South Africa would lower import costs for SADCC, give them greater choice of suppliers, and increase their economic independence from South Africa.

In economic terms, the nontransport costs of South African destabilization are greater but more concentrated. The key elements are the direct costs of violence and sabotage, especially in Mozambique and Angola, and the indirect costs of diversion of government resources to security forces and combat with insurgents and South African–supported forces. Among the SADCC states, probably only Tanzania could wholly escape these costs, although it in fact does have troops stationed in Mozambique. The size of these costs, both absolutely and relative to the national economy, varies widely. Even in states such as Botswana, Lesotho, Swaziland, and Zambia, however, it is clear that both threats and actions by South Africa have resulted in police and military expenditures greater than would otherwise be needed, in a period when there are urgent alternative uses for government funds. Putting a dollar value on these costs is difficult, if not impossible, because of the problem of specifying the appropriate hypothetical alternatives with respect to, for example, security expenditures. Even less tangible and amenable to quantification are the costs attributable to the diversion of effort and attention of government and its policymakers from development efforts to dealing with South Africa, as well as the lost investment that must be occurring because of the insecurity, instability, and uncertainty about the future caused by South African destabilization, which must affect both foreign and local investors. A 1985 SADCC estimate of the direct costs of destabilization suggested $2 billion a year, larger than annual disbursements of foreign aid in the region and close to 10 percent of SADCC GDP (Lewis 1987). Another estimate (Hoskins 1987:20) of the inclusive costs to the Southern African region from South Africa's campaign of aggression and destabilization comes from a memorandum at the July 1986 meeting of the Organization of African Unity (OAU) in Addis Ababa. For the period 1980–85, the figure came to approximately $48.5 billion in these categories:

	(in $ billions)
direct war damage	7.7
extra defense expenditure	14.7
higher transport and energy costs	4.7
lost exports and tourism	1.1
smuggling	0.9
refugees	3.2
reduced production	3.8
lost economic growth	9.6
boycotts and embargoes	1.2
trading arrangements	1.6
Total	$48.5

South African belligerence continued to increase during the later 1980s, so these estimates represent a reasonable order of magnitude to assume for more recent years. It is also worth noting that this cost is very likely substantially larger than any conceivable level of sustained costs to SADCC countries from the imposition of comprehensive sanctions against South Africa by the rest of the world. This makes SADCC support for sanctions entirely rational economically, despite allegations to the contrary from some observers and political leaders in countries such as the United States and Britain.

Effects on SADCC of Economic Developments in South Africa

The imposition of sanctions against South Africa by countries outside SADCC can have both positive and negative spillover effects on the SADCC states. Partial sanctions, or sanctions by only some countries, have already had some documented negative effects. For example, South Africa's loss of North American markets for canned pineapple resulted in South African canners diverting their output to Europe, undercutting Swazi prices, and taking over traditional Swazi markets (Central Bank of Swaziland 1987). On the other hand, there can also be positive effects: both Lesotho and Swaziland have benefited from investment by firms seeking to evade restrictions on imports from South Africa while continuing to operate within SACU (Booth 1990; Cobbe 1990). Similarly, Botswana and Swaziland have gained from investment by U.S. firms, such as Colgate-Palmolive and Coca-Cola, seeking to "divest" from South Africa while maintaining access to its market from within SACU (Booth 1990; Parson 1990). Overall, at this point there is insufficient information to estimate with any confidence precisely what the net impact of either existing sanctions or possible future sanctions packages may be on the various SADCC states. It is clear, however, that a large net negative impact is unlikely except as a result of explicit South African retaliation or punishment, and such behavior by South Africa is likely to be short-lived for reasons of South Africa's own economic advantage; nevertheless it could be devastating in the short run even if unlikely to be sustained for the long run.

An interesting aspect of the recent period is the widespread misconceptions about the effects on SADCC states of South Africa's recent economic difficulties. As first cogently pointed out by Stephen Lewis (1987), the way things have worked out is that most of the SADCC states (Lesotho and those without trading relations with South Africa being the exceptions) have actually benefited from South Africa's problems. The reasoning is quite simple: South Africa runs a large trade surplus with SADCC, from which it benefits. The surplus is there, however, because SADCC states import more from South Africa than they sell there, since the bulk of SADCC exports go overseas. South Africa's balance of payments is supported by this surplus because South Africa earns foreign exchange. But in the recent period (from 1980 through early 1987) when the external value of the South African rand was declining faster than South African export prices in rands were rising, SADCC states were benefiting by obtaining their imports from South Africa at a lower dollar cost (or cost in terms of units of exports) than before. Lewis calculated that between 1980 and 1985, the dollar price of South African goods fell by almost one-third, and at least six of the nine SADCC states must have gained from these lower prices. Of course, when the dollar value of the rand had roughly stabilized in 1987 and 1988, and given that South African inflation continued apace, this terms-of-trade effect operated in the reverse direction.

Prospects for the Future

Rather than attempting to predict the future in economic terms, it seems more appropriate to make some observations about effects on SADCC of various possibilities. First, there is the issue of further sanctions against South Africa of various types and severity and the possibility of South Africa trying to pass on, or divert, their costs to SADCC. Basically, this would be economically irrational from the perspective of South Africa, except as a short-term strategy to achieve specific aims. Currently, South Africa gains from its trade, migrant labor, service, and transport relations with SADCC, and therefore actions to reduce such links would hurt South Africa economically. This, of course, does not mean that the South African government would not take such actions; the historical record is replete with economically irrational actions by the South African government in pursuit of its political aims, and short-term interruptions may have low costs for South Africa. It does reduce the probability of such actions, however, and particularly of such actions over extended periods of time. It is interesting to note that the majority of South African economic actions against SADCC states in recent years have been carefully structured to reduce costs to South African parties while increasing them for the SADCC victim, and they have usually been temporary in nature: once the point of economic power has been demonstrated and (usually) the particular current objective secured, the action has been withdrawn (Lewis 1987).

One special case that deserves some mention is that of Lesotho. Lesotho is overwhelmingly dependent on the export of migrant labor to South Africa and on the importation of goods and services from and through South Africa. There is no short- to medium-term alternative for Lesotho, although early next century the balance of dependence may shift somewhat toward reliance on export of water rather than labor. As I have argued at length elsewhere (Cobbe 1986, 1988), although this suggests Lesotho has no choice but to be totally compliant with South African wishes, the reality is not quite that extreme. The Chamber of Mines has, and will continue to have, very good reasons to want to continue to use a substantial cohort of Lesotho miners for the foreseeable future, although the continued prominent participation by Basotho miners in union activity could change that (see Crush 1989 for further discussion). Chaos in Lesotho would not be advantageous to Pretoria under any scenario that is at all likely. Hence, if we credit the South African government with a minimal amount of rationality, it is clear that Lesotho does have some freedom of action if its government is brave enough to risk the inevitable brinkmanship involved. The Lekhanya regime that replaced Leabua Jonathan's government in January 1986 is turning out to be highly pragmatic in its economic dealings with South Africa and has thereby secured substantial economic advantage. Although the new regime is also more politically compliant than Jonathan's regime was, it is not reliably Pretoria's puppet (Cobbe 1988).

For the rest of the region, the key issues remain transport and destabilization. Restoration of the independent rail links to the sea would lower trade costs, increase options, and reduce dependence on South Africa. It would also lower South Africa's leverage over the region and reduce the substantial economic benefits South Africa derives from the current situation. There is thus every reason to suppose that South Africa will do all it can, including by military means, to prevent the rehabilitation of the rail lines and ports in question, as it has for the past dozen years. All the more reason why the outside donors should increase their efforts to restore these transport links and why there is a case for outside participation in the maintenance of security along these railways. All these issues intersect in the current efforts to restore to fully operational status the highway, railway, and pipeline of the Beira corridor linking Zimbabwe to the Indian Ocean along with the port and storage facilities of Beira itself. The undertaking involves more than $450 million in pledged aid from Western donors, technical assistance and personnel from the United States, the Netherlands, Sweden, Italy, and Canada, and the military presence of 3,500 Zimbabwean troops. The results are already being felt as Beira now handles about 20 percent of Zimbabwe's exports. At the same time, RENAMO forces (most probably with continued South African backing despite denials to the contrary) continue to attempt to disrupt the flow of traffic and goods through constant attacks, making travel uncertain during the day and virtually impossible at night (*New York Times*, 21 February 1989).

Destabilization is enormously costly to the victims in other direct and indirect terms as well; it must, for example, have a marked negative effect on levels of private investment throughout the region. The prospects here would seem to be dependent on political developments in South Africa rather than economic ones, however, and there is little cause for optimism.

One particularly interesting set of issues concerns the probable consequences of what might be termed "maximalist" actions by South Africa. For example, it is suggested above that South Africa may well be willing to use military means if need be to maintain SADCC reliance on its own transport system. Suppose this were to include South African bombing of the port of Beira and the rail line in the Beira corridor once the rehabilitation work has been completed and the foreign technicians have left: what would the consequences be, and in particular, what would be the response of international actors from outside the region? The European Community and its member states, and more recently if less certainly also the United States, appear to have a genuine and long-term interest in relations and economic interaction with SADCC, and several European countries are currently providing Mozambique with military assistance. Would the West acquiesce in South African military bullying of SADCC to that extent, or would an action such as that result in the West finally having to make a choice between Pretoria and SADCC, rather than trying to keep in with both sides as at present? And if so, on which side would the West come down?

By mid-1990, with the released Nelson Mandela on a triumphal tour of North America, the African National Congress (ANC) again legal within South Africa, and substantive negotiations anticipated between it and F. W. de Klerk's reformist government, such speculations might seem unduly pessimistic. But just as it has been a mistake throughout this century to assume nothing will ever change in South Africa, so it would now be a mistake to assume that a satisfactory and peaceful solution to South Africa's internal problems is just around the corner. The ANC's position is clear: sanctions should be retained until real progress has clearly been made, and this position appears to be accepted by both the U.S. administration and the majority of European states (the major exception was Margaret Thatcher's government). It is, of course, entirely possible that there will be a rapid and peaceful movement to a constitutional settlement in South Africa that will result in wholly normal relations between the new South Africa and the rest of the world. If that happens, the biggest problems for SADCC will probably be that South Africa will be very concerned with its own economic problems, may be less hospitable to migrants (who will likely be perceived as taking jobs away from South African blacks), and may be so attractive to foreign investors that investment is diverted to it from other SADCC states.

On the other hand, it is also entirely possible that conditions within South Africa may again deteriorate, because of a breakdown in negotiations between de Klerk and the ANC, or because the ANC fails to deliver sufficiently wide black acceptance of what it is able to negotiate, or because de Klerk reverses himself, or—perhaps the most likely, if the most unpredictable in terms of its detailed consequences—because de Klerk's government falls and is replaced by one intent on restoring and preserving white supremacy. In any of these circumstances, South Africa's relations with SADCC could again become hotly antagonistic, and the issues discussed in this chapter would remain salient.

In the meantime, South Africa's economic instability continues to raise other economic problems for SADCC states. If South Africa succeeds in continuing to divert the bulk of SADCC trade through its borders, South African inflation, exchange rate policies, and trade regime policies will continue to pose difficult macroeconomic management problems for its SADCC trading partners (Lewis 1987). For example, rapid changes in the external value of the rand, which have occurred in the past and are quite likely to occur again, pose awkward exchange rate choices for countries such as Botswana and Zimbabwe in particular. Overall, it is unhappily clear that the great economic potential of the SADCC region is unlikely to be realized until the South African situation has been resolved. Perhaps the only positive note one can grasp for in conclusion is that finally "sound opinion" in the West (as represented by the *Economist*, 30 January 1988) is beginning to recognize this fact, and to see that neither the other countries of the region nor the West need have much to fear from sanctions or an ANC-ruled South Africa—and might have much to gain.

REFERENCES

Booth, Alan. 1990. "South African Sanctions-Breaking in Southern Africa: The Case of Swaziland." In *Sanctioning Apartheid*, ed. Robert E. Edgar, 323–38. Trenton, NJ: Africa World Press.

Central Bank of Swaziland. 1987. *Annual Report for 1986*. Mbabane: Central Bank of Swaziland.

Cobbe, James. 1986. "Consequences for Lesotho of Changing South African Labour Demand." *African Affairs* 85(338): 23–48.

———. 1988. "Economic Aspects of Lesotho's Relations with South Africa." *Journal of Modern African Studies* 26(1): 71–89.

———. 1990. "Sanctions Against South Africa: Lesotho's Role." In *Sanctioning Apartheid*, ed. Robert E. Edgar, 339–56. Trenton, NJ: Africa World Press.

Crush, Jonathan. 1989. "Migrancy and Militance: The Case of the National Union of Mineworkers of South Africa." *African Affairs* 88(350):5–23.

Economist. 1988. "A Sanctions Puzzler." 30 January, 30.

Economist Intelligence Unit, 1987. *Country Report: South Africa.* No. 3. London: Economist Intelligence Unit.

Hoskins, Linus A. 1987. "Dependency and Destabilization: South Africa's Sub-Imperialist Tools." *Africa and the World* 1, no. 1 (October):17–20.

International Bank for Reconstruction and Development. 1984. *Toward Sustained Development in Sub-Saharan Africa: A Joint Program of Action.* Washington, D.C.: International Bank for Reconstruction and Development.

———. 1986. *World Development Report, 1986.* New York: Oxford University Press.

———. 1987. *World Development Report, 1987.* New York: Oxford University Press.

———. 1988. *World Development Report, 1988.* New York: Oxford University Press.

Lewis, Stephen R. 1987. *Economic Realities in Southern Africa (or, One Hundred Million Futures).* Discussion Paper no. 232. Brighton, U.K.: Institute of Development Studies. June.

Murray, Colin. 1988. "Displaced Urbanisation." In *South Africa in Question*, ed. John Lonsdale. Portsmouth, NH: Heinemann.

Parson, Jack. 1990. "The Potential for South African Sanctions Busting in Southern Africa: The Case of Botswana." In *Sanctioning Apartheid*, ed. Robert J. Edgar, 293–321. Trenton, NJ: Africa World Press.

Relly, Gavin. 1986. "Chairman's Address, Anglo American Corporation of South Africa." Johannesburg: Anglo American Corporation.

South African Institute of Race Relations. 1987. *Race Relations Survey, 1986, Part 1.* Johannesburg: South African Institute of Race Relations.

———. 1988. *Race Relations Survey, 1987–88.* Johannesburg: South African Institute of Race Relations.

Standard Bank Investment Corporation Limited. 1990. *Standard Bank Economic Review.* Johannesburg: Standard Bank Investment Corp. May.

Van der Berg, Servaas. 1989. "Long Term Economic Trends and Development Prospects in South Africa." *African Affairs* 88, no. 351 (April):187–203.

Volkskas Bank. 1987. *Economic Spotlight.* December. Johannesburg: Volkskas Bank.

———. 1989. *Economic Spotlight.* May. Johannesburg: Volkskas Bank.

9

Conflict in Southern Africa: The Case of Mozambique

ALLEN F. ISAACMAN

The Fifth Party Congress, held in July 1989 by Mozambique's ruling party FRELIMO (Front for the Liberation of Mozambique), marked a major turning point in Mozambique's political history. National consensus and unity replaced class struggle and Marxism-Leninism as the dominant political idioms. The country's socialist project came to an abrupt halt. FRELIMO, which had previously described itself as a vanguard party of the worker-peasant alliance, became a "vanguard party of all the people." The celebration of ethnic and cultural diversity was highlighted by the addition of three new members to the party's Political Bureau from underrepresented regions of the country. Businessmen previously excluded from membership were permitted to join the party, and Christian and Muslim religious leaders received enthusiastic applause after addressing the congress. Finally, the FRELIMO Central Committee report, presented at the congress, staunchly defended the controversial Economic Recovery Program (ERP, or PRE in Portuguese) negotiated by the International Monetary Fund and the World Bank.

The theme that dominated the congress and underscored FRELIMO's renewed nationalist agenda, however, was the need for unity and peace in the face of the decade-long war with the South African–backed Mozambique National Resistance (MNR), known more commonly as RENAMO. This war, part of Pretoria's broader campaign of regional destabilization, has devastated the Mozambican countryside. More than 100,000 Mozambicans have lost their lives; 2.5 million peasants have been left homeless. The nation's economy has been paralyzed and the rural health and educational infrastructure destroyed. In his opening address President Joaquim Chissano emphasized that the survival of the Mozambican nation depended on "the active involvement of all classes and strata in society." Above all else, he stressed the need for peace and outlined the diplomatic offensive his government has initiated to end the cycle of death and destruction.

Even as Chissano spoke, a delegation of Mozambican religious leaders, with his approval, was preparing to leave for Nairobi to continue exploratory negotiations with RENAMO leaders.

The decisions made at the Fifth Party Congress and the economic and military crises that they are intended to alleviate need to be placed within a broader historical and regional perspective. At the root of the young nation's problems are an inherited colonial economy excessively dependent on South Africa, a set of misguided or poorly implemented state and party policies, and, above all else, Pretoria's aggressive economic, military, and political offensive designed to maintain South Africa's regional hegemony.

Portuguese Colonialism and South African Economic Hegemony, ca. 1900–1975

Although Lisbon imposed its political domination on Mozambique shortly after the turn of the century, it was South African capital that quickly came to dominate the colony's economy. From the outset the most salient feature of Portuguese colonialism was the absence of development capital. This lack of financial resources provided South African and British investors with a strategic entry point from which their capital would come to exert predominant influence in the Mozambican economy.

Without substantial investments, Portuguese interests in both the metropole and Mozambique could only hope to extract a portion of the colony's resources by transforming the rural area into a labor reserve. This transformation would, through state intervention, generate a large bound and ultracheap labor force. An 1899 government commission (quoted in Cunha 1949:144), whose task was to analyze the prospects for development in Mozambique, concluded: "We need native labor, we need it in order to better the conditions of these laborers, we need it for the economy of Europe, and for the progress of Africa. Our tropical Africa will not grow without the Africans. The capital needed to exploit it, and it so needs to be exploited, lies in the procurement of labor for exploitation. Abundant, cheap, solid labor . . . and this labor, given the circumstances, will never be supplied by European immigrants." Colonial officials anticipated that by forcing male members of the rural population to pay a tax in European currency and by imposing artificially low prices that strangled peasant initiatives, Africans would be compelled to seek employment on Portuguese and foreign-controlled plantations, in the embryonic light-industry sector, and in the port towns of Lourenço Marques (now

Maputo) and Beira. While the tax laws did provide the state with a new source of revenue, they failed at first to generate a sufficient cheap labor force, requiring the colonial state to resort to undisguised coercion known as *chibalo*. But just as the lack of Portuguese capital provided an opening for South African investors, so the forced-labor policy, designed to remedy this situation, drove thousands of Mozambican migrant laborers to the relatively better-paying South African gold mines. The result was to reinforce Mozambique's dependence on its southern neighbor.

As early as 1897, Lisbon sought to maximize short-term potential revenue by "renting" labor to the expanding South African mining industry. Under interstate agreements specific portions of the workers' salaries were paid directly to the Portuguese government in gold at a fixed rate of exchange well below the market price. Between 1912 and Mozambican independence in 1975, the number of Mozambican mineworkers in South Africa ranged from 73,000 to 118,000, providing the major source of colonial income.[1] Moreover, the country's southern provinces had been transformed into a South African labor reserve in which the wages earned in South Africa played a critical role in the cycle of reproduction for rural households. Returning migrant laborers brought with them not only food and clothing but plows and other agricultural implements as well.

The labor treaties also laid the foundation for another form of dependence on South Africa. In return for the right to cheap labor, South Africa agreed to divert a substantial portion of traffic to and from the Transvaal through the Mozambican port of Lourenço Marques. Lisbon's capitulation in 1928 to South African demands that the congested port be managed more efficiently and that Mozambique continue to export a prescribed number of mineworkers suggests the extent to which the country had already become an economic satellite of its southern neighbor.

At the same time that the 1928 agreement was signed, an obscure professor of economics, António Salazar, became Portugal's finance minister and shortly thereafter prime minister, heralding forty years of fascist rule. Salazar's colonial policy rested on two interdependent propositions that theoretically placed him in direct opposition to South Africa. Fiercely nationalist, he insisted that the colonies had to remain under the firm grip of Lisbon. Second, the human and natural resources of Mozambique had to be more effectively and directly exploited for the benefit of the metropole and the nascent Portuguese capitalist class rather than for the benefit of foreign investors, including the South Africans. To achieve this goal he promoted a neo-mercantilist policy in which state intervention figured prominently at all levels of the economy. At the same time he continued the prior practice of denying any educational or economic opportunities to Mozambicans.[2]

Yet despite Salazar's rhetoric of economic nationalism and his neo-mercantile policies, which had the effect of further distorting the Mozambican economy by blocking virtually all industrial development in the colony, his regime failed to extract Mozambique from South Africa's economic hegemony. To the contrary, as the colony's balance-of-trade problems expanded (see Table 9.1), Mozambique's dependency on "invisible income" from South Africa—generated by wage remittances from the miners and port and transit fees—increased proportionately.[3] And despite continued complaints from representatives of settler agriculture about the lack of cheap African labor, the Salazar regime permitted an increasing number of Mozambicans to work in South Africa's mines.

Table 9.1.   Balance of Trade, 1960–73 (in thousand contos)

YEAR	IMPORTS	EXPORTS	BALANCE	BALANCE BETWEEN IMPORTS AND EXPORTS
1950	1,753	1,221	- 522	0.70
1960	3,646	2,099	- 1,547	0.58
1961	3,720	2,548	- 1,172	0.69
1962	3,908	2,616	- 1,292	0.67
1963	4,075	2,896	- 1,079	0.71
1964	4,488	3,042	- 1,446	0.68
1965	4,984	3,106	- 1,878	0.62
1966	5,967	3,223	- 2,753	0.54
1967	5,725	3,500	- 2,225	0.61
1968	6,735	4,450	- 2,276	0.66
1969	7,491	4,081	- 3,410	0.54
1970	9,363	4,497	- 4,866	0.48
1972	8,912	4,768	- 4,144	0.54
1973	11,425	5,541	- 5,874	0.49

Source: Estatística do Comercio Externo: Mozambique, Economic Survey (Lourenço Marques, 1975).

The formation of Mozambique's liberation movement FRELIMO in 1962 and its initiation of armed struggle two years later increased the South African presence in Mozambique. In order to finance its military operations against FRELIMO and against liberation movements in Angola and Guinea-Bissau, the Salazar regime was forced to reverse its protectionist policies and seek foreign investments in its colonies. Beginning in 1965, generous tax holidays and liberal terms for repatriation of the profits were offered. A UN study completed in 1973 found that these incentives enabled foreign investors to enjoy some of the highest profits in the world. Given such favorable conditions,

Mozambique became increasingly attractive to South African and other Western investors. By 1973, South Africa had replaced Portugal as the principal supplier of imported goods and had become an important investor in several major development projects, including Cahora Bassa Dam, the largest in Africa.

Expanding economic ties and a shared racist ideology motivated Pretoria to provide military assistance as the threat from FRELIMO increased. Although South African assistance was never as great as that provided by Rhodesia, there is evidence of overt security ties between South Africa and Portugal (Martin and Johnson 1982; Henriksen 1983:179). Whatever the degree of direct South African military involvement, it was certainly increasing in April 1974, when the Armed Forces Movement launched its successful coup in Portugal, thus ending forty years of fascism and raising the possibility of Mozambican independence.

In the aftermath of the coup, policymakers in Pretoria, who had been forewarned by their own intelligence services of the deteriorating war situation in Mozambique and the growing antiwar sentiment in Portugal, had to confront the difficult decision of whether or not to intervene militarily. The Lusaka Agreement in September 1974, in which the new Portuguese government reluctantly acceded to FRELIMO's demand for independence after a nine-month transitional phase (ending in June 1975), precluded a neocolonial solution that would have allowed Pretoria to exercise maximum leverage without intervening (Leonard 1983:13–14; *Observer*, 4 August 1974). With this option denied to it, Pretoria faced a difficult decision. Powerful forces within both the military and the right wing of the National party called for intervention. The chief of the defense forces, Admiral Hugo Bierman, voiced concern about the threat that FRELIMO posed (*Times*, 12 July 1974): "There certainly has never been a precedent to the current vast number of events with its potential impact, individually and collectively, on our national security." Moreover, the South African government provided sanctuary and support for ex-Portuguese secret police officials and former settlers who had fled Mozambique and organized FICO ("I Stay"), a right-wing movement to prevent FRELIMO from coming to power (*Observer*, 4 August 1974). On 7 September 1974, FICO supporters seized the radio station in Lourenço Marques and urged all Portuguese to rise up while appealing for direct South African intervention. Although Pretoria is reported to have mobilized some troops on the Mozambican border, no military assistance was forthcoming and a joint FRELIMO-Portuguese force, to the dismay and disbelief of the insurgents, crushed the coup (*Star Weekly*, 19 September 1974; *Observer*, 15 September 1974).

The South African government under Prime Minister John Vorster had resisted the immediate temptation of direct intervention when it became clear that there was no real "moderate alternative" who could guarantee political stability on its northern border. Vorster acknowledged this sober reality (*Financial Times*, 30 May 1974): "All that we are really interested in is good rule. It is not in our interest that there should be chaos in any neighboring country. We want stability. It is not for us to prescribe what sort of rule."

Short of direct intervention, however, Pretoria could still exercise enormous economic and military leverage in order to perpetuate its own regional domination and to narrow FRELIMO's more radical options. Vorster (*Guardian*, 30 April 1974) warned FRELIMO leaders that despite Mozambique's economic potential, "it cannot stand on its own legs without the cooperation of South Africa." And he was right. By the end of the first half of 1974, Mozambique's faltering economy derived half of all its hard currency from economic relations with South Africa. Moreover, Vorster did not preclude future military intervention (*Star Weekly*, 5 October 1974): "We have no plans to invade Mozambique as is being alleged in some quarters. All South Africa will ever do is to defend itself with its full striking power if it is ever attacked. This is South Africa's right and no country and no organization can deprive us of it."

FRELIMO's leaders, despite an increasingly revolutionary ethos, were not in a position during the transition to independence to confront South Africa or even to begin to extract Mozambique from the historic web of dependency. Although President Samora Machel tried to negotiate substantial aid agreements with the USSR, China, and the United Nations to achieve greater economic autonomy, nothing significant ever materialized from these initiatives (*Observer*, 18 August 1974). Before independence FRELIMO had to devote almost all of its energy to the immediate problems of consolidating its power over the southern half of the country—where its presence had been minimal—and establishing the structures of government, and therefore relations with Pretoria assumed secondary importance.

Independent Mozambique: The Deteriorating Economic and Military Situation, 1975–1982

With independence and state power, FRELIMO was theoretically positioned to set policies in motion that, over time, might transform Mozambique's distorted economy, address pressing social problems, and reshape its relations with South Africa. Even before such policies could be considered, however, forces beyond the government's control foreclosed such options. A combination of natural calamities that destroyed much of the nation's agricultural output, extensive sabotage of factories, trucks, and farm equipment by Portuguese settlers, and a massive exodus of technicians and professionals left Mozambique's fragile economy in disarray. With more than 90 percent of the citizenry illiterate, the new government lacked the expertise to manage the economy. There was, for example, only a handful of economists and not a single agronomist in the entire country.

Despite these problems, during the first five years of independence the new government did implement a number of policies that improved the quality of life for most Mozambicans and held out hope for the future. Between 1975 and 1982, the number of children in school doubled from 672,000 to 1,330,000 and illiteracy was reduced by 20 percent. The government introduced free national health care, infant mortality in the urban areas was cut in half, and more than 95 percent of the population was vaccinated against smallpox. Despite extensive sabotage of factories, trucks, and farm equipment by fleeing Portuguese settlers, the massive exodus of European technicians and professionals, and repeated attacks by the Rhodesian army, the economy stabilized and even showed modest growth (Comité Central de Partido FRELIMO 1989:11–12). These gains notwithstanding, the problems facing the new government were overwhelming. The pressure to take immediate action to reverse the long history of national impoverishment combined with inexperience, lack of expertise, and revolutionary zeal prompted a number of poorly conceived and improperly implemented political, economic, and military programs.

In the political sphere FRELIMO's decision at the Third Party Congress in 1977 to become a Marxist-Leninist vanguard party stifled popular participation. As a national front open to all but dominated by a radical core, FRELIMO successfully waged a war of liberation that empowered millions of Mozambicans who opposed colonialism and exploitation. By abandoning this historical stance, the party effectively removed the masses from political life. As one leading ideologue (who requested anonymity) noted, with "96 percent of the population composed of illiterate peasants such a policy was not only premature but excessively romantic." By the early 1980s, only about 100,000 Mozambicans had been selected for party membership. Moreover, after the first flush of political mobilizing, party cells increasingly became bureaucratized and, in some parts of the country, isolated from the grass roots. Repeating guidelines and slogans often took the place of debate and self-criticism. At the Fifth Party Congress, President Chissano (Comité Central de Partido FRELIMO 1989) acknowledged the shortcomings of trying to impose an orthodoxy from abroad: "Experiences of other countries, while they constitute extremely valuable reference points, cannot, however, be copied and mechanically transposed." He called on party delegates to reject sectarianism and mechanistic thinking and to forge a new political culture in which there will be "space for greater popular participation."

FRELIMO's initial economic policies suffered from many of these same problems as the party sought to take command of the distorted, dependent, and deteriorating economy it had inherited.[4] The new government faced the dilemma of trying to keep existing structures functioning in order to sustain a viable level of life while simultaneously restructuring critical sectors to achieve its socialist agenda.

Because 90 percent of Mozambicans were peasants who, with rudimentary tools, cultivated less than five acres each, agricultural transformation rather than industrial development was at the core of FRELIMO's long-range economic program. "The socialization of the countryside," to use FRELIMO's lexicon, rested on the creation of a network of Eastern European–style state farms and the organization of communal villages with agricultural cooperatives serving as their economic base. Although there was some debate, which carried important ideological and developmental implications, about which of the two should receive higher priority, proponents of state farms prevailed. At the Third Party Congress in 1977, they argued for grouping together the most accessible of the abandoned settler farms and modernizing production under the direction of the state. This offered the quickest way to resolve the country's historic food shortages, and to ensure that between 150,000 to 200,000 rural workers who had been left idle when the settlers fled would again be employed in productive labor. By 1982, the state had invested more than 50 million pounds sterling in agricultural machinery, including 3,000 tractors and 300 combine harvesters, and had incorporated 35,000 acres of choice land into the system (Moçambique 1982; Hanlon 1984:100–101).

For all the fanfare and elaborate projections, the experiment was a dismal failure. Although receiving the lion's share of the agricultural budget, state farms by 1982 accounted for only 20 percent of the total output. The minister of agriculture was forced to admit that not one state farm was profitable. Poor planning, a tendency to rely on seasonal labor, lack of management skills, a dearth of technical experts to organize production on these large complexes, inappropriate and expensive foreign equipment, and an unwillingness or inability to mobilize rural workers all contributed to the failure. Moreover, in the fertile Limpopo Valley, home of the largest state farm complex, and in other regions as well, peasants were not prepared to be agricultural laborers disconnected from their own land for low wages (Bowen 1989).

Underfunded communal villages did not fare much better, particularly in war zones. Although FRELIMO was able to forge a network of almost 1,400 communal villages in which 1.8 million Mozambicans resided by 1982, less than 25 percent of the communal villages had agricultural cooperatives. And even on these, interest in collective plots declined precipitously. The problem was simple. There was no incentive to engage in collective labor and, despite promises of aid, technical input and training from the state were minimal. Forced villagization, which occurred in some regions, and other arbritrary and capricious administrative measures further dampened peasant interest (Geffray and Pedersen 1985; Hermele 1988: 46–49). Frustrated participants also found that they could earn far more by cultivating cash crops in their own gardens. Although there were a few notable successes, production on collective fields declined by almost 50 percent between 1979 and 1981. By 1982 cooperatives provided less than 1 percent of production. Thus, five years after the "socialization of the countryside," the family sector still provided over 75 percent of the total agricultural output (Moçambique GODCA 1980; Hanlon 1984:103–13).

Inspired by both ideological considerations and the sudden exodus of rural merchants and urban industrialists, the state also intervened to take control of the marketing and manufacturing sectors. This strategy, however necessary to prevent paralysis, also proved ineffectual. FRELIMO attempted to replace the network of abandoned rural stores with state-run "People's Shops," but the provision of consumer goods to stock these shops received lower priority than importing capital goods. This decision, as well as the acute shortage of trucks, meant that shelves were often bare and that there was little incentive for peasants in the family sector or working on agricultural collectives to increase production in order to sell their commodities to the state. The industrial sector, 85 percent of which had been nationalized by 1982, experienced similar difficulties. In that year, it was operating at only 40 percent of capacity.

Mozambique's deteriorating economy left it increasingly vulnerable to economic sanctions from South Africa. The simplest way for Pretoria to squeeze the FRELIMO government was to reduce the number of Mozambicans working in South African mines. Between 1975 and 1982, Mozambique lost $3.2 billion because South Africa slashed the number of Mozambican mineworkers from 120,000 to 45,000 and discontinued its long-standing practice of remitting their wages to the Mozambican government in gold at a preferential rate. At the same time, South Africa reduced the level of commerce moving through the port of Maputo from approximately 600 million to 100 million tons, which cost the young nation $250 million in transit fees (Azevedo 1980:571; Murray 1981:30; Moçambique Ministério, 1980:3–4).

At the Fourth Party Congress held in 1983, FRELIMO announced several steps aimed at reversing the economic crises. Whereas the prior congress was primarily concerned with establishing state control over strategic sectors of the economy, new policies were introduced to reverse this trend by decentralizing power and resources. In a characteristically self-critical assessment, FRELIMO's leaders acknowledged that heavy-handed statism was stifling local peasant initiatives and grass-roots impulses. Instead of continuing to privilege Eastern European–style state farms, President Machel declared that "the family sector in the countryside warrants immediate priority." The congress endorsed Mozambique's economic opening to the West and emphasized the critical role of the interregional alliance of independent Southern African states, known as SADCC (Southern African Development Coordination Conference), as an instrument to challenge Pretoria's economic hegemony.[5]

The deteriorating military situation, however, made it difficult for FRELIMO to implement these new policies. By 1982, RENAMO was operating in six of the country's ten provinces. It is now clear that FRELIMO's leaders had underestimated the destructive capacity of RENAMO, had failed to develop an effective strategy to contain it, and had misread Pretoria's long-term objectives.

Within six months of Mozambique's independence, South African security forces working with their Rhodesian counterparts had recruited Portuguese settlers and mercenaries, black and white secret police agents, and former African members of the elite special forces of the colonial army Grupos Especiais (GE) to form RENAMO. Several former agents of the Portuguese secret police Policía Internacional E do Defesa do Estado (PIDE), including Orlando Cristina who became the secretary-general of RENAMO, also figured prominently. To this initial group were added ex-FRELIMO guerrillas who had been expelled for corruption or who had left because of unfulfilled personal ambition or political disagreement. Andre Matzangaiza and Afonso Dhlakama, two former FRELIMO soldiers, received senior positions to give RENAMO visible black leadership (Isaacman and Isaacman 1983:176–78).

From 1976, the Rhodesian government provided RENAMO with arms, bases along the Mozambican border, and logistical support. In retaliation for Mozambique's imposition of UN-backed sanctions against Rhodesia, the latter repeatedly sent RENAMO bands into Mozambique to burn villages, plunder agricultural cooperatives, attack railroad lines and road traffic, disrupt commerce, and raid re-education camps from which they also recruited additional members. Between 1976 and 1979, Mozambique suffered more than 350 Rhodesian and RENAMO attacks.

In the face of these attacks and the threat of a full-scale Rhodesian invasion, Mozambique disbanded most guerrilla units and began to organize a conventional army. Military strategists believed that the Soviet-supplied tanks, artillery, and jets, however antiquated, would be a more effective deterrent against a frontal assault by the Rhodesian army. Whatever the merits of the argument, by the time this new policy was implemented Ian Smith's regime had been defeated and the most immediate threat came from RENAMO guerrillas who, left without their Rhodesian patron, did not crumble as FRELIMO had expected.

Instead, the South African military transferred RENAMO head-quarters and bases to the Transvaal, South Africa's northern province adjacent to Mozambique. South African special forces at Phalaborwa reorganized RENAMO's command structure, trained new recruits, and planned major operations within Mozambique. Indeed, RENAMO commander Afonso Dhlakama (quoted in Legum 1983:13) boasted to Portuguese journalists that South African Defense Minister Magnus Malan had made him a colonel and assured him that "your army is now part of the South African Defense Force."

Mozambique was thus unprepared for RENAMO's surprising resurgence in late 1980. FRELIMO, which had been effective as a guerrilla force, found itself transformed into a relatively inexperienced, poorly equipped conventional army unable to contain RENAMO guerrillas who enjoyed the full backing of the South African military.

South African Destabilization: Escalating the Conflict, 1980–1986

Pretoria's decision to take direct control of RENAMO was a critical component of a broader regional policy that came to be known as "total strategy." This policy began to take shape in a 1977 defense ministry white paper. As Angola and Mozambique achieved independence, powerful forces within the South African military and security apparatus had argued that the prevailing *laager* (circled wagon train) mentality was defeatist and inflexible. They were joined by important financial interests concerned about the growing crises facing South African capitalism (Davies and O'Meara 1985:185). "Total strategy" called for an aggressive economic, political, and military offensive to ensure Pretoria's hegemony over the region in order to defend the internal interests of the apartheid state and to isolate the African National Congress (ANC). The white paper emphasized "a solid military balance relative to neighboring states." Harking back to the earlier notion of a "constellation of states" subordinate to Pretoria, the new strategy called for expanded economic and political relations that would link the surrounding countries to South Africa (Davies and O'Meara 1985:191–93). Thus, from the outset apartheid strategists envisioned a combination of coercive techniques and selective incentives to achieve their regional objectives. The defeat of the Smith regime in 1979 and the formation of the SADCC shortly thereafter created a new sense of urgency for the apartheid government.

Almost immediately after becoming prime minister in September 1978, P. W. Botha began to implement the policy of "total strategy." Key elements of the military apparatus were reorganized and the powerful new State Security Council was given the responsibility for overseeing this policy. To enhance South Africa's ability to strike at its neighbors, the state initiated a major arms development program, organized new commando units, and doubled the military budget between 1977 and 1984 (Davies and O'Meara 1985:194). To demonstrate further its resolve, Pretoria escalated its support for insurgents fighting the Frontline governments of Zimbabwe, Lesotho, and Angola, and it also imposed a variety of economic sanctions against its neighbors.

It was Mozambique, however, that was to be the principal terrain of struggle and RENAMO the principal instrument for implementing Pretoria's policy of regional domination. At a meeting between RENAMO leader Dhlakama and Colonel Charles van Niekerk of the South African security forces in 1980, the latter ordered RENAMO to "interdict rail traffic from Malverne-Gwelo [southern Mozambique], establish bases inside Mozambique adjacent to the South African border, open a new military front in Maputo province, and provoke incidents in Maputo and Beira" (R.N.M. 1980).[6] Pretoria's strategy was clear: RENAMO must extend its activity to the strategic central and southern provinces, thereby discouraging Zimbabwe and other landlocked countries from exporting their commodities through Maputo and Beira.

South Africa initially trained RENAMO forces at military bases in the Transvaal, air-dropped supplies, and provided logistical assistance to the guerrillas inside Mozambique. Mozambique's long coastline is also ideally suited for naval landings, which became more frequent. Captured RENAMO documents suggest that coastal landings were the preferred resupply route since Mozambique's fledgling navy could not patrol effectively. In addition to small arms, mortars, mines, and anti-aircraft weaponry, Mozambican officials reported that RENAMO received communications equipment that was far more sophisticated than that available to their own forces. This enabled the guerrillas to maintain contact with South African reconnaissance planes flying inside Mozambique and providing valuable information on Mozambican troop movements (R.N.M. 1980).

By 1983, Western diplomats in Maputo estimated the number of RENAMO forces at between 5,000 and 10,000 men. Most knowledgeable observers believe that this figure has doubled in the past five years. The overwhelming majority of these recruits were forced to join the movement. Accounts from Western journalists who have traveled throughout Mozambique and visited refugees in neighboring countries reveal a consistent pattern of abduction. A 1988 State Department report based on extensive interviews conducted by Robert Gersony concludes that "forced recruitment was...the principal mechanism through which these men had been impressed into service" (Gersony 1988:123). A recent Ford Foundation–funded study conducted by sociologist William Minter (1989) estimates that as many as 90 percent of the RENAMO rank and file had been press-ganged. Both reports also document a wide array of coercive mechanisms used by RENAMO to prevent desertion and intimidate the population under their control.

Unpopular government policies aided RENAMO recruitment efforts. FRELIMO's initial tendency to dismiss many aspects of "traditional culture" as reactionary, its removal of all local chiefs, and its disdain for religious leaders offered a strategic entry point for RENAMO leaders who called for a return to "authentic" African society.[7] The government's failure to provide significant support for the family farming sector and its 1982 forced resettlement of unemployed urban dwellers in the countryside brought the rebels additional followers.

Whatever the movement's initial attraction, RENAMO's plundering, brutality, and terrorism quickly alienated most of the rural population, who above all else wanted to be left alone. The rebels' brutal tactics, lack of coherent political agenda, and failure to mobilize the peasants in those areas in which they operate belie RENAMO's claim that it is a serious movement of nationalist freedom fighters disillusioned with FRELIMO's Marxist strategy. According to a 1987 State Department report, "RENAMO draws most of its adherents from the Shona tribal group of central Mozambique. It has shown little capability to expand its political influence in other areas of the country or to create a cohesive political organization, even in areas where it has some ethnic support. Credible reports of RENAMO atrocities against the civilian population have undercut its popular appeal, as have increasingly apparent divisions among its military and political leaders" (U.S. Department of State 1987).

If RENAMO made few political inroads, it nevertheless proved to be an effective force in Pretoria's undeclared economic, political, and psychological war against Mozambique and its SADCC allies. Roving bands repeatedly attacked strategic economic targets by cutting railroad lines, mining roads, and bridges; interdicting traffic; plundering communal villages, state farms, and shops; and sabotaging key development projects. Mineral prospecting and geological surveys in the provinces of Sofala, Manica, and Zambesia were also disrupted, and a number of technicians from both Eastern and Western European countries were captured or killed.

South Africa's principal economic target, however, was not Mozambique itself but rather the SADCC transportation network, especially the railway lines from Mozambique to Zimbabwe, which came under repeated attack. Between 1980 and 1983, Zimbabwe had redirected 50 percent of its exports from South African ports to Mozambican ports. By 1985, this figure was less than 10 percent (Martin and Johnson 1986:5). Despite the appreciably lower cost of shipping through Maputo and the ten-day shorter turnaround time there, escalating RENAMO attacks culminating in the destruction of the Zimbabwe-Maputo railroad line had forced Zimbabwean companies to continue relying on the South African port of Durban. Beira, historically Zimbabwe's major international outlet, has suffered the most.

As the economic stakes increased, South African commandos no longer even bothered to maintain their facade as instructors. For example, they destroyed the strategic bridge across the Pungue River, blocking road communications to Beira, and periodically mined the railroad lines linking that port city to Zimbabwe. On 9 December 1982, they blew up thirty-four oil storage tanks in Beira valued at more than $40 million. This caused severe shortages in Zimbabwe (*Financial Times*, 6 January 1983; *Observer*, 20 February 1983; *Washington Post*, 7 January 1983).

While South Africa intensified its military pressure it also expanded its larger political objectives. Fearing both the increasing popularity of the ANC and the liberation movement's ability to attack strategic points within South Africa, Pretoria embarked upon a campaign to compel Mozambique to deny sanctuary or support for the ANC. The first indication of this policy was the 1981 attack on the homes of South African refugees, some of whom were ANC members, living on the outskirts of Maputo. More ominous was the explicit warning of South African Defense Minister Magnus Malan in August 1982 that his country might find it necessary to initiate a "Lebanese-type invasion" of Mozambique to rid it of "ANC terrorists" (*Reuters*, 22 August 1982).

By 1984 Pretoria's destabilization campaign had taken its toll. Mozambique's leaders were forced to admit that they lacked the military capacity to counteract South African aggression and that the socialist countries were either unwilling or unable to provide military assistance on the scale necessary to blunt the escalating RENAMO attacks. Soviet weapons—with the exception of the MIG-21s, MI-24 helicopter gunships, and SAM-7s—were out of date and costly. Moreover, there was growing dissatisfaction with the quality of the conventional military training provided by Eastern-bloc advisors, which proved ineffectual against the guerrillas.

South Africa's undeclared campaign of economic strangulation, together with RENAMO sabotages, decimated Mozambique's ailing economy. Prodded by promises of Western economic and military support in March 1984, Mozambique signed an agreement with South Africa known as the Nkomati Accord. Each party promised "not to allow its territory to be used for acts of war, aggression or violence against the other." But whatever diplomatic and economic benefits Mozambique may have derived from this agreement, the Nkomati Accord did not end South African support for RENAMO. From the outset, Pretoria violated both the spirit and the substance of the accord. Documents captured at RENAMO headquarters inside Mozambique, which became known as the "Documentos de Gorongosa," reveal that shortly before the Nkomati agreement Pretoria provided RENAMO with sufficient arms to pursue military activities for several months. An entry in one of the captured diaries noted that RENAMO leader Afonso Dhlakama met "on February 23, 1984, at 10 a.m. in Pretoria... [with] the general of military intelligence." The purpose of the meeting was to "plan the war in the face of the situation taken up by the South African Republic"—a euphemism for the impending Nkomati agreement. General "Wessie" van der Westhuizen is quoted as reaffirming the commitment of the South African security apparatus: "We the military will continue to give them [RENAMO] the support without the consent of our politicians in a massive way so that they can win the war."[8]

While it is possible, even likely, that differences existed among policymakers, these differences seem to have centered on the level of support South Africa should continue to provide to RENAMO and the extent to which the cycle of destabilization should be escalated. Davies (1986:13–17) has argued convincingly that the debate was between minimalists who viewed escalation as a means of changing political behavior and maximalists who believed that the time was right to overthrow the FRELIMO government. At no time after the Nkomati agreement did Pretoria move to disarm RENAMO, dismantle its South African bases, or close down its communication centers. South African planes and ships repeatedly violated Mozambique's airspace and territorial waters to resupply RENAMO. An entry from one of the captured diaries dated 19 October 1984—approximately six months after the Nkomati agreement—suggests the extent to which Pretoria was committed to rearming RENAMO. The document notes that during the week ending 28 September, South African Dakotas and DC-3s airdropped supplies to RENAMO forces operating in the provinces of Sofala, Maputo, Inhambane, and Zambesia ("Documentos de Gorongosa"). South Africa's refusal to rein in RENAMO effectively undercut the Joint Security Commission set up to implement the terms of the Nkomati Accord. In October 1985 President Machel suspended his government's participation in the commission and announced that Mozambique would intensify military efforts against RENAMO.

Machel's decision, coupled with his highly visible Western diplomatic offensive in the fall of 1985, posed a serious problem for the Botha regime. On the one hand, Western governments—especially the Reagan administration, which had brokered the Nkomati Accord—exerted pressure on Pretoria not to violate the agreement. On the other hand, powerful domestic forces, including key sectors of the military and security apparatus, the right wing of the National party, and the increasingly powerful Portuguese community within South Africa, all demanded that Botha escalate support for RENAMO.

One way to accommodate these potentially contradictory pressures was for South Africa to curtail some of the more visible aspects of its destabilization campaign. Pretoria's shift in strategy rested on the expanded involvement of the Malawian government, which, since 1981, had periodically allowed RENAMO to launch attacks across its frontier. Military bases in southern Malawi, on the border with Mozambique, provided an ideal way to resupply the guerrillas surreptitiously. They also offered easy access to strategic economic targets in central and northern Mozambique. The existence of a South African embassy in Malawi, moreover, facilitated the collection of intelligence information, allowing South African security to coordinate strategic military planning for RENAMO.

In a rare interview Mozambique's former army chief of staff and deputy defense minister, Sebastião Mabote (1986), claimed: "Malawi is helping South African–backed guerrillas materially, logistically, and is also providing them with travel documents and airport access so that they can move around the world." When pressured for specifics, he cited "the presence of RENAMO training bases in southern Malawi" and the fact that "South African helicopters and DC-3s were using airstrips in Malawi to resupply RENAMO forces in Niassa, Zambesia and Tete provinces." Ample evidence subsequently emerged to support these charges. Zimbabwean intelligence officers who returned from Mozambique confirmed the existence of RENAMO bases run by South Africans in Malawi. In the fall of 1986, a journalist for the London *Observer* (24 August 1986) witnessed Malawian troops fraternizing with RENAMO forces at the frontier post of Muloza. The Malawian commander was quite candid: "We are with them all the time and we help them against FRELIMO." And when President Machel, Prime Minister Mugabe of Zimbabwe, and President Kaunda of Zambia confronted President Banda of Malawi with this irrefutable evidence at their September 1986 meeting, threatening economic and military sanctions, Banda conceded that there could be clandestine bases in the south operating without his authorization (Chissano 1986).[9]

On the face of it, Malawian support for RENAMO seemed inexplicable. Not only did such a policy further isolate the Banda government from its African neighbors, but guerrilla attacks had disrupted Malawian commerce, which relied heavily on Mozambican rails and ports. As a result, Malawian businessmen have had to use more costly transport routes via South Africa and Tanzania. The cost of the extra mileage was estimated at $100 million a year, which is approximately one-third the total value of Malawi's exports (*International Herald Tribune*, 30 December 1986).

Despite his government's repeated public denials, there are several possible explanations for Banda's policies. Some observers suggest that because of close economic and security ties to Pretoria, Malawi's life president may have been simply closing his eyes and giving Pretoria a free hand. Others point to Banda's long-standing claim that much of northern Mozambique had historically been part of a greater Malawian empire. Control over this territory would give landlocked Malawi direct access to the Indian Ocean. In the early 1960s, Banda proposed to President Julius Nyerere of Tanzania that the two countries divide northern Mozambique. Banda subsequently aided a tiny separatist movement (União Nacional Africana de Rombézia) as part of a plan to integrate northern Mozambique into a greater Malawi (Johnson and Martin 1986:23–24). Banda also has well-documented historical ties to Portuguese investors and secret police officials who fled Mozambique after independence and who were bankrolling RENAMO and playing important roles within the rebel movement.

Whatever Banda's motives, the Malawian connection assumed an increasingly important role in Pretoria's destabilization campaign. By 1985, a string of RENAMO bases with South African and reportedly Israeli advisors had been established in southern Malawi. RENAMO incursions into central and northern Mozambique increased dramatically over the next year. In the fall of 1986, several thousand RENAMO forces penetrated deep into the strategic province of Zambesia and adjacent regions. The poorly armed and inadequately supplied Mozambican army was totally unprepared for an attack of this magnitude. The invaders captured a string of rural towns, destroyed important economic centers, and reinforced their holdings in the strategic lower Zambezi Valley.

There is evidence that the invading RENAMO forces had broader objectives. By pushing southward they hoped to gain control of the coastal towns of Chinde and Pebane, which would have facilitated South African efforts to resupply them by sea. Their drive may also have been designed to capture a major administrative center, which would have given them the option of installing a provisional government. Such a policy would be consistent with their concerted effort to gain legitimacy in the West by demonstrating that they represent a serious political force.

The invasion also seems to have been part of South Africa's broader strategy of sabotaging the Beira corridor. As rehabilitation of the corridor advanced and traffic from Zimbabwe and Beira increased, the apartheid regime was forced to act. It sent a substantial number of RENAMO forces across the Zambezi River to operate in areas immediately adjacent to the Beira corridor as part of a concerted effort to disrupt traffic and discourage future investment. Zimbabwean troops, whose numbers have increased threefold since 1984 to approximately 10,000, thwarted this drive.

Despite Zimbabwean military assistance, the cycle of destruction and terrorism unleashed by Pretoria has been devastating. Even before the 1986 RENAMO offensive, a decade of war had cost Mozambique more than $5.5 billion in economic losses (Chissano 1986). In addition, the destruction of roads, bridges, and other infrastructure paralyzed key sectors of the economy not directly affected by the attacks. Thus, the inability to transport coal from the Moatize mines cost Mozambique $24 million in potential income, while the destruction of several hundred pylons linked to Cahora Bassa, Africa's largest hydroelectric plant, brought production to a virtual standstill (*Christian Science Monitor*, 1 January 1987; *Times*, 12 March 1987). Work at the Morrua tantalite mines in Zambesia had also ceased. A U.S. geological team estimated the total value of Morrua's mineral deposits at approximately $1 billion (Newton 1986).[10] To make matters worse, the most recent raids destroyed more than $100 million worth of agro-industrial equipment, devastated the tea industry, killed thousands of head of cattle, and destroyed the strategic hydropower plant at Monapo.

The cumulative impact of this economic sabotage was staggering. Cash crop production, which had experienced modest growth in the late 1970s, plummeted. Between 1980 and 1984 cashew and cotton production, two of the nation's major cash crops, fell by more than two-thirds (see Table 9.2). Tea output declined by almost half. Without capital generated from the sale of agricultural commodities and without raw material from the countryside, industrial production declined precipitously. Between 1980 and 1985, the gross value of industrial output dropped from 32,569,834 contos to 14,346,017 contos (Moçambique Commissão Nacional 1985:58; 1986:41–43). Between 1982 and 1986, gross domestic production declined by one-third, and Mozambique's foreign exchange earnings plummeted to a mere

$180 million. By the fall of 1986, the country's foreign debt was esti-
mated at $3 billion, and its debt-service ratio was 170 percent, which
meant that even if it used all of its 1986 earned foreign exchange, it
could not meet its debt obligation for the year (Gunn 1986:3; Johnson
and Martin 1986:30; Moçambique Commissão Nacional 1986). In
October 1986, the apartheid regime tightened the economic squeeze.
Pretoria announced that it would expel 68,000 mineworkers and prohibit future recruitment of Mozambicans, depriving the country of
desperately needed foreign currency plus South African–manufac-
tured consumer goods and farm implements critical to southern
Mozambique's peasantry. This move also meant the Mozambican government faced the problem of reintegrating a large pool of unemployed workers into the country's moribund economy.[11]

Table 9.2   Agricultural Commodity Production, 1975–85

PRODUCT	1975	1976	1977	1978	1979	1980	1981	1982	1983	1984	1985
Cashew	160.0	120.0	102.0	90.0	62.6	87.6	90.1	57.0	18.1	25.3	30.4
Cotton	52.0	36.8	52.0	72.4	36.8	64.9	73.7	60.7	24.7	19.7	5.7
Rice	94.0	75.0	60.0	44.0	56.3	43.6	28.9	41.5	17.3	19.1	17.9
Maize	95.0	90.0	34.0	70.0	66.0	65.0	78.3	89.2	55.8	82.6	58.6
Sunflower	8.0	7.0	10.0	7.0	4.8	11.8	12.1	10.8	7.3	5.0	5.7
Potatoes	40.0	30.0	15.0	25.0	15.2	9.0	13.9	9.4	8.3	3.1	1.5
Beans	14.8	14.0	14.0	10.1	13.0	9.6	14.9	6.9	4.7	3.5	3.6
Copra	50.4	72.0	48.0	60.0	51.0	37.1	54.4	36.6	30.7	24.8	24.0
Citrus	34.0	30.0	25.0	38.6	39.0	37.3	36.7	38.1	33.5	24.6	31.5
Cattle	14.7	10.6	11.0	7.0	8.3	8.3	7.9	7.2	5.8	4.7	3.2
Pigs	2.3	1.0	0.4	2.0	2.6	3.3	3.9	3.7	1.8	1.1	2.7
Chickens	2.8	2.8	2.9	4.0	4.5	6.4	5.7	3.4	1.5	1.5	0.6
Eggs	12.5	12.0	14.1	19.9	33.6	45.9	48.0	49.7	29.0	37.0	34.7
Milk	5.1	4.7	3.4	5.2	5.1	5.7	5.5	5.3	5.3	4.5	3.9
Wood											
Production	199.0	100.0	52.0	77.3	83.7	138.1	93.3	53.8	33.5	44.5	—
Tea	59.1	67.3	77.3	67.6	86.0	90.2	99.2	109.7	51.1	59.8	25.0
Sisal	340.0	325.0	325.0	375.0	424.1	298.0	233.8	139.9	122.4	136.6	78.8

Source: Moçambique Commissão Nacional (1985, 1986).

The social costs of destabilization were even more staggering. Food
shortages and famines were widespread as more than 1 million
Mozambican peasants sought to flee the ravages of war. In the words
of Agency for International Development Director Peter McPherson
(*Washington Post*, 19 February 1987), the situation in Mozambique "is a
political disaster, not a natural disaster made by mother nature...
Food has not been planted because of the war in many places and distribution has been greatly inhibited because of the war again." By the
middle of 1986, more than 3.5 million Mozambicans, roughly 25 percent of the population, were suffering from acute food shortages. In
addition, more than 500 clinics had been destroyed or abandoned,
paralyzing the government's rural health program (*Weekly Mail*, 2
March 1987). And between 1983 and 1986, RENAMO attacks were

responsible for closing more than 1,300 schools and the displacement of 313,000 students (Johnson and Martin 1986:30).

The Chissano Government: The Narrowing Set of Choices

It was against this backdrop of economic collapse and public despair, heightened by the devastating death of President Machel in a suspicious plane crash,[12] that Joaquim Chissano came to power in November 1986. Reports of a deep-seated succession crisis involving as many as five senior Mozambican officials proved to be unfounded. This is not to diminish ideological and personality differences among the leadership but rather to suggest that there was a broad consensus that Chissano was the most viable choice. His highly visible role in the independence struggle, his ability to pull the party together through a series of factional crises in the late 1960s, the unifying role he played after the assassination of party founder Eduardo Mondlane, his position as prime minister during the 1974–75 transitional government, and his effective performance as a foreign minister from 1975 to 1986 gave him a clear edge over any other potential rival. So did the fact that he was regarded, according to Western diplomats, as the most popular public official after Machel. Despite Chissano's popularity, the deteriorating situation and limited options left him little space in which to maneuver. Nevertheless, he has pursued a vigorous, if controversial, policy to revitalize the economy, end the war, and bring the nation together.

In a desperate effort to salvage the economy, the Chissano administration implemented the IMF–World Bank structural readjustment program known in Mozambique as the PRE. At the heart of the policy was a radical devaluation of the national currency (see Table 9.3), loosening of state control over the economy, reduction of public expenditures and state subsidies, and expansion of the role of the private sector (Moçambique 1987). The first two years of the readjustment policy have produced mixed results at best. The economic programs and infusion of foreign loans did end the precipitous decline of the economy that had averaged 8 percent per year since 1982. Between 1986 and 1987 Mozambique's gross domestic product increased by 3.6 percent, and in 1988 overall economic growth was 4.6 percent. The economy is expected to grow by 5 percent in 1989, despite serious debt-repayment problems. Foreign loans played an important part in this growth, allowing for the purchase of raw materials and parts needed to revitalize Mozambique's moribund industrial sector.[13] The continuing war in the countryside, however, has meant that agricultural increases were less than projected and that output varied sub-

Table 9.3.   Exchange Rate: Meticais to US Dollar, 1981–89

YEAR	NO. METICAIS TO $1 U.S.	
1981	35.35	
1982	37.37	
1983	40.18	
1984	42.44	
1985	43.18	
1986	40.43	
1987	200.00	(first devaluation, January)
	400.00	(devaluation, June)
1988	450.00	(devaluation, January)
	580.00	(devaluation, July)
	620.00	(devaluation, October)
1989	645.00	(January)
	663.00	(February)
	682.00	(March)
	702.00	(April)
	715.00	(May)
	728.00	(June)
	742.00	(July)

Source: Bank of Mozambique.

stantially between and within regions. Security problems have also limited efforts to redistribute state farmlands to peasants and to put into place a rural extension service in the most productive districts of the country (Comité Central de Partido FRELIMO 1989:169–211).

If key sectors of the economy have made small but significant gains, the austerity programs have imposed new hardships on the poorest and most vulnerable strata of society. Cutbacks in state subsidies for medicines, a sharp increase in the price paid for medical consultations, and a new housing policy that no longer ties rents to income have all hurt low-paid workers and the urban poor. Most devastating was the decision in April 1988 to lift subsidies on essential foods. The price of rice, maize, and sugar increased between 300 percent and 500 percent in that year alone (see Table 9.4). Two wage hikes of 50 and 15 percent respectively and an additional increase to cushion the loss of food subsidies have proven inadequate. One exasperated party delegate complained, "We cannot tighten our belt too much more" (author's per-

Table 9.4.   Prices of Basic Goods, 1988

	MARCH	APRIL	% INCREASE
Rice	40 MT	271 MT	575
Maize (kg)	27 MT	112 MT	317
Maize flour (kg)	38 MT	145 MT	287
Wheat flour (kg)	178 MT	190 MT	7
Bread (250 grams)	20 MT	30 MT	50
Sugar (kg)	50 MT	264 MT	428
Cooking Oil (litre)	360 MT	540 MT	50

Source: National Commission on Wages and Prices.

sonal observation). As if to underscore this point, a recent ministry of health study concluded that the rising cost of living jeopardized the health and nutritional status of many urban dwellers (*S.A. Economist*, April 1989). At the same time, merchants, well-placed farmers, private entrepreneurs, and corrupt officials are prospering, fueling a process of social differentiation—a phenomenon that FRELIMO had sought to combat since independence.

In the final analysis, the security crisis poses the most immediate and serious challenge for Chissano, as it did for Machel. The new president devoted almost a quarter of his inaugural address to this issue and, as he had in the past, took an intransigent position toward the South African–backed RENAMO (*Tempo* 1986:6–9): "This is a struggle in which there cannot be compromise... we will continue the war to finish the war," he promised members of the Central Committee. In words reminiscent of his predecessor, Chissano noted that "banditry is an integral part of the regional destabilization carried out by the South African apartheid regime." At the same time, he held out an olive branch to the Banda government, emphasizing that "we want to develop relations of friendship and cooperation with the brother people of Malawi" but noting that "these relations are seriously affected by the support that the bandits have received from Malawian territory." This conciliatory policy, coming on the heels of the Mozam-bican-Zimbabwean ultimatum, seems to have borne some fruit. In an apparent reversal of policy, Malawi signed a security agreement with Mozambique at the end of 1986. The agreement included the dismantling of RENAMO bases in Malawi, Mozambique's right to hot pursuit across the border, and the dispatching of several hundred Malawian troops to help guard the strategic Nacala-Malawi railroad line. Although not fully implemented, Mozambican officials consider the agreement a major diplomatic victory. It transformed an adversary into an ally, and today a contingent of Malawian forces is fighting inside Mozambique against the guerrillas (*Observer*, 22 March 1987; *Guardian*, 7 March 1987).

In the short run, Chissano has also been able to count on military assistance from Zimbabwe and Tanzania. The latter, whose own resources are limited, had provided training and some logistical support. For Zimbabwe in particular, the defense of Mozambique is critical. Prime Minister Mugabe has declared publicly on numerous occasions that "the survival of Mozambique is our survival. The fall of Mozambique will almost certainly be our fall." Minister of State for Security Emerson Munangagwa has indicated that the smooth functioning of the Beira corridor is so important that Zimbabwe will keep it open at any cost. Completion of the corridor, a several-year, $280 million project funded primarily by the Netherlands and Sweden, will triple the port of Beira's handling capacity to 3.5 million tons. This, in turn, would free Zimbabwe and the other Frontline states from their dependence on South African ports and railroads. In the short term results have been encouraging, despite problems of congestion and shortages of transportation and handling facilities. From 1986 to 1987 the total cargo handled by the Beira port increased 40 percent to 1.96 million tons. By the end of 1987 Beira was handling 27 percent of Zimbabwe's exports and preliminary data from 1988 suggest the figure was even higher (*Africa Insight* 1989:22–23; U.S. Department of Commerce 1989).

Within a month after Chissano assumed control, the Mozambican army, bolstered by increased support from its neighbors, moved to blunt the RENAMO offensive in central Mozambique. In rapid succession, FRELIMO forces, reinforced by a contingent of Tanzanian troops, retook much of eastern Zambesia, in the process reopening a major highway between the provincial capital of Quelimane and the central town of Mocuba and thwarting a major South African effort to resupply RENAMO units through the coastal port of Pebane and Chinde in Zambesia. In adjacent Sofala and Tete provinces, across the Zambezi River, a joint Zimbabwean-Mozambican force recaptured five river towns as well as a key railroad bridge that spans the waterway. Mozambican officials claim that their counteroffensive killed more than 2,200 RENAMO forces (Mozambique Information Office 1987). These victories notwithstanding, RENAMO forces are still well entrenched in parts of Zambesia adjacent to Malawi, and others escaped north into Nampula and Niassa provinces where they continue to plunder the countryside. Moreover, they maintain a varying military presence in the remaining seven provinces, and the threat they pose in the south has actually increased as new troops have poured in from South African bases.

FRELIMO's failure to eliminate RENAMO reflects not only Pretoria's continued commitment to its allies but also Mozambique's inability to upgrade substantially its poorly trained and ill-equipped army. At FRELIMO's 1989 Fifth Party Congress, one irate delegate demanded to know why the battalion in his area of Meluca "had not received food, transport or their salaries in months." He insisted "that they must have their basic needs met since they are the ones who defend us" (author's personal observation). His criticism, similar to that made by other delegates, had obvious merit. There is ample evidence—from successful battalions in Inhambane and Gaza, from the experiences of the special forces in Zambesia, and the British-trained units guarding the southern railway line—that whenever Mozambican soldiers have received appropriate training and adequate supplies and logistical support, they have more than held their own against RENAMO forces. Conversely, where government troops have been isolated without

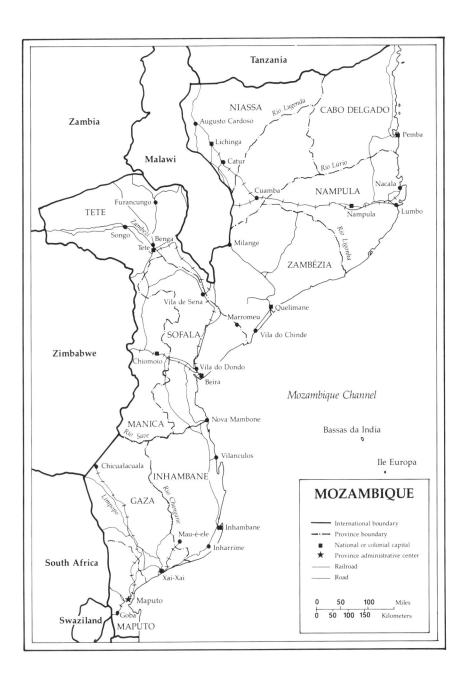

appropriate provisions and salary, they have frequently degenerated into a ragtag army. In such situations soldiers have often fought poorly and, on occasion, have plundered the peasantry.

Senior Mozambican officials, as well as Zimbabwean officers and foreign military diplomats, contend that the only way for the army to be transformed into an efficient fighting force is to overhaul the command structure. This requires retiring a number of senior officers who have political clout and replacing them with better-trained younger commanders. Chissano has appointed a new chief of staff and commander of the army and there are reports circulating in the capital that other major changes are imminent. While essential, such an overhaul will not alleviate the pressures brought about by the Soviet Union's decision to cut its military support, the unwillingness of the West to provide anything more than symbolic military aid, and the growing opposition in Zimbabwe to the continued use of its troops in Mozambique (*Washington Post*, 3 June 1989; *Africa Confidential*, 9 June 1989).

With the war grinding on and no military solution in sight, Chissano has intensified diplomatic efforts to end the conflict. Although still in a relatively early phase, Mozambique's efforts have produced several tangible gains. Every major Western country including the United States has denounced RENAMO as nothing more than a group of South African–backed terrorists. Italy, France, Portugal, Spain, and the United Kingdom have even provided security assistance to Mozambique on a limited scale. Although less well publicized, FRELIMO has strengthened diplomatic ties with conservative African nations such as the Ivory Coast, Zaire, Senegal, and Morocco who, under other circumstances, might have been attracted to RENAMO's anti-Marxist rhetoric (interview with Foreign Minister Pascoal Mocumbi, 7 August 1989).

With the help of Great Britain and the United States, Mozambique is also pressing Pretoria to adhere to the 1984 Nkomati Accord and to pursue a policy of détente rather than confrontation. In a series of high-level negotiations, culminating in a July 1989 meeting between Chissano and National party leader F. W. de Klerk, South Africa agreed to back Mozambique's peace efforts and called for an end to the conflict. Despite this pledge, Western intelligence sources report that support is still coming from powerful forces within the South African military as well as from right-wing extremists (*Africa Confidential*, 23 June 1989; interview with U.S. ambassador Melissa Wells, 14 August 1989). While publicly expressing support for de Klerk's intentions, Mozambican officials remain privately skeptical. They are closely following events in Namibia and Angola to ascertain de Klerk's regional strategy. Meanwhile, they press South Africa to demonstrate its peaceful intent by introducing legislation prohibiting any group from providing support for RENAMO.

In a reversal of the public position he took upon assuming office, Chissano has begun to prepare his war-torn country for a political solution in which RENAMO forces would be reintegrated into the country. Beginning in 1988, his government adopted a policy of amnesty that passed after heated debate in the National Assembly. The policy provides the legal mechanism through which guerrillas in the bush can turn themselves in without risk of prosecution and with guarantees of basic material support for their life. As of July 1989, 3,000 RENAMO members had accepted amnesty. The president has also used his frequent meetings in the countryside to prepare the nation for the idea of direct negotiations with RENAMO. At the Fifth Party Congress he outlined twelve broad principles aimed at ending the violence and beginning peace negotiations. While continuing to condemn RENAMO atrocities, Chissano for the first time referred to the guerrillas as "our brothers in the bush." Behind the scenes he authorized a delegation of Mozambican religious leaders to begin exploratory peace talks with RENAMO. Out of the most recent discussions in July 1989 came a rebel counterproposal which, although rejected by the government, represents the first tentative steps toward negotiations.

The peace process is still at a very precarious stage, with many possible pitfalls ahead. Only time will tell if the shifting regional balance of power, marked by the independence of Namibia, growing popular unrest and economic problems in South Africa, and increased diplomatic pressure on Pretoria, will convince de Klerk to abandon his nation's policy of regional destabilization. Even then, it is not certain that de Klerk can control the powerful elements in the military and security apparatus who oppose détente. RENAMO's long-term agenda also remains unclear. Over the past two years it has attempted to Africanize its leadership.[14] In addition, for the first time in its fifteen-year history, RENAMO held a party congress. At the June 1989 meeting, internal military officers expelled several external representatives closely linked to ex–Portuguese colonialists and South African security, and there appears to have been a conscious effort to broaden the ethnic base of the leadership. According to the highly influential journal *Africa Confidential* (7 July 1989), this move was probably supported by the CIA and other interest groups in Washington as a means of enhancing RENAMO's political credibility.[15] With the well-armed rebels still receiving aid from both South Africa and right-wing religious groups in the United States, serious negotiations are likely to be long and drawn out. A July 1989 Mozambican-Zimbabwean military offensive in which RENAMO's command center and a number of other bases in Sofala were overrun was designed to demonstrate to rebel leaders that there is no meaningful alternative to negotiations.

While the future remains uncertain, it is clear that the success of

Chissano's peace initiative depends on factors over which Mozambique has only limited control. A Western policy providing increased military aid to Mozambique and simultaneously intensifying economic and diplomatic pressures on South Africa would go a long way toward redressing the imbalance of power and enabling Mozambique to protect its national sovereignty and begin to reconstruct the very fabric of its society. For its part, FRELIMO must open up the political system to produce greater accountability in government in order to avoid many of the problems of the past.

NOTES

This paper was written in 1986 and updated in September 1989. Since then East-West relations have been transformed, Nelson Mandela has been freed, and the African National Congress has been legalized. The impact of these events falls outside the scope of this paper.

1. For a discussion of Mozambican labor migration to South Africa, see First (1983) and Minter (1986).

2. For the broad outlines of Salazar's policy, see Smith (1974), Isaacman and Isaacman (1983), and Munslow (1983).

3. Until 1957, "invisible income" offset the colony's negative balance of payments, and subsequently this income reduced it to a few million dollars.

4. Although much has been written about these policies, it should also be noted that substantial gains were made in health, housing, and education. See Saul (1985), Hanlon (1984), and Isaacman and Isaacman (1983:103–13) for further details.

5. See Isaacman and Isaacman (1983:189–200) for an English translation of the major economic policies that came out of the Fourth Party Congress.

6. This is one of a number of captured RENAMO documents referred to in this chapter (see note 8). Western intelligence considers them to be authentic.

7. FRELIMO's campaign against polygamy, bride-price, female initiation rites, and other customs that either exploited women or reproduced "obscurantism" was bitterly opposed by a number of chiefs and male elders. RENAMO was able to appeal to this dissatisfaction with some success. For a discussion of RENAMO's efforts to win over local chiefs in one region of Northern Mozambique, see Geffray and Pedersen (1987).

8. The diary was among a collection of documents and diaries, known as "Documentos de Gorongosa," which were subsequently reproduced and distributed to foreign governments and journalists. *Gorongosa* refers to the captured RENAMO base where they were discovered. For further information, see Johnson and Martin (1986:36–37).

9. Joaquim Chissano was, at the time of this interview, minister of foreign affairs.

10. At the time of this interview, Anthony Newton was the economic officer at the U.S. embassy in Maputo.

11. In January 1987, Pretoria apparently bowed to pressure from mining companies and agreed to expel only half of the Mozambican workers (*Guardian* (London), 17 January 1987).

12. Immediately after the crash, it was the general consensus that Machel's death was an accident. News accounts, coming primarily from South Africa, emphasized some combination of human error and bad weather. Shortly thereafter, South Africa's foreign minister, Pik Botha, offered several alternative explanations that laid blame for the crash on drunken Soviet pilots and antiquated Russian navigational equipment. His speculation received substantial play in the Western press. Subsequent evidence called the initial reports into question, and Botha admitted before an international commission of inquiry on 26 January 1987 that his initial charges were groundless.

    To date, the exact cause of the crash remains unknown. While there is no firm evidence linking South Africa to the crash, Western journalists raised a number of questions that, given the fragmentary nature of the data and Pretoria's strict censorship policy, may never be answered. Why were South African security forces placed on full alert the night before Machel's crash? Why did South African controllers not inform the Soviet pilot that he had entered South African territory? The controllers' silence is particularly puzzling since the South African journal *Business Day* (21 October 1986) reported that they had tracked Machel's plane with a sophisticated computer-assisted radar system for hundreds of miles before it entered the militarily sensitive region of the eastern Transvaal. Finally, what was the origin of the radio beacon which, experts believe, drew the plane off course? Pretoria opined that it may have come from an airport in Swaziland, but Swaziland used a different frequency from that of the Maputo airport, which was the plane's destination. An article published in the *New York Times* (27 January 1987) suggested that decoy beacons from South Africa may have lured Machel's plane off course. Reports from witnesses that a large tent, which could have housed mobile electronic equipment, stood 150 yards from where the plane went down and was dismantled the day after the crash and the failure of the South African authorities to inform Mozambique of the crash for fifteen hours while they rifled through confidential documents have fueled speculation about their involvement. So too have accounts of implicit threats against Machel made by South African Defense Minister Magnus Malan shortly before the crash and Machel's own revelation that there had already been an attempt on his life.

13. On 22 April 1987 a number of aid-donor countries undertook a $209 million relief effort. The United States and Italy were the largest donors. With regard to rescheduling or forgoing loans, Mozambican officials were optimistic that both the socialist countries and Western nations would respond sympathetically to their requests as they had in the past. As of 1987, 40 percent of Mozambique's debt was owed to the West, 27 per-

cent to the socialist nations, and 21 percent to OPEC members (*Southscan*, 11 March 1987). Subsequently, a number of nations have reduced or renegotiated Mozambique's debt payment. In 1989 the debt payment was projected to be more than twice the value of exports (Mozambique Information Agency 1989:6). Mozambique's debt was estimated at $4.2 billion (*Southscan*, 28 July 1989).

14. RENAMO's president, Afonso Dhlakama, at the urging of South African officials and anticommunist lobbies in the United States, has attempted to Africanize the movement's image by removing highly visible whites and Asians previously associated with the Portuguese colonial regime. The principal casualties of this Africanization campaign were Evo Fernandes, former RENAMO secretary-general who was subsequently murdered, and Jorge Correia. Nevertheless, the main RENAMO lobbyist in the United States remained a white American, Thomas Schaff (see *Washington Times*, 20 August 1986; *Africa Confidencial*, 18 March and 22 April 1987).

15. The RENAMO congress chose a new four-member cabinet and a ten-person national council. Gone were Arturo Janeiro da Fonseca, longtime head of external relations, who had very close ties to South African security, and Canadian-based Francisco Nota Moises, who was responsible for information and propaganda. They were respectively replaced by Raul Manuel Domingos, formerly commander of the rebel forces, and Vicente Zacarias Ululu, secretary for internal administration. Neither Domingos nor Ululu come from the Shona-speaking Ndau who have dominated the RENAMO leadership (*Africa Confidential*, 7 July 1989; *Indian Ocean Newsletter*, 24 June 1989).

REFERENCES

Africa Confidencial (Lisbon). 1987.

Africa Confidential (London). 1989.

Africa Insight. 1989.

Azevedo, Mário. 1980. "A Sober Commitment to Liberation: Mozambique and South Africa, 1974–1979." *African Affairs* 79(317):567–84.

Bowen, Merle L. 1989. "Peasant Agriculture in Mozambique: The Case of Chokwe Gaza Province." *Canadian Journal of African Studies* 23(3):355–79.

Business Day (Johannesburg). 1986, 1987.

Chissano, Joaquim. 1986. Interview with author. 10 October.

Christian Science Monitor. 1987.

Comité Central de Partido FRELIMO. 1989. *Por Um Consensão Nacional de Normalização de Vida*. Maputo: Sede de Comité Central.

Cunha, J. M. da Silva. 1949. *O Trabalho Indígena: Estudo do Direito Colonial*. Lisbon: Agencia Ceral das Colónias.

Davies, Robert. 1986. "Mozambique: What Is South Africa's Strategy?" *Southern Africa Report*. 2, 13–18.

Davies, Robert, and Dan O'Meara. 1985. "Total Strategy in Southern Africa: An Analysis of South African Regional Policy since 1978." *Journal of Southern African Studies*, 11(2):183–211.

Financial Times (Johannesburg). 1974, 1983.

First, Ruth. 1983. *Black Gold*. Sussex: Harvester Press.

Geffray, Christian, and Mögens Pedersen. 1985. *Transformação da Organização Social e do Sistema Agrário do Campesinato no do Erati: Processo do Socialização do Campo e Differenciação Social*. Maputo: Universidade de Eduardo Mondlane and Minesterio de Agricultura.

———. 1987. "Sobre a Guerra na Província de Nampula." *Revista Internacional de Estudos Africanos* 4–5:303–20.

Gersony, Robert. 1988. "Summary of Mozambican Refugee Accounts of Principally Conflict-Related Experience in Mozambique." Report submitted to U.S. Department of State.

Guardian (London). 1974, 1987.

Guardian (New York). 1987.

Gunn, Gillian. 1986. "Mozambique after Machel." *CSIS Africa Notes* 67.

Hanlon, Joseph. 1984. *Mozambique: The Revolution under Fire*. London: Zed Press.

Henriksen, Thomas. 1983. *Revolution and Counterrevolution*. Westport, CT: Greenwood Press.

Hermele, Kenneth. 1988. *Land Struggle and Social Differentiation in Southern Mozambique*. Uppsala: Scandinavian Institute of African Studies.

Indian Ocean Newsletter. 1989. Paris.

International Herald Tribune. 1986.

Isaacman, Allen, and Barbara Isaacman. 1983. *Mozambique: From Colonialism to Revolution, 1900–1982*. Boulder: Westview Press.

Johnson, Phyllis, and David Martin, eds. 1986. *Destructive Engagement*. Harare: Zimbabwe Publishing House.

Legum, Colin. 1983. "The Counterrevolutionaries in Mozambique: The Challenge of the Mozambique National Resistance." *Third World Reports*. March.

Leonard, Richard. 1983. *South Africa at War*. Westport, CT: Lawrence Hill Press.

Mabote, Sebastião. 1986. Interview with author. 2 July.

Martin, David, and Phyllis Johnson. 1982. *The Struggle for Zimbabwe*. New York: Monthly Review Press.

———. 1986. "South Africa Imposes Sanctions on Its Neighbors." UN Conference on Sanctions against South Africa. 16 June.

Minter, William. 1986. *King Solomon's Mines Revisited*. New York: Basic Books.

———. 1989. "The Mozambican National Resistance (RENAMO) Described by Ex-Participants." Report submitted to the Ford Foundation and the Swedish International Development Agency.

Moçambique. Gabinete de Orgnização e Desenvolvimento das Cooperativas Agrícolas (GODCA). 1980. "Documento Final." 15 August.

———. Ministério de Porto e Transportes, Departamento de Estatísticas. 1980. *Informação Estatística*. Maputo.

———. 1982. *Linhas Fundementais do Plano Prospectivo Indicativo para 1981–1990*. Maputo.

———. Commissão Nacional do Plano. Direcção Nacional de Estatística. 1985. *Informação Nacional de Estatística, 1975–1984.* Maputo.

———. Commissão Nacional do Plano. Direcção Nacional de Estatística. 1986. *Informação Nacional de Estatística, 1985.* Maputo.

———. 1987. *Strategy and Program for Economic Rehabilitation 1987–1988.* Maputo.

Mocumbi, Pascoal. 1989. Interview with author. 8 August.

Mozambique Information Agency. 1989. *Mozambiquefils.* July.

Mozambique Information Office. 1987. *News Review.* Vol. 98.

Munslow, Barry. 1983. *Mozambique: The Revolution and Its Origins.* London: Longman Press.

Murray, Colin. 1981. *Families Divided.* Cambridge: Cambridge University Press.

Newton, Anthony. 1986. Interview with author. 14 June.

New York Times. 1987.

Observer (London). 1974, 1983, 1986, 1987.

Resistencia Nacional de Moçambique (R.N.M.). 1980. "Relatório Referente a Sessão do Trabalho de R.N.M. e do Representativo do Governo Sul Africano." 25 October.

Reuters. 1982.

Roesch, Otto. 1986. "Socialism and Rural Development in Mozambique: The Case of Aldeia Comunal 24 de Jullo." Ph.D. Thesis. University of Toronto.

S.A. Economist (Zimbabwe). 1989.

Saul, John, ed. 1985. *A Difficult Road: The Transition to Socialism in Mozambique.* New York: Monthly Review Press.

Smith, Alan. 1974. "António Salazar and the Reversal of Portuguese Colonial Policy." *Journal of African History* 15(4):653–68.

Southscan. 1987, 1989.

Star Weekly (Johannesburg). 1974.

Tempo. 1986. Vol. 844.

Times (London). 1974, 1987.

United Nations. 1973. General Assembly A/AC. 109/L.919. July.

U.S. Department of Commerce. 1989. "Foreign Economic Trends and Their Implication for the United States and Mozambique." Washington, D.C.

U.S. Department of State. 1987. "Mozambique: Charting a New Course." *Current Policy* no. 980. Washington, D.C.

Washington Post. 1983, 1987, 1989.

Washington Times. 1986.

Weekly Mail (Johannesburg). 1987.

Wells, Melissa. 1989. Interview with author. 14 August.

10

South Africa's Contradictory Regional Goals

PATRICK O'MEARA

This chapter focuses on key dimensions of the political, economic, and military interaction between South Africa and the Southern African region. Different South African governments have employed contrasting strategies such as the idea of a "constellation of states," destabilization, nonaggression pacts, sanctions, and diplomatic initiatives in order to maintain South Africa's regional economic and political hegemony. There was one overriding regional political objective: the survival of white power within South Africa. At times there were contradictory policies because regional economic integration had limited the effectiveness of South Africa's attempts at regional political domination. From this perspective, Timothy Shaw and Ibrahim Msabaha (1987:4) are correct in their assessment that regional studies "have rarely examined modes and relations of production; rather, they have concentrated on exchange, infrastructure, and communication. Thus they overlook patterns of regional social contradiction and coalition: why do trade and migration continue despite repeated destabilization and sanction." Because of South Africa's dominance in the region, there is a tendency to regard it as the primary political and economic actor. In many ways the economies of the Frontline states are intrinsically bound to South Africa whether through migratory labor systems, transport grids, or customs agreements.[1] South Africa has significant advantages over its neighbors, but it also needs them economically since they are the primary markets for a large percentage of South Africa's exports, albeit covertly in some cases.

South Africa's responses to the nations that constitute the Southern African regional system have differed over time. For analytical purposes it is convenient to group these responses into four historical periods. During the first period, which ran from the Act of Union (1910) until 1959, South Africa's internal racial policies were consistent with the white settler regimes of the region and international capital fully accepted South Africa's internal policies and regional initiatives. In the second period, between 1959 and 1975, divergence began to occur. South Africa's homelands policy sharply contrasted with the decolonization process that was taking place regionally, and the independence of Mozambique and Angola posed new political and economic threats to South Africa. The Sharpeville crisis in 1960 and South Africa's expulsion from the British Commonwealth in 1961 marked the beginning of divergence on the international level. In the third period, from 1975 to 1980, the gap widened between South Africa and its neighbors. Internally South African oppression in the 1976 Soweto crisis highlighted the difference between its regressive internal policies and regional moves toward self-determination. Internationally South Africa's political isolation grew, as did doubts about the country's long-term economic stability. During the fourth period, from 1980 to the present, the lines were more sharply drawn. This was a period of outright disconsonance between South Africa and the region. With Zimbabwe's independence, South Africa responded to the demise of the white redoubt, the ring of white-ruled states that surrounded it, with a policy of destabilization aimed at protecting its regional economic and political interests. Internationally this was the period in which there was a move from the threat of economic sanctions to the actual imposition of such sanctions.

Historically South Africa's internal economic and political policies, its involvement in the region, and the concerns of overseas capitalist interests have all coincided. By the early 1970s, however, the divergence that began following World War II gathered momentum after the independence of Angola and Mozambique. South Africa's primary interest was now the internal viability of white power despite the regional economic costs caused by its destabilization policy.

From Union until 1959

For indigenous peoples the Southern African region has been a "battleground" ever since the arrival of the Dutch at the Cape of Good Hope in 1652. South Africa has been seen as the center of imperialist operations in the region since the Cape was first recognized as a vital strategic center on the route to India and the Far East. This prominence has remained constant through successive stages of the region's history. Indeed, it was from South Africa that the colonization of many of the other countries of the region (particularly the former British colonies) emanated.

Historically the development of capitalism in Southern Africa led to the formation of a regional subsystem in which the principal sources of capital accumulation were located in South Africa. The other territories of the region became subordinated to serve the needs of capital accumulation in South Africa in various ways—as a source of labor reserves (supplying 300,000 migrant workers for the mining industry alone in 1973), to supply cheap raw materials and/or specific services such as transport, and to serve as markets for South African–produced commodities (Shaw and Msabaha 1987: 242).

In the case of Southern Rhodesia (now Zimbabwe), for example, the country had been colonized largely from the south. Its legal system was fundamentally the same as that of the Cape of Good Hope (with both based on Roman Dutch law), there was a continuous railway between the two countries, and Southern Rhodesia's trade was mainly with the town and ports of South Africa. This historical connection, grounded in geographical proximity, continues into the present to maintain Zimbabwe's dependence on South Africa. In the 1980s, 60 percent of Zimbabwe's external trade was shipped via South African railways and ports. Twenty-five percent of Zimbabwean imports originated from South Africa and 22 percent of its exports went to South Africa. South African–based mineral companies, such as Anglo American Corporation, remain significant in the mineral sector of Zimbabwe's economy. Botswana, Lesotho, and Swaziland are in even worse positions in terms of their dependence on South Africa. While South Africa was the source for the development of many of the countries of the region, it must not be forgotten that it was itself part of a larger overseas context of international trade and production.

From the early twentieth century until World War II, South African interests were predominant in the region despite minor conflicts with even some of the nearby white-ruled colonies. Within South Africa, the end of the Boer War in 1902 resulted in the clear dominance of British interests in the economic sphere, and this in turn sustained a regional stability that lasted through the 1940s and in which South African needs took precedence over those of the rest of the region. Since 1948, however, fundamental changes have taken place. Immediately after World War II, the decolonization process began in sub-Saharan Africa. Just as the major colonial powers were thinking about granting self-determination to their former colonies, South Africa launched its policies of institutionalized racial segregation. The policies of apartheid were, in turn, reflected in South Africa's responses to the region. Even before the National party took power in 1948 its leaders expressed their ideas about South Africa's place in Africa and their suspicions about the demands for independence that were emerging in other parts of the continent. The National party's first prime minister, Daniel F. Malan, often reaffirmed the significance of Western values and called for the preservation of white civilization.

Decolonization in the region was thus a major threat: "In the decade or so following the Second World War, South African governments, seeing the dangers that might follow from decolonization, sought increased influence on imperial policies in Africa. The National Party, from the moment it took power in 1948, struggled to halt or slow down the decolonization of the continent and conceived of defense arrangements in which Pretoria would have an important role with the imperial order" (Bender, Coleman, and Sklar 1985:53). Thus South Africa tried to use its historical ties with Western powers in order to influence the decolonization process, particularly by emphasizing its vital role in defending Africa from the supposed threat of a Communist takeover.

The Beginning of Divergence: 1959–1975

In the Southern African region it is possible to identify two forms of independent states: those territories that acquired independence after being protected by Britain from Afrikaner annexation in the nineteenth century, and independent states that resulted from twentieth-century national liberation struggles. The former were relevant to new regional policy initiatives in South Africa in the late 1950s. Prime Minister Hendrik F. Verwoerd's new emphasis on separate development, codified in the Bantu Self-Government Act of 1959, had implications not only for South Africa but for the region as well. The act introduced the possibility that black ethnic "homelands," or bantustans, might eventually exercise some form of independence. In order to foster the illusion of self-governance, South African citizenship was taken away from millions of rural and urban blacks and replaced with the citizenship of a particular homeland. Africans were thus to vote and participate in politics only in their respective homelands. By these moves the government ensured that the South African white minority would become the majority in the newly defined geopolitical entity of South Africa. A familiar pattern emerged in which the white South African government provided "foreign aid" to the homelands, thus perpetuating the fiction that they were independent states.

The evolving homelands policy also anticipated a new form of regional interaction. The irony of the situation was that while South Africa was busy trying to create moderate ethnically based states both inside the country and in the surrounding region, black opposition groups in South Africa saw themselves involved in a revolutionary struggle that opposed all forms of regional colonial domination. Verwoerd hoped that the homelands model would be exportable, particularly with the impending independence of Bechuanaland (Botswana), Basutoland (Lesotho), and Swaziland. He thought that these countries might be drawn into a homelands-type relationship to South Africa, with an emphasis on economic, not political, independence. As Alexander Hepple has noted about Verwoerd's plans: "The three territories constituted a vital part of his grand design of separate development. In 1956 he had urged the incorporation of the protectorates, so that all land in Africa south of the Limpopo should be divided into separate white and black states. To overcome the objection that South Africa's Blacks were allotted a mere 13.7 per cent of the land in the Republic, Verwoerd hoped that the protectorates could be included as additional 'Bantu' areas, bringing the African share of the land to forty-five percent" (1967:195)

The 1960s also saw changes in the significance of external economic and political influence highlighted by the flight of international capital from South Africa after the Sharpeville massacre in 1960. South Africa's withdrawal from the British Commonwealth in 1961 and world criticism surrounding the Sharpeville crisis were early indications of the new international context within which South Africa would henceforth have to operate. International condemnation of its repression during the 1976 Soweto uprising and the emphasis on sanctions, disinvestment, and divestment are subsequent landmarks in this process. In its diplomatic interactions as well as on many other levels, including, for example, international sports competitions, South Africa has drawn inward or been shunned by the world community. South Africa, however, has not been able to isolate itself nor be isolated from a region with which it is so viscerally connected. At the heart of the international strategies designed to end apartheid is the recognition that while South Africa is a pariah state it remains centrally linked to the Western political economy.

Beginning in 1966 Verwoerd's successor, Prime Minister John Vorster, established different, and at times contradictory, internal and external political policies and goals. For example, Vorster's "outward movement," which began in 1967, called for rapprochement with African nations to the north, while his internal policies showed little evidence of reaching out to blacks within South Africa's own boundaries. This was fundamentally different from the Verwoerdian design, which attempted to develop a domestic policy that was consistent with external policies (Geldenhuys 1986:85). Internally Vorster set about imposing stringent controls on black political activity, but at the same time he established diplomatic relations with Malawi and in 1969 renegotiated the Southern African Customs Union Agreement with Botswana, Lesotho, and Swaziland, which remains in effect today.

Increasing cooperation among the minority white-ruled states of the region was another characteristic of the late 1960s. These were the declining years of Portuguese rule in Angola and Mozambique and the period of the Unilateral Declaration of Independence (UDI) by the Ian Smith regime in Rhodesia. South Africa became involved in counterinsurgency operations in Angola and Mozambique, and in 1967 it cooperated with Rhodesian authorities in a campaign against the Rhodesian African National Congress guerrillas who were operating in southern portions of that country. In the early years of UDI, South Africa became essential to the survival of the Smith regime. This was also the period when a variety of liberation forces were beginning to engage in coordinated strategies, and an important part of South Africa's regional political policy developed from the necessity to divide and weaken these organizations.

The Widening Gap: 1975–1980

With the independence of Angola and Mozambique in 1975, South Africa became acutely aware of its regional vulnerability. Rhodesia was by this time almost totally dependent on South Africa for trans-shipment of its exports and imports and for military supplies. South Africa was gradually forced to recognize the inevitability of African independence in Rhodesia and began to implement plans designed to enable black moderates to win power. By 1975 the South African government wanted to avoid further involvement in the unpopular and drawn-out guerrilla war in Rhodesia. It considered that its best interests would not be served by continuing to back the illegal Smith regime but by finding a solution to the conflict and ensuring that a conservative black government would succeed the white settler government. To this end, it withdrew its paramilitary support from Rhodesia in July 1975 and made it increasingly difficult for Rhodesian exports and imports to move through its port facilities. South Africa saw itself as a principal actor in negotiations to bring about the settlement of the Rhodesian crisis. For example, meetings were held between South Africa and Zambia concerning Rhodesia in October 1974 and again in August 1975 at Victoria Falls. The failure of the 1975 conference and the inability of other regional initiatives to bring about a settlement brought an end to such joint ventures; however, the meetings between Prime Minister John Vorster and President Kenneth Kaunda of Zambia led South Africa to explore a broader means of cooperation among the states of the region. But these efforts too were ultimately doomed to fail.

The Soweto uprisings of 1976, the demise of the Portuguese empire, and the increasing likelihood that matters in both Namibia and Rhodesia were not going to be settled rapidly or in a way in which

South Africa's interests would be paramount all contributed to a changed political context. It was becoming clear that South Africa would have to increase its military capabilities. South Africa had believed that Portuguese rule of Mozambique and Angola would survive into the future and that, by one means or another, other black states in the region would come to terms with South Africa economically. When P.W. Botha took power in September 1978, he initiated new domestic and external policies. The regional dimension played a significant part in his "total strategy," which soon came to be adopted as official policy. This strategy was ultimately very different from Vorster's regional diplomacy. It called for an aggressive economic, political, and military offensive to ensure Pretoria's hegemony over the region and to cripple liberation efforts by the African National Congress (ANC) and other antiapartheid forces. It also naively hoped to "win the hearts and minds" of blacks inside South Africa by a series of cosmetic reforms.

To enhance South Africa's ability to strike at its neighbors, the state initiated a major arms development program, organized new commando units, and doubled the military budget between 1977 and 1984. In an influential paper published by the Institute of Strategic Studies at the University of Pretoria in 1981, Deon Geldenhuys laid out the objectives for the total strategy and destabilization, including the use of economic relationships to impose political goals. Geldenhuys called for neighboring states not to be used as springboards for the liberation of South Africa and even went on to demand that they ensure that these incursions did not take place. Specifically, Geldenhuys (1981:20) insisted that the neighboring countries should not provide training facilities for the liberation movements.

1980 to the Present

Prior to 1980, South Africa's attacks on the countries in the region were relatively restrained. P.W. Botha's "total strategy," however, reflected a change in South Africa's internal power structure. The prominence and influence of the military in South African policy-making increased significantly from 1980 onward. Under Botha, the State Security Council (SSC) became the most important decision-making body in regard to foreign policy issues. This cabinet committee, with a number of military representatives, had been set up by an act of Parliament in 1972 and remained a purely advisory body until South Africa's aborted military invasion of Angola in 1975–76. The policy of destabilization with which it has been closely identified had several goals, but it was primarily designed to preoccupy the Frontline states with internal economic and strategic problems so that they would not be able to serve as effective bases for liberation movements such as the ANC. Geldenhuys sums up the basic purpose of destabilization: "South African actions amount to destabilization if they are deliberately intended to create new or exacerbate instability in a target state. The object of destabilization is, then, to promote [or force] profound political change in the target country. These may or may not involve structural change—in effect toppling the regime in power and seeing it replaced by a 'moderate one'—but would certainly involve a major change in the target state's behavior toward the destabilizer" (1981:20).

The range of military acts of destabilization include the violation of boundaries, bombings, sabotage, air strikes, commando raids, and other such incursions or threat of them. As part of the carrot-and-stick dimension of the "total strategy," South Africa sought to promote joint economic projects with neighboring states in an effort to show the superiority of the South African capitalist model, and, above all, it made efforts to draw the moderate states into nonaggression pacts as a means to contain ANC activities in neighboring countries. In addition, just as the South African government sought to bring the moderate Bishop Abel Muzorewa to power in Zimbabwe, it also recognized that it could align itself with dissident movements or factions in other parts of the region.

At the same time, Botha's new idea of a "constellation of states" was being developed, which, it was hoped, would lead directly to mutual cooperation in the solving of regional problems. An underlying premise was that the "moderate" countries of Southern Africa were all supposedly facing similar threats of Communist incursion and that by working together they would be able to resist this attack. Ultimately, South Africa anticipated cooperative regional interaction among the independent homelands, a moderate government in Zimbabwe, an independent Namibia ruled by a group that had won the approval of Pretoria, and such states as Botswana, Lesotho, Swaziland, and Zambia. In retrospect, the constellation idea was naive and may only have been intended as a public relations effort to convince the Western powers of South Africa's goodwill. South Africa's assumption was fundamentally flawed in that it presumed that simple economic linkages would override more fundamental political questions, especially those internal to South Africa.

South Africa used more than military power in its regional destabilization efforts. Despite its strident condemnation of the idea of sanctions it politicized regional trade and transport relations, thus imposing its own form of sanctions. Tactics included delaying or restricting the payment to neighboring governments of the remittances earned by migrant workers. For example, South Africa reduced the number of Mozambican migrant workers within its borders by some 60 percent since Mozambique's independence, and it terminated the agreement under which a portion of the wages of the migrant workers was remitted in gold at a fixed rate to the Mozambican government. The destruction of crucial transport links in Mozambique and Angola by South Africa–backed dissident movements dramatically increased the dependence of these countries on South Africa's more expensive transport network, which in turn provides South Africa with enormous economic leverage while opening up the constant threat of reprisals.

In very real terms the cost of South Africa's "total strategy" was enormous. Between 1980 and 1983, Zimbabwe had redirected 50 percent of its exports from South African to Mozambican ports, but by 1985 the figure was less than 10 percent. The total cost to the countries of the region has been estimated at more than $10 billion for the years 1980–1984, a sum that is the equivalent of all member states' export earnings during the same period. In addition, the Commonwealth Secretariat's Eminent Persons Group report, *Mission to South Africa* (1986:129), placed the loss of life in the region as a result of destabilization at 100,000 and indicated that the number of refugees far exceeds this figure. Furthermore, destabilization led neighboring states to allocate excessive portions of their budgets to their own military buildup at the expense of vital social programs.

Destabilization was a particularly effective technique against countries which themselves have weak political institutions, such as Lesotho, or countries with severe disadvantages in the economic sector that have been magnified because of South Africa's covert or overt activities, such as Mozambique. There have been some diplomatic advantages for South Africa from the "total strategy"—for example, the 1982 Non-Aggression Pact between South Africa and Swaziland and the Nkomati Accord signed with Mozambique in March 1984. South Africa, however, achieved many more of its goals through violence and disruption, thus emphasizing the continuing division between its economic and political objectives. Ironically, it became a country that was forced to destabilize its major regional trading partners.

A Regional Response: Southern African Development Coordination Conference (SADCC)

The formation of the Southern African Development Coordination Conference (SADCC) in Lusaka on 1 April 1980 coincided with two other regional changes, the new South African regional offensive and the coming into being of the independent nation of Zimbabwe. SADCC, which consists of the six Frontline states (Angola, Botswana, Mozambique, Tanzania, Zambia, and Zimbabwe) and three other regional members, Lesotho, Malawi, and Swaziland, aims to develop the self-sufficiency of its nine members by mutual agreements, to foster joint international activities, and to support cooperative projects to reduce the dependence of member nations on the apartheid regime. The independence of Zimbabwe brought about an increasing realization by the states of the region that economic cooperation should be formalized. Cooperation on regional economic development allowed states with a variety of political relations with South Africa to come together. Each of the member nations has adopted a particular area for special concern. Angola, for example, deals with energy; Lesotho with soil conservation; Malawi with fisheries, wildlife, and forests; Mozambique with transport and communications; Zambia with mining; Zimbabwe with food, security, and so forth.

The efforts of the group are coordinated through regular meetings of the standing committee of permanent secretaries and through a council of ministers. The secretariat is housed in Botswana. SADCC is a direct outgrowth of the collaboration of the Frontline states Botswana, Tanzania, Zambia, Mozambique, and Angola in the liberation process of Zimbabwe, which then became a member of the group. Despite differences in ideology, the Frontline states became a decisive force, both within the region and within such international organizations as the Organization of African Unity (OAU), because of a shared common goal. Since the independence of Zimbabwe, there has been a shift away from the "Frontline" concept to that of SADCC. Thandika Mkandawire (1987:160–61) maintains that while SADCC started off well, having emerged directly out of the Frontline states' cooperation and support of the liberation forces of Zimbabwe and Namibia, and while there remains a political commitment to the liberation struggle and resistance to South Africa, under "the guise of pragmatism" there is a growing tendency to keep politics out of SADCC affairs and to technocratize dealings among SADCC states. Indeed, donors appear to have been impressed by the depoliticization of SADCC and have "in a rather paternalistic way" praised SADCC for this pragmatism (Mkandawire 1987:168).

The contribution of foreign donors towards the depoliticization of SADCC has meant that frequently cooperation has taken place only over the least controversial projects. For some commentators SADCC is a cause for optimism because of its economic potential rather than its political or strategic focus. Timothy Shaw emphasizes the advancement toward collective self-reliance and collective cooperation and notes that "Southern Africa has begun to achieve more autonomy in design and direction than ever before, the prospects for which will grow in both conception and content as Namibia and South Africa are liberated" (Aluko and Shaw 1985: xii–xiii). Some writers have been particularly critical of the U.S. role in regard to SADCC. Sam Nolutshungu maintains that "the United States could develop stronger economic and political relations with the rest of the region. It could more directly support the efforts of SADCC countries at regional integration and discourage South African military attacks" (Bender, Coleman, and Sklar 1985:61). SADCC may also be seen at the center of a debate on how the United States is to best promote its national interests—specifically, whether U.S. interests are better served through regional or national development aid. Congress consistently pushed the Reagan administration to appropriate more money directly to SADCC-approved projects. There were thus two major issues that were debated between Congress and the Reagan administration— how much aid, and to whom in Southern Africa should it be sent?

Effects of Regional Destabilization

South Africa's destabilization program, in the form of concrete measures or as a looming implicit threat, remained the major regional problem through the 1980s, with Angola and Mozambique being the principal countries affected. In addition to backing rebel movements such as the Union for the Total Independence of Angola (UNITA), South Africa placed special emphasis on attacking railway routes to the sea through Angola and Mozambique. For example, the Benguela Railway line, which was of considerable importance for the movement of goods, products, and minerals from Zaire and Zambia, was shut for nearly ten years. Activities in Mozambique by the South African–backed Mozambique National Resistance movement (MNR, or, more commonly, RENAMO) were directed at cutting the important linkage of the Beira rail line from Zimbabwe to Mozambique. Transport-route sabotage became one of the easiest and most successful ways of ensuring that aid not be given to ANC guerrillas in neighboring countries, especially those without access to the sea.

Ironically, in practice, all states in the region accommodated to the reality of South African dominance by maintaining normal commercial relations with and military neutrality toward the apartheid state. In simple terms, the dependency of the member nations of SADCC was explicit: Mozambique, with a clear dependence for foreign exchange from migrant labor in South Africa; Swaziland, overwhelmingly dependent for transport and energy; Lesotho, totally enclosed by

South Africa and 100 percent dependent on transport; Botswana, 100 percent dependent for transport; Zimbabwe, 80 percent dependent for transport, with South Africa as its largest trading partner; Zambia, 40 percent dependent on South Africa for transport, with South Africa as its major supplier of imports especially for its mining sector; Malawi, 40 percent dependent on transport and heavily engaged in trade, aid, and technical cooperation with South Africa. Thus, throughout the 1980s South Africa remained in firm command of its most significant weapon—the control of regional transportation (Martin 1987). In addition, the weakness of the South African rand in this period has meant that South African commodities have been cheaper than those from abroad, thus increasing regional economic dependence on South Africa.

One of the most significant threats has been the tactic of border closures or border delays. South Africa has demonstrated its ability to delay rail and road transit traffic, without acknowledging any political intention, simply by introducing more rigorous customs inspections, import licenses, and packaging standards. Using these "legal means" South Africa was able in January 1986, to topple the government of the late Chief Leabua Jonathan of Lesotho. South Africa periodically caused severe inconvenience to the Zimbabwe government by closing the Beit Bridge. Instead of using the term *Frontline states* in discussing this period, it might be more appropriate to introduce the notion of *contiguous states*, i.e., those states who share borders primarily with South Africa and are directly subject to its intervention and interference. In the 1980s the contiguous states were well aware of the range of weapons available to South Africa.

How far could South Africa have gone? In the extreme scenario, the ports of Beira or Maputo or even the port of Dar es Salaam could have become targets. Bridges, oil storage facilities, and other installations could all have been bombed. Indeed, Roger Martin (1987) maintains that there were some military voices in South Africa who advocated a "maximalist" solution, proposing that aggressive military actions be taken sooner rather than later in order to neutralize opponents and complete the ring of friendly governments around South Africa. Zimbabwe balked at imposing sanctions against South Africa, in part because the pragmatists in Mugabe's government were able to put forward such arguments as the fact that in a ten-month period in 1986–87 Zimbabwe's trade with South Africa was well over $400 million and the negative effects of sanctions on the Zimbabwean economy would have been devastating (*Star*, 15 August 1987). Mozambique, Malawi, Zaire, Botswana, Lesotho, and Swaziland also made it clear that for pragmatic reasons they would not impose sanctions against South Africa. As the 1980s drew to a close, South Africa continued to trade normally with all the member states of SADCC, and acts of destabilization were reduced, a sign of a more relaxed regional environment.

It would be misleading to assume South Africa bore no economic costs for its own regional policies. Indeed, South Africa was well aware that it was as dependent on the region as the region was dependent on it. Closing of borders, delays in transportation networks, and loss of markets for South African products all had serious effects on the South African economy. Moreover, South Africa benefits significantly in foreign exchange earnings from its trade with the region and this trade surplus is of vital importance. Furthermore, the country needs migrant labor from the region because foreign labor is more controllable than South Africa's domestic labor force. It is noteworthy that South Africa's border reprisals were only of short duration so as to cause minimum economic damage.

Regional destabilization coupled with severe internal political and economic problems also resulted in limitations on South Africa's access to foreign capital. South Africa's position in relation to the world economy was altered by the withdrawal of large numbers of U.S. corporations and increasing numbers of British and European interests. Its value to Western capitalism had simply decreased. Until 1960 South Africa's internal policies of regional hegemony were seen as consistent with the interests of overseas capitalists. In 1960, however, a progressive change began to occur that came to a head with the destabilization policy. Capitalist interests were simply not served by the policy of destabilization. In fact the growing alienation between business interests and the South African state was also reflected in the regional arena. From an economic point of view regional economic growth was stymied, returns on investments were lower, risks were greater, and sanctions and criticism took a heavy toll. Thus, South Africa's place, both within the region and within the larger world economic system, was itself undergoing a transformation. "South Africa may confront fundamental structural problems based on apartheid in advancing beyond semi-industrialization because its pattern of polarized accumulation is so accentuated. Paradoxically, therefore, South Africa needs regional markets because its national level of consumption is limited artificially by institutionalized racism" (Aluko and Shaw 1985:301).

Conclusion

In a recent essay Michael Clough and Jeffrey Herbst point the way to the beginning of a new era for the region: "But southern Africa is changing. Regional battlelines, which previously seemed so clear-

cut—black versus white, pro-Soviet versus pro-Western—are blur-
ring. New strategies are being pursued by the most important regional
powers. A postcolonial, post–Cold War, postdestabilization, postapartheid era is slowly beginning to dawn" (1989:4). Given the dramatic internal changes taking place, South Africa's policy of regional
destabilization to ensure the survival of the apartheid state is outmoded. The smooth transition to independence for Namibia, prospects
for a resolution to the Angolan crisis and for a more stable Mozambique, and a more benign regional role played by South Africa imply
the beginning of a new regional economic and political configuration.
Destabilization was thus a policy reflecting the needs and times of the
1980s, while the 1990s will undoubtedly present different options,
possibilities, and strategies. Increases in trade and investment and an
end to regional violence might point the way to a regional Southern
African economic common market. Even a noncapitalist independent
South Africa would probably continue to play the role of regional
power, even if there were to be changes in the very basis on which
this power is operated. But an independent South Africa could produce significant shifts in the order of production and in the restructuring of economic priorities. Ultimately, regional economic integration
might even lead to some form of political union. On the other hand,
South Africa, even under black rule, might be increasingly perceived
as a regional economic hegemonic power. It would be wrong to
assume that changes within South Africa will lead to balanced growth
in the region. Indeed, SADCC might very well continue as a vehicle
for reducing economic dependence on the southern giant.

On a more positive note, it is possible to foresee a situation in
which foreign corporations and investors reinvest vast sums into
South Africa because they consider it to have the necessary infrastructure for expanding regional exports and trade. The less-developed
countries of the region could offer new markets and new opportunities, thus providing South Africa itself with the means to redress some
of its own social and economic inequities. Increased demands for
goods and services from the region might ameliorate South Africa's
bleak unemployment situation. An increase in revenues could help
pay at least a part of the bill for new housing for the country's increasing black population and help to underwrite a minimum wage, better
health care, and educational and other social programs. Regrettably,
unresolved problems within South Africa, such as the ongoing violence between the ANC and the predominantly Zulu-based Inkatha
movement, and the real danger of anomic violence on the part of the
white radical right will not only delay South Africa's economic renais-
sance but bring their own negative impacts on the region.

Ideally, the 1990s might herald a new period for South Africa and
the region—one of mutual respect and cooperation. An observation

made by the vice president of Botswana, Peter Mmusi, provides a perspective on how South Africa's self-interest has stunted the region and on what the future might hold: "The abolition of apartheid could be the greatest single contribution which could be made to the economic development of the region" (*Mission to South Africa: The Commonwealth Report* 1986:129). This could have far-reaching consequences for a postapartheid South Africa and the future of the Southern African region.

NOTES

1. The Frontline states initially consisted of Angola, Botswana, Mozambique, Tanzania, and Zambia, which joined together to promote the liberation of Zimbabwe, Namibia, and, ultimately, South Africa. They later constituted the core states, along with Zimbabwe, of the Southern African Development Coordination Conference (SADCC), as discussed later in the chapter.

REFERENCES

Aluko, Oladje, and Timothy M. Shaw. 1985. *Southern Africa in the 1980s*. London: George Allen and Unwin.

Bender, Gerald J., James S. Coleman, and Richard Sklar, eds. 1985. *African Crisis Areas and U.S. Foreign Policy*. Berkeley: University of California Press.

Clough, Michael, and Jeffrey Herbst. 1989. *Beyond Destabilization: South Africa's Changing Regional Strategy*. New York: Council on Foreign Relations.

Geldenhuys, Deon. 1981. "Some Strategic Implications of Regional Economic Relationships for the Republic of South Africa." *Strategic Review for Southern Africa* (Institute for Strategic Studies, University of Pretoria).

———. 1986. "South Africa's Fruitless Quest for Neighboring Friends." *Energos* 14:85.

Hepple, Alexander. 1967. *Verwoerd*. Hammondsworth, U.K.: Penguin Books.

Martin, Roger. 1987. "Southern Africa Brief 1." *Front File* (London).

Mission to South Africa: The Commonwealth Report. 1986. Hammondsworth, U.K.: Penguin Books.

Mkandawire, Thandika. 1987. "Conflict in Southern Africa." In *African Perspectives on Peace and Development*, ed. Emmanuel Hansen, 160–61. London: Zed Books.

Nolutshungu, Sam C. 1985. "South African Policy and United States Options in Southern Africa." In *African Crisis Areas and U.S. Foreign Policy*, eds. Gerald J. Bender, James S. Coleman, and Richard L. Sklar, 49–63. Berkeley: University of California Press.

Shaw, Timothy M., and Ibrahim S. R. Msabaha, eds. 1987. *Confrontation and Liberation in Southern Africa*. Boulder: Westview Press.

Star (Johannesburg). 1987. 15 August, 3.

CONTRIBUTORS

KARL S. BECK is a State Department officer presently on detail with the International Organization for Migration in Germany. He wrote his chapter while he was a senior associate at the Carnegie Endowment for International Peace. He first went to Southern Africa in 1967 as a Peace Corps volunteer in Lesotho. Since then he has lived and worked in several countries of the region. From 1985 until 1988 he covered South African extraparliamentary opposition politics for the U.S. embassy in Pretoria.

JAMES COBBE was educated in the United Kingdom, receiving a B.A. in economics with first-class honors from Trinity College, University of Cambridge. His Ph.D., in economics, is from Yale. He was a lecturer in economics at the University of Botswana, Lesotho, and Swaziland, and then at the National University of Lesotho from 1973 to 1976. He returned to the National University of Lesotho in 1981–82 as associate professor and head of the Research Division of the Institute of Southern African Studies. He is currently professor of economics at Florida State University, where he has been a faculty member since 1976. He is the coauthor with John E. Bardill of *Lesotho: Dilemmas of Dependence in Southern Africa* and has written a number of other publications dealing with economic issues in Lesotho and the Southern African region.

R. HUNT DAVIS, JR., holds a Ph.D. in history from the University of Wisconsin. He is currently professor of history and African studies at the University of Florida, where he also previously served as director of the Center for African Studies. He is also the former editor of the *African Studies Review.* His research and writing have focused primarily on South Africa, with particular attention to the history of education, African politics, and U.S. policy toward Southern Africa. He recently co-authored with Gwendolen M. Carter a chapter titled "Case Study: South Africa" in the edited volume *Intervention in the 1980s: U.S. Foreign Policy in the Third World* (1989) and is coeditor with Sheridan Johns of *Mandela, Tambo and the African National Congress: The Struggle Against Apartheid, 1948–1990* (1991).

CHARLES JONATHAN DRIVER is a South African novelist, poet, and biographer, now living in the United Kingdom as a British citizen. He is master of Wellington College in Berkshire, U.K. He holds degrees from the University of Cape Town and Trinity College, Oxford. In the early 1960s, he was president of the National Union of South African Students. In July 1964, he was detained without charge under the Ninety-Day Detention Act in South Africa and was denied renewal of his South African passport in 1966. His biography, *Patrick Duncan* (1980), is a study of a leading figure in the South African Liberal party in the 1950s.

KENNETH W. GRUNDY received his Ph.D. from Pennsylvania State University in 1963 and is M.A. Hanna Professor of Political Science at Case Western Reserve University. He has served as visiting senior lecturer at Makere University College, visiting scholar at the Institute of Social Studies, the Hague, and visiting Fulbright professor at the University of Zambia and at University College, Galway, Ireland. His books include *Guerilla Struggle in Africa* (1972), *Confrontation and Accommodation in Southern Africa* (1973), *Ideologies of Violence* (coauthor, 1974), *Evaluating Transnational Programs in Government and Business* (coeditor, 1980), *Soldiers Without Politics: Blacks in the South African Armed Forces* (1983), and *The Militarization of South African Politics* (1986; rev. ed., 1988).

C.R.D. HALISI received his Ph.D. in political science from UCLA and is assistant professor of political science at Indiana University. He has undertaken extensive field research on black politics in South Africa. He is coauthor with James S. Coleman of "American Political Science and Tropical Africa: Universalism vs. Relativism" (1983), which appeared in the *African Studies Review,* and is the author of chapters and articles on South Africa. These include: "Popular Struggle: Black South African Opposition in Transformation," *Radical History Review,* (1990); "Racial Proletarianization and Political Culture in South Africa," in Edmond Keller and Louis Picard (eds.), *South Africa in Southern Africa,* (1989); and "Soviet–U.S. Cooperation for Southern African Development and Regional Security," in Anatoly Gromyko and C.S. Whitaker (eds.), *Agenda for Action: African–Soviet–U.S. Cooperation* (1990). Halisi is currently completing a book on black political thought in South Africa.

ALLEN F. ISAACMAN holds a Ph.D. in history from the University of Wisconsin and is currently professor of history at the University of Minnesota and director of its MacArthur Program on Peace and International Cooperation. He previously held the chair in Mozambique history at the University Eduardo Mondlane in Maputo. Isaacman was a distinguished lecturer at the 1989 annual meeting of the African Studies Association, where he presented his Social Science Research Council–commissioned paper titled "Peasants and Rural Social Protest in Africa," subsequently published in the *African Studies Review* (1990). His study *Mozambique: The Africanization of a European Institution, the Zambezi Prazos, 1750–1902 (1972)* won the Melville Herskovits Award of the African Studies Association in 1973 as the most distinguished book of the year in African studies. He has published three other books as well as numerous scholarly articles on Mozambique. He has also written on contemporary Mozambique for the *Christian Science Monitor,* the *Los Angeles Times,* and *Africa Report.*

PEARL-ALICE MARSH is coordinator of the Stanford-Berkeley Joint Center for African Studies. She received her Ph.D. in political science from the University of California at Berkeley. She has published several articles on South African trade unions, has completed a book manuscript titled *Antagonistic Partnership: South African Industry and African Labor, 1968–1982,* and has lectured widely on South African labor, women under apartheid, and U.S. foreign policy toward Southern Africa. Currently she is researching the international sanctions movement against South Africa.

ANTHONY S. MATHEWS holds an LL.B. and a Ph.D. from the University of Natal and is James Scott Wylie Professor of Law at the University of Natal. He has been a visiting scholar at Harvard, has held a Butterworths Overseas Legal Fellowship and a visiting fellowship at Cambridge, and has twice served as visiting professor of law at the University of Florida. He is the author of *Law, Order and Liberty in South Africa* (1972), *The Darker Reaches of Government* (1978), and *Freedom, State Security, and the Rule of Law: Dilemmas of the Apartheid Society* (1986). He has also authored numerous book chapters and articles in scholarly journals.

PATRICK O'MEARA is a graduate of the University of Cape Town and received his M.A. and Ph.D. degrees from Indiana University, where he is currently director of the African Studies Program and professor of political science and public and environmental affairs. He has long been involved with research, teaching, and writing about the politics of Southern Africa. Among his publications are *Rhodesia: Racial Conflict or Coexistence?* (1975) and several books coedited with Gwendolen M. Carter, including *Southern Africa: The Continuing Crisis* (1979; 2d ed., 1982), *International Politics in Southern Africa* (1982), and *African Independence: The First Twenty-five Years* (1986).

ROBERT SHANAFELT received his Ph.D. in anthropology from the University of Florida. He is currently an instructor in anthropology at Florida State University. A Peace Corps volunteer in Lesotho from 1982 to 1984, Shanafelt returned there in 1987 with the support of a Fulbright-Hays dissertation research grant. Based on thirteen months of fieldwork with Sotho and Xhosa speakers, his doctoral dissertation examines political identity in Lesotho and in South Africa. He has also written on Sotho literature and on human rights.

INDEX

Accountability, of security forces, 23–28, 30

Act of Union, 5, 213. *See also* Union of South Africa, formation of

Adam, Heribert, 38, 50, 93

Admission of Persons to the Union Regulation Act No. 22, 150

Africanism. *See* PAC (Pan-Africanist Congress)

African National Congress. *See* ANC

African National Congress Youth League (ANCYL), 6

African Resistance Movement (ARM), 62, 68

Africans, black: black states, 69; class relations of, 80; deaths of, 22, 25, 28; income of, 172; population of, 2, 4; poverty of, 3; resurgence of, 2; vs. blacks, 68; working class, 90; youth, 105, 106, 107. *See also* Baca; Blacks; Hluvi; Mpondo; Mpondomise; Nguni; Shangaan; Shona; Sotho; Tswana; Venda; Xhosa; Zulu

Afrikaner Leases, 123

Afrikaner Nationalist party, 63

Afrikaners: arrival of, 214; England and, 144, 147; intransigence of, 63–64, 67; and racialism, 66

Afrikaner Weerstandsbeweging. *See* AWB

Agriculture, 149, 165; in Mozambique, 189–91, 199–200, 201, 202; in southern Africa, 166

Air force, South African, 196, 197, 220

Alexander, Neville, 79, 83, 84

Alexandra, government withdrawal from, 105–6

Alexandra Action Committee, 95

Aliens Act, 150, 162n.12

Alton, Mhlamvu, 133

AmaMpondo. *See* Mpondo

Ameliorism, 65–67, 69

Amnesty, for RENAMO insurgents, 207

ANC (African National Congress), 36, 55, 62, 69, 72, 100, 154, 170, 219; banning of, 13, 87; BCM and, 89; Communist support of, 31n.3; and Congress movement, 60; de Klerk and, 63; dilemma of, 180; dissension within, 75; DP and, 38; Freedom Charter of, 80; future of, 180; ideological strains within, 87; and Inkatha, 15, 226; isolation of, 192; and KwaNatal plan, 49; legalization of, 2, 6, 14, 179, 208; militancy of, 6; Mozambique and, 195; NECC and, 101; PAC split from, 85; and revolution, 93, 94; Rhodesian, 218; and SACP, 84; and Sharpeville massacre, 94; and socialism, 87, 96n.4; outside South Africa, 220; training camps of, 23; and UDF civic associations, 110. *See also* Congress movement; Mandela, Nelson; Sisulu, Albertina; Sisulu, Walter; South African Congress of Trade Unions; Tambo, Oliver; *Umkhonto we Sizwe; Umzabalazo*

ANCYL (African National Congress Youth League), 6

Anglo American Corporation, 66, 121, 122, 161n.4; and Bregman commission, 138n.5; Zimbabwe and, 215. *See also* Vaal Reefs

Anglo-Boer War. *See* Boer War

Angola, 53; agriculture in, 166; civil war in, 30, 193 (*see also* UNITA); and energy, 222; as Frontline state,